A JOURNEY OF FAITH
BOOK ONE

THE GIRL IN THE LITTLE WHITE DRESS

KASIA NIMOCKS

THE GIRL IN THE LITTLE WHITE DRESS
COPYRIGHT © 2020 BY KASIA NIMOCKS

All rights reserved. No part of the book may be reproduced or transmitted in any form or by any means without written permission from the author.

All Scripture quotations, unless otherwise marked, are taken from the King James Version of the Holy Bible, public domain.

Scripture quotations marked NKJV are taken from the New King James Version®. Copyright © 1982 by Thomas Nelson. Used by permission. All rights reserved.

Scripture quotations marked WEB are taken from the World English Bible, public domain.

Scripture quotations marked ESV are taken from the ESV® Bible (The Holy Bible, English Standard Version®), copyright © 2001 by Crossway Bibles, a publishing ministry of Good News Publishers. Used by permission. All rights reserved.

Scripture quotations marked NIV are taken from the Holy Bible, New International Version ®, NIV®, Copyright © 1973, 1978, 1984, 2011 by Biblica, Inc.™ Used by permission. All rights reserved worldwide.

Scripture quotations marked AMP or Amplified Bible are taken from The Amplified® Bible (AMP), Copyright © 2015 by The Lockman Foundation. Used by permission. www.Lockman.org.

Scripture quotations marked (NLT) are taken from the Holy Bible, New Living Translation, copyright ©1996, 2004, 2015 by Tyndale House Foundation. Used by permission of Tyndale House Publishers, a Division of Tyndale House Ministries, Carol Stream, Illinois 60188. All rights reserved.

"When I Think About The Lord" © 1998 by James Huey used with permission

AUTHORED BY:
Kasia M. Nimocks – www.kasianimocks.com
EDITED BY:
Steven A. Nimocks – steven@stevennimocks.com
Erika Mathews – Resting Life Editing – www.restinglife.com
COVER DESIGN:
Cherie Foxley – Cheriefox Book Design - www.fiverr.com/cheriefox

Published in Garfield, New Jersey USA
Hardback ISBN 978-1-7343427-0-3
Paperback ISBN 978-1-7343427-1-0
eBook ISBN 978-1-7343427-2-7
Library of Congress Control Number: 2020906435

I write this book in honor of my Lord and Savior, Jesus Christ, whom I love with all my heart. At the tender age of seven, I found myself crying out to Him because of my poverty-stricken life. In His love, He came to me and made Himself known to me. He responded to my cry by guiding me purposely to the Psalms and promising to be a Father to me:

"When my father and my mother forsake me, then the LORD will take me up" (Psalm 27:10).

He has continued to keep His promise to me.

I also write to encourage those of you who are struggling to believe God and struggling with your faith. To all those who are going through similar circumstances to what I've gone through. If you're questioning whether God truly cares and whether He really exists, I hope that as you read each page of this book, you, too, will feel Him close. I pray that you feel the presence of God and that you begin to experience the supernatural in your life through the power of your faith.

DEDICATION

I dedicate this book to my dear mother, Ms. Leila. I was your seventh child. When you were all alone with no help, you could have gotten rid of me, but you chose to love me unconditionally anyway. You gave me life and love as best as you could. For this, I'll always honor and love you.

To my dear husband, Jacob, I can never forget how much you sacrificed for me. Shortly after we got married, you used our income tax returns to purchase my shiny MacBook Pro even though we had other pressing bills. Since then, you have been willing and happy to buy every other writing device I have needed to help my writing evolve. You devoted endless hours to help me proofread every chapter of this book. Thank you so much. I love you.

To my sister, Shelly, one of my best friends and hero: I dedicate this book to you. You sacrificed your own lunch money countless times so that I would have money for transportation and a little lunch in my stomach so I could earn an education. I could never forget your kindness and love towards me.

To Sister P., Ms. Ivorene Pitters: thank you for allowing me to come to your house. If it hadn't been for your book, I wouldn't have known anything about my woman issues.

To Ms. Norma Plummer, former Vice Principal of Bridgeport High, you stepped in as a mother and gave me valuable lessons in wisdom, lunch passes, books and newspaper clippings to study for my exams. Thank you!

To Brother Beckford and Joseph Dempster my Sunday school teachers from Wildman Street: thank you for believing in me, for listening to my every cry, and for always giving me a word of encouragement.

CONTENTS

Foreword vviii
Acknowledgments iix
Introduction x

THE GIRL IN THE LITTLE WHITE DRESS

Chapter 1
My Mother's Cloak of Poverty 2

Chapter 2
I Didn't Have Any Shoes 22

Chapter 3
The Day I Wore My Mother's Underwear to School 39

Chapter 4
Poverty Almost Stole My Good Hair 47

Chapter 5
I Only Had One Dress 58

Chapter 6
My Imaginary Closet and My Little Red Sweater 79

Chapter 7
My Bed Was Broken 89

Chapter 8
We Only Had One Door 96

Chapter 9
From Going in the Bushes to Having Three Toilets 101

Chapter 10
I Went to School Barefoot 104

Chapter 11
Thank You, Mass Charlie 121

Chapter 12
Growing Up Fatherless 128

Chapter 13
God Baptized Me with the Holy Ghost and Fire! 147

Chapter 14
Miracle Money 167

Chapter 15
The Death of My Sister Restarted the Struggle 185

Chapter 16
God Sent Me to Listen to the Radio 192

Chapter 17
I Had to Leave My Mother 197

Chapter 18
My Journey to Kingston 211

Chapter 19
A Call to Faith 232

Chapter 20
The Work of the Holy Spirit 238

Chapter 21
The Holy Spirit Gave Me a Phone Number 243

Chapter 22
My New Home 255

Chapter 23
God Called Me to Bridgeport High 271

Chapter 24
How the Holy Spirit, Faith, and Prayer Can Get You the Answers You Are Looking For 282

Chapter 25
Author's Note: To Encourage You to Pray, Fast, and Exercise Your Faith 296

Chapter 26
The Faith of Kasia 308
References 315

Foreword

This book will awaken all your senses like drinking a hot cup of herbal tea laced with menthol from the pungency of the essence of eucalyptus, the tanginess of lemon and sweetness of pure honey. I caution you to have a full box of Kleenex handy because you will experience nostalgia, a giddiness of laughter, somberness of awe, and the wonder of knowing if she can survive this life's journey of pure faith, then you can find hope and true love, by seeing life through a different lens.

This masterpiece, *The Girl in the Little White Dress* is well written and will leave you longing for more. Plunge in! You will thoroughly enjoy the ride.

Margaret M. Banks

THE GIRL IN THE
LITTLE WHITE DRESS

Acknowledgments

First, let me acknowledge and give honor to my Father, the Lord Jesus Christ. He has been a good, good Father to me. When James Huey penned the lyrics for this song: *When I think about the Lord, How He saved me, How He raised me. How He filled me with the Holy Ghost. How He healed me to the uttermost. When I think about the Lord, How He picked me up and turned me around. How He set my feet on solid ground.* He wrote all the gratitude my heart felt towards the Lord.

If I were to write and declare all my love and adoration for my sweet Lord and Savior, this book would have no end.

I want to thank Don Dixon, Angella Clarke, Dr. Chiagozie Fawole, Camille Laird, Steven Nimocks, Minister Racquel Jones, Shavonne Shaw, Talina Pyne, Margaret Banks, Mouya Belford, and Ava Lynch. Thank you for all your love and support. Thank you for believing in me.

Thanks to all my friends on social media who shared and commented on every testimony I put out there. Thank you for encouraging and motivating me to write down all my testimonies, stories, and reflections into this body of creative work.

THE GIRL IN THE
LITTLE WHITE DRESS

Introduction

All of us have our pasts. Some of us have good ones and others not so much. As for me—Kasia Nimocks, Kacey, Sophia, the girl in the little white dress—I came from a background painted with the ugliest colors of poverty. Today, I know without a doubt that God is the one who orchestrated every one of my steps—and every single one of my struggles—for His will, purposes, and glory in my life. He has designed every single one of us to live a worthy life full of joy and purpose from a place of wholeness and abundance.

> *I first discovered my mother's old Bibles one day in 1988*

But what happens when you have absolutely nothing with which to cultivate that life—because you were born poor and insignificant? What then can you do to cultivate a good life for yourself?

The Journey

I am in total amazement of God and how He has used poverty to inspire my life and every chapter I record in this book. John, the author of Revelation, wrote, "And they overcame him by the blood of the Lamb, and by the word of their testimony" (Revelation 12:11a).

So why then did I pen this book? I wrote it to testify, encourage, and bring hope to every single one of God's people everywhere.

When I first began to share snippets of these testimonials during speaking engagements, with friends, with family, and especially on my social media platforms, I was amazed at the impact the word of my testimony had on so many people. Thousands of people have watched my testimonial videos and shared my stories, and I'm blown away by the responses I got. I've received hundreds of emails and direct messages from people around the world who are looking for the answer to walk away from poverty and find a better life. I promise you I don't have all the answers, but in every chapter, I will tell you who has them.

In all honesty, I never imagined myself being an author. As a little girl, the only books we had to read were Bibles. With nothing else on hand, I devoured my mother's old Bibles from book to book and chapter to chapter to feed my insatiable appetite for knowledge.

I first discovered my mother's old Bibles one day in 1988 while I was home healing from a toe injury I had suffered on my way home from school the previous day. That day, I cried out to God for hours because my life of poverty had incapacitated me. The cumbersome burden of pervasive hopelessness completely cocooned and deeply depressed me. It was so, so overwhelming. It felt like my tiny little self was being crushed on every side. The pressure was so visible; I could see and feel it as it coursed through my mind and left a painful trail that I scrabbled my thoughts on—wishing I could be emancipated from its stigma so that I could be free to actually have and live a better life. Have you ever experienced moments like that?

Every day, this poverty added more turmoil and an ugly conflict in my life. Have you ever felt like all odds were against you and you could no longer see the light of day or a way out? I saw that poverty wanted to annihilate my dreams from the inside, so it was totally up to me to find a way to do something about it. I lived in a place that did nothing to shape me, so I had to go out and shape myself, and I chose to shape myself and my future with God.

I lived in a world filled with dread and doubt—and did I mention how I suffered in invisible ways? Some days, I felt whipped by it like a little child who was sent to school wearing extra clothing in an effort to hide the scars.

I must admit, that I didn't learn very much during my elementary school days. As I walked around and played among my friends, I wore invisible scars in my heart. I'm just the poorest child, I thought. I looked happy, but I felt morose. I often cried a lot, especially at night. Mama always asked me, "Sophia, what's wrong? Why are you crying?" The burden of it crushed me—it crushed and clashed with my dreams. But it was God who gave me my life's dream in the first place—He wouldn't let what seemed like the curse of poverty rob me and swallow them up, would He?

Each day, poverty sucked away at my life like a leech. I often wondered if I would have any life by the time I was twenty. I felt like the whole world was on my seven-year-old shoulders, and I just didn't see how I could escape its yoke.

And it was during that time that I began to grapple with these questions about my life and existence. I asked God:

"Why am I poor?"

"Why was I born out of wedlock?"

"Why don't I have a father?"

"Why don't I have any clothes?"

"Why don't I have any shoes?"

He only answered one of my questions. He gave me Psalm 27 and told me that He was going to be a father to me. (I was really tired of going barefooted, and I would've preferred Him to answer my question about the shoes instead... God, I'm still mad. Just kidding!)

This was the encounter that gave my life a one-hundred-and-eighty-degree turnaround.

From that day forward, I began to read my Bible religiously. At seven, I started in the book of Psalms, and the next thing I knew, I had read all four gospels. Every day, I spent any time I could spare in the book of John. I fell in love with Paul's epistles. I would wake up just so I could take lively walks in the book of Acts. I got lost in Romans and I wanted Hebrews 11:1 to become my life's reality: "Now faith is the substance of things hoped for, the evidence of things not seen."

I didn't have parents who could buy me the things I hoped for or even what I needed to live—so I had to put all my faith in God, and I had to "hope for" everything! As you read this book, you will understand how the entire book of Hebrews became a catalyst for me. You will see how Acts 2:38 eventually changed the entire course of my life. My faith in God will always be the most important part of who I am today.

By the time I was thirteen, I had conjured up five more questions to add to the list. I asked God:

"Why am I here?"

"Who am I?"

"Where is my life going?"

"Where did I come from?"

"What is the purpose of my life?

God answered these questions by leading me on a wild journey of faith. By fifteen, I had read through the entire Bible from Genesis to Revelation several times. Although I wanted to write about the truth I was devouring, I lacked writing materials. I constantly walked around with my little green New Testament Bible because, in it, I was happy. I fell madly in love with the author and His written Word. The Bible and God became my world, my mold.

In the church, in school, and on my own, I managed to memorize several verses. These implanted verses became the weapon and energy that fueled me—and as a teenager, my entire inner life and spirit exploded. My soul matured as an adult before my time because, by seeking God's Kingdom, I learned key principles from the Bible which adults around me were clueless about.

I knew something had changed internally, but externally; poverty still slept on our doorstep like one of my mother's dogs—except that I despised poverty but loved the dogs. Poverty's most crushing pain struck in 1997 through the sudden death of my sister Juju. This nailed me, took the wind out of my sails, and pushed me to the edge of my life. The brokenness and pain traumatized me in the deep recesses of my soul, the place no one could see. Does life ever fill you with such despair that you just want to die, but deep down, you know God needs you to live? The truth is that I *love* life, and because God dwells inside me, the vigor of life is always vibrant in me—but when she was gone, I secretly wanted to die too.

Somewhere on this journey called life, I came to understand that when God presents His will for our life, He never puts a map anywhere in the blueprints explaining that His will would be easy, but He promises to be there with us all the way—even in hell. (Psalm 139:8).

This is a reminder of what God said to me, and what He's saying to you. No matter what life throws at you, "I will never leave thee, nor forsake thee." (Hebrews 13:5b) and "...lo, I am with you always, even unto the end of the world." (Matthew 28:20b).

Despite all the struggles, I took the biggest risk of my life. We decided I was going to leave my mother (by we, I mean

God and I—it was a mutual decision). What made this move risky and dangerous is that I was only fifteen years old, and I had no idea where or to whom I was going. All I had was a little mustard seed of faith — and I knew the Holy Spirit would keep me safe. If I hadn't left my mother's house, poverty might have had the last word.

Sometimes, you're going to have to get up, square your shoulders, and leave from wherever you are. Just make up your mind to obey God and leave. Naomi left Bethlehem with her husband and her two sons because they were searching for a better life during a famine. The risk cost her family, but in Moab, she met Ruth. Ruth took a risk also when she left her family behind in Moab to follow Naomi and the God she didn't know to Bethlehem of Judea. What Naomi didn't realize is that all was not lost—because her daughter-in-law, Ruth, was going to change her family lineage and her entire life forever.

Ruth also lost her husband, and when she took that risk following Naomi and her God, she had no idea she was going to meet and marry Boaz—possibly one of the richest men in Bethlehem of Judea as at the time. Isn't this most single women's dream? It's fascinating how Ruth ended up in the greatest lineage on earth, all because she took one risk — or you can call it a leap of faith. (You can read the full story in the book of Ruth in the Old Testament.)

So, with these examples before you, will you take the risk?

The Hope

I write this book for those of you who are being crushed by your situation and saying, "Where is God?" I want to tell you that God is in the poverty, the pains, the depressions, the disappointments, trauma, the scars, the loss, the turmoil, the darkness, the weakness, the divorce, the hardships, and the loneliness you're going through. And He's going to get you out just the way He got me out.

Some of you have been crushed in your heart. Failed expectations overwhelm you. You thought you should be much further along in your life, and you're not. You feel stuck—stuck in life, sabotaged by poverty like I was.

As I unpack my early life in the chapters of this book, I pray you'll hear me think and hear my voice. I hope something in these pages impregnates your thoughts, strengthens you, and stretches your faith and imagination to help to change your narratives. I pray that God will give you a seasoned word from a passage—a word that will become like a *destiny helper*…a word to give birth to your purpose and lead you into your God-designed destiny.

I feel in my spirit that God will use this book to break through some deep-seated personal things in your life. He wants to place you back in the Kingdom where you belong and give you the Kingdom's authority to break generational curses from over your life. To many of you, I believe your time has come! I believe He wants you to have the abundant life that He always had in mind…I believe God is ready to show you how to break free from whatever it is that is holding you captive. For me, it was poverty—and God, through the divine help of the Holy Spirit, freed me from its grotesque bondage. God wants to free you right now!

Let me finally take a moment to share with you the substratum of this book. It's to help you unstick your faith…and stretch it to its greatest measure in God. It's to help free you from your current place of deterioration to the Ephesians 3:20 life. It's to stop you from giving up on yourself and your dreams and show you how to live by faith and not by sight. It's to help you pray more fervently and to believe in what you've prayed for—for prayer and fasting are the key to many of the answers we are in search of today. It's for you to reject the thought that because you have many setbacks, you can't achieve true success. You need to know that you're not a mistake. There are 7.5+ billion people on the planet, and God has equipped and wired every last one of us with talents and gifts to succeed in life. You need to know that God has you here on earth for a purpose. You were made in His image and likeness; therefore, you're not designed to fail. God designed you to win and have good success. Proverbs 18:16 says, "A man's gift makes room for him, and brings him before great men" (WEB). Your God-given gift is the key to your success.

I would not be here or writing to you if I believed in my past narrative. When I allowed God to possess my spirit, the gift of His Holy Spirit changed my narrative (Acts 2:38). David was intimately acquainted with the Spirit of God and in Psalm 16:11, he said, "You will show me the path of life. In your presence is fullness of joy. In your right hand, there are pleasures forever more" (WEB). God has made known the path of life to me, and He wants you to know it, too.

The location of your birth doesn't define your destiny. It doesn't matter where you start; what matters is how you finish. You have to believe in your dreams. It's God who placed my dreams and yours inside us as little children. By rejecting ourselves and our dreams, we declare that God isn't good, isn't wise, isn't powerful, and doesn't know what He's doing. Even though I suffered so often as a child, He called to me from way down deep and told me that it doesn't matter how I suffer, or how much I was ridiculed for having only one dress, no shoes, and no father...or for being an illegitimate child. Even when people turned up their noses on me and said that I wasn't going to amount to anything, and that I would only end up having eight children or more out of wedlock like my mother—none of it was true!

If you are reading this book, and you delivered your baby out of wedlock, God will be by your side. God has a purpose and plan for your baby's life. He can lift your life up and turn it around. Your circumstances are not who you are...you have to believe that. You are enough as a person in Him, and God has more in store for you. None of the evil and pain you've suffered can define who you are in Christ. None of it matters because "And after you have suffered a little while, the God of all grace, who has called you to his eternal glory in Christ, will himself restore, confirm, strengthen, and establish you" (ESV). If you are going through this, please hold on to I Peter 5:10. None of what people says about you matters. It's not true. You're what God said you are. And when all hell is breaking loose in your life, hold on to the truth inside of you—and know that He who began a good work in you will finish it

(Philippians 1:6). God will perform what He said over your life until the day of Jesus Christ. Hallelujah!

If you can relate to my story—poverty almost took my life, but I survived—remember that God can turn your struggle into a beautiful testimony. He can turn your scars into stars, your trials into glory. He will take your pain and turn it into victory!

I want to tell you that I'm here for you. I'm nothing special, but God called me out of obscurity for your sake. These collections of inspirational testimonies are very personal to me and have been written and compiled for your benefit.

I seek to offer uplifting and insightful biblical principles and answers to many of life's difficult questions. If it feels like I try to engage with you at times, it's because I'm consciously thinking of you and have felt that I was in conversation with you at some point.

If you are in your suffering season or a storm right now. Nadia Nembhard-Hunt, author of *The Purpose of this Storm*, alluded to that when she said, "God sends storms into our lives, to get our attention, to mature us, to build us and to get the glory out of us." To you who are facing the worst storms of your lives right now, it is to you that I was called. It's for you that I wake up every day—to let you know that God hasn't abandoned you. He won't let you die until you've fulfilled His purpose and total calling for your life. He won't let you fall off the edge of your life, and when you decide to jump, even if the landing crushes, cuts, and bruises you, He is there to hold you up and sustain you.

I write to people who have been feeling stuck for a long, long time. People who are orphans. People who were born in a single-parent home. People who long for the presence of a father. People who longed to be genuinely loved. People who long to experience a supernatural breakthrough. I pour out my heart into this book because I believe I'm supposed to give you what was deposited inside me to make your life so much better.

Thank you for indulging me. It is my sincere desire that these pages would bless, encourage, enlighten, and strengthen you for the journey ahead. I hope I can pass on some wisdom that will help to cultivate your thoughts and fuel you. As you journey with me through The Girl in the Little White Dress, how about pulling up a comfy chair, grabbing a cup of your favorite coffee, tea, or any other beverage of your choice, sitting back, throwing your legs up, and taking some time to enjoy an array of inspirational and uplifting anecdotes. As you digest these words, may the Lord and Savior Jesus Christ draw you nearer and deeper unto a divine wholeness and into a closer walk with Him.

~~ With love, your Kacey! ~~

THE GIRL
IN THE LITTLE WHITE DRESS

THE GIRL
IN THE LITTLE WHITE DRESS

CHAPTER 1

My Mother's Cloak of Poverty

What a darkness I was born into. My mama wore a cloak of poverty that was like a transferable mantle that beckoned to me. This was one mantle that I detested so much.

Have you ever experienced something that tried to choke the life out of you? The condition of her life unsettled me. At such a tender age, I found it painful to witness her heart-wrenching struggles. We were a family of impecunious circumstances. Without any form of support system, she was financially unstable. She didn't have a lot of hope, and we all know that, "Hope deferred makes the heart sick, but when longing is fulfilled, it is a tree of life."(Proverbs 13:12 WEB). The stench of poverty

> *Since we had to carry water from miles away, we couldn't afford to lose any water around the house.*

increased every single day. It was worse than the stink of Lazarus, and I say that with humility. It was like a slow, choking death.

I watched her rise at daybreak five days a week. The crowing of the roosters between 5:30 and 6:00 was her morning alarm clock. Seriously, how can anyone go through life every single day, depending on a rooster to crow? I guess my mama thought that since Jesus used the crowing of roosters, she could use them, too.

But the simple truth is that she couldn't afford an alarm clock or a watch. I don't know how mama was so sure about those roosters. I was convinced she had more confidence in the roosters waking her up than confidence in any of us (her kids) waking her up.

As further evidence of our poverty, these roosters did not even belong to us. My mama depended on our neighbors, one hundred feet away, to keep her alarm clock fed. How fortunate she was to have the neighbor's roosters wake her up!

Once she was awake, I watched her go through her mundane morning rituals: prayer and washing, discretely and silently so as not to wake us up. I would hardly sleep (I still don't) because I was her most fastidious child — or maybe I am just chosen like Joseph was. Somehow, the responsibility to look after her was thrust upon me, so I watched her like a hawk.

She would wash herself behind the door, in the little corner space beside the table and the cabinet. Most of the time, she would sit a little while, rubbing her hands in a circular motion around her knees for warmth. Then she would quietly move her lips. Sometimes, her breath puffed in frosty clouds as she talked softly to Massa God before she got started because without indoor plumbing, the water was ice cold.

I would watch as she carefully reached for our broken bath pan. The pan had a crack at the bottom, and most of the rim was broken off. With necessary delicate care, she daintily rested the bath pan against the wall in the corner on top of some old floor rags for support. I would pray intently to God and ask Him to please help me to grow up fast so I could buy a new bath pan for my mama. What a prayer. Now, sometimes, I wish I was still little.

If the bath pan shifted accidentally, water would soak the floor. Since we had to carry water from miles away, we couldn't afford to lose any water around the house.

Did you ever have to carry water on your head as a child? When it didn't rain, that was our necessary daily task. The rain barrel at the back of the house sat in one place for several decades. We had to be gentle with moving it because it had a hole at the bottom — or was it its side? If we moved or shifted the barrel, we would lose all the rainwater. I think God often refilled it on purpose. Sometimes, I watched the water level lowering in the evenings, but when I checked back in the morning, the water level would be way above the mark, and it didn't rain.

Drinking water was a scarce commodity. Without money or property of our own, we couldn't afford to purchase or build a water tank. We never owned enough buckets to collect water for long term storage. My most unfavorable water memory is carrying a bucket of water from miles and miles away one late evening for us to drink. Then I'd hear splish-splash in the middle of the night because a rat had decided to take a midnight bath or maybe it was going for a swim. I don't know if I should confess to drinking rat water. Grotesque! We depended on the rain, springs, and rivers. Occasionally, the neighborhood pipes would be turned on for a few days but then, be turned off for several months. This was entirely out of our control. I don't know—maybe the "water people" took us for elephants with storage trunks!

Often, my little sister and I ended up using our mother's leftover bathwater from the night before or that morning. We used it for bathing before school or at bedtime because that's all we had.

Once my mama finished tidying up herself, she would sing old spiritual songs of Zion. I used to question her about every song she sang. The songs seemed to bring her some sort of mental stability, comfort, peace, and strength. She was the first person I ever heard sing many of the old hymns:

- When the Roll is Called Up Yonder
- Meet Me by the River
- Goodbye World, I Stay No Longer With You
- Swing Low, Sweet Chariot
- In the Sweet By and By
- Precious Memories
- We're Marching to Zion
- Telephone to Glory, Oh What Joy Divine!
- I Must Tell Jesus
- It Soon Be Done
- O It Must Be the Breaking of the Day
- The Old Rugged Cross

My mother loved the Lord. If it was raining in the morning, she would sing "Nearer My God to Thee." She was the first person from whom I heard the story of the Titanic and what songs the orchestra played while it sank. By the time I was fully immersed in my Apostolic Faith, these songs were deeply ingrained and held true meaning for me.

By the time we prepared for school, she had already swept the yard with her makeshift broom that she crafted from sticks. She had some qualities of a Proverbs 31 woman as she proudly did her best to keep her room and the yard clean and pristine for over forty years. She was humble, and she had learned how to make do with whatever she had.

Have you ever had to live any period of your life without electricity? Since we didn't have electric power or a gas stove, any cooking and heating required the use of the fireplace. That was by far the most difficult part of her morning routine.

Some folks were fortunate enough to afford fire coal. Fire coal was sold by the bag or pan, but most of the time, my mother couldn't find twenty dollars to purchase even a half bag—so we had to rely on firewood. Since my mother was alone, she had to do everything by herself with little help from the children. Like a good hunter, she always ensured that firewood was available.

In the rainy hurricane season, I prayed to God all the more. I asked him to send angels ahead of her to cut down trees so she could easily find firewood. When it poured rain, my petition became, "Please, Lord, make that firewood dry." Sometimes I would go to the kitchen to help her blow and give her some relief. I can't forget how strong and unbearable the smoke was for our eyes and throats. Unfortunately, the smoke mildly damaged her eyesight. Just imagine spending decades upon decades of your life taking in deep breaths of smoke and blowing firewood with your mouth. I don't know how she did it. It almost drove me mad.

If she didn't have any kerosene oil for making a good fire, she had to improvise with paper or plastic. I watched silently—sometimes, with tears streaming from my eyes, caused by the increased smoke. I watched and wishfully prayed and dreamed of the day when I could afford to personally purchase a four-burner gas stove for her.

Breakfast, the first meal of the day, was always a challenge. Sometimes, mama struggled to find something nutritious to prepare for breakfast and lunch. The truth is we didn't know what nutrition meant. Most times, breakfast was whatever we had left from the previous night. If we were fortunate enough to have what they called "hard dough bread" for breakfast instead of leftovers, that was always a royal treat. Sometimes, we had no choice but to carry the leftovers to school for lunch. I never did enjoy tire-wheel dumplings for lunch, but I was grateful. (We called them tire-wheel because they were huge and round like a tire.)

Normally, I left for school before mama left for work. Other times, if I ended up missing a day of school for sickness or for other reasons, it gave me an opportunity to spend time with mama.

One day, I stayed home because I had caught the measles. I decided I would watch her attentively as she got ready to go off to her farm. It was pitiful to watch her trying to sharpen her cutlass (machete) on a rusty old file. Sometimes, she was fortunate enough to borrow a file from one of the men she worked for. A file wasn't that expensive, but she couldn't come up with a single ten-dollar bill to spare to buy one for herself. Man, I thought her life was rough, and that made me dread my own life journey ahead sometimes. This part of my early life made me think of Much-Afraid from the book *Hinds' Feet On*

High Places and her travels to the High Places with the Shepherd amid all the hardships she encountered.

After mama sharpened her cutlass, I watched intently as she struggled to put on her cracked galoshes (water boots). She grabbed her worn-out crocus bag and placed either a bulla cake or the same leftover food for her lunch inside it along with a cup. She never had a proper water bottle. If she forgot her cup, she would use a folded coca leaf instead. She lived a very primitive life. Her drinking water during the day depended on whether she found a spring nearby. Somehow, she always did.

She then picked up her machete, her hoe, and maybe a fork if she was fortunate enough to borrow one. She threw them over one shoulder with her crocus bag over the other shoulder or on her head. Sometimes she worked miles from home, and her journey was always tedious on foot because she had no donkey. I was constantly praying and asking God to protect her life.

I watched until her shadow vanished up the hill and melded with the other shadows. Even though I was so young, I realized the harshness and bitterness of my mom's life, and I couldn't fully articulate the reasons. She struggled through so much to keep us fed. But I also felt that my life would be greater than the poverty that surrounded us.

She rented a single bedroom in a tenement yard, so she left me there with the rest of the women and little children.

Mama often told me that when she couldn't come up with her rent, she would have to work it off in farm labor. She cut grass and dug yam hills as any man could. She said Mass Cyrus was one of those kindhearted merciful humans who saw her destitution and showed her much needed empathy and mercy.

This life became her livelihood, but there was no way under the sun I wanted this life to be mine. No siree, Bob! She lived this life religiously for over fifty years. She did it for my siblings and I, and she never murmured one day while doing it. Once God and those roosters woke her up, she was going out to toil. She never stayed home for a day, not even if she didn't feel like going. Even when she was sick, I would still see her roll out of bed and struggle to get out to do as much as she could. I call this love. She loved us all with every fiber of her being, wouldn't you agree?

I often think of how the story of blind Bartimaeus in the tenth chapter of Mark resembles mama's story. According to the Scripture and some scholars, because of Bartimaeus's blindness, his cloak was his only material possession. I saw my mother's poverty in the same way as Bartimaeus's blindness. Her poverty hindered her as his blindness had hindered him—and this rendered them poor.

Because of Bartimaeus's blindness, he had no choice but to live poverty-stricken. He was totally unable to properly provide for himself. Some studies have stated that Bartimaeus's cloak may have been his only shelter and warmth. Others have said he used the cloak to collect alms. Since he was a beggar, he had to spread out his cloak on the ground to receive coins or food from passersby. The cloak served as his daily salvation—it was used to help him survive his desperate situation.

Like Bartimaeus, I saw her, living in low status, a single woman with absolutely no one beside her, no financial or emotional help, a stranger in the district, with no one of kin to turn to, no one to depend upon in the community. She was alone, and that bothered me. No one gave her anything for free. She wasn't a beggar and was never lazy; she worked tirelessly and hard.

I wondered about my mama every day. God never created women to fight and struggle alone. Think of how hard it is to mother two or three children today—let alone mothering eight fatherless children all by yourself.

After seeing my mama off that day, I retreated to our room and closed the door behind me. I sat on her bed and wept profusely because my heart was stricken with grief. It churned my stomach and burned into my young soul.

At that moment I noticed, for the first time, how broken our bed was. Her bed was the best place to sit and think since we had no chairs. As I sat examining her life and how her decisions had affected her and all of us, I was daunted by the reality of her life.

You must understand that my mother didn't just one day decide that she too wanted to wear this cloak. Absolutely not! She inherited it from her mother, who inherited it from her own mother. Mama started wearing this cloak from way before the early passing of her mother.

After mama completed school, she worked as domestic help for a teacher and her family, but after a little while she became pregnant. (Mama was fortunate to learn how to speak proper English). I am number seven, so by the time she gave birth to me, the cloak of poverty had submerged her deeper in severe destitution. She had little or no hope of freeing herself from its bitter bondage.

Have you ever felt like you were carrying the weight of your family? I knew I wanted to help her. But how could I help? I was only seven.

I quickly realized that this cloak touched the lives of my siblings. The cycle almost repeated itself with my eldest sister. And this same cloak now chased after me, but I refused to let it catch and conquer me.

It was as though God purposefully removed the veil from my young eyes to show me her life of poverty up close and personal. He was intentionally using it to teach me and to warn me about my own life choices. Truly, the preview was mind-blowing, heart-wrenching, and very real.

As I sat on my mama's broken-down bed, I began to zero in. I took stock of everything my mama owned. The word of God says, "Houses and wealth are inherited from parents." (Proverbs 19:14a, NIV), but none of us had anything to inherit from her—no inheritance, no heirlooms, nada! This discovery disturbed my spirit.

However, thoughts of decorating and rearranging the room before my mother returned home perked me up slightly. I touched her champagne color lace curtain hanging at the window. It had hung there for as long as I could remember. Every major holiday she removed the curtain, washed it, and rehung it. I could see so vividly how much the color had faded. I took a closer look and noticed patches of all different sorts of threads sewn into it like an expression of art to keep it from falling apart. I realized just how old and dry rotted that curtain was. Yet I had a grand plan: I would stir up the house and search every nook and cranny to find a better piece of curtain.

In our room, we had two medium size beds directly beside each other up against the walls. Against the adjacent corner, we had our table. The foot of the bed had a trunk attached that slightly overlapped the table. When we were little and could fit in the space, we sat on the trunk like a bench and ate there at the table. As we grew, we sat on the floor. This was the scene I contemplated rearranging as I looked over our little matchbox room.

First, I wanted to look inside the trunk. I crawled under the table to try with all my strength to open the trunk, yet very quickly I discovered that it was a difficult task. At last, I was able to strain the lid open. But about halfway, I caught a glimpse of uncountable crawling creatures, and, in horror, I slammed it shut as fast as I could. The table became unstable due to the movement of its supporting trunk. It shifted its weight onto me, preventing my rapid flight away from the disgusting vermin. I'm not exaggerating. It was grotesque.

I laughed so hard. I thought to myself, "We are seriously destitute, and I am in deep trouble." When I tallied up stocks and trunk, we truly had nothing. Everything was broken.

I must confess, the table hadn't been moved from its place in decades, and that put a damper on my decorating spirit. I murmured because I couldn't move anything. So I opened everything else we had. I found no curtains. I couldn't make any changes to the room. I was livid. My mother was much poorer than any church mouse. She was the poorest woman I knew in our community. I still haven't met any other woman today who was as poor as she was. She had no status and no personal possessions other than her quiver full of eight fatherless children.

Is it possible to feel depressed and optimistic simultaneously? When I pondered her situation, I gave myself permission to hope a little because of how her life was made so bitter without much sweetness. I suppose we brought her some joy, but how sweet can the joy of children be when you don't have anything much to offer to them?

I reflected on the life of Naomi returning home from Moab and how very distraught she was about the bad hand life had dealt her. "I went out full, and the Lord hath brought me home again empty," murmured Naomi (Ruth 1:21a). She felt her name should be changed to Mara, which means bitter. A season of her life was bitter, but in reality, it was bittersweet because of Ruth. She had no idea that her life was fully sweet from the beginning—and sweeter than the honey in the honeycomb.

Sometimes, our circumstances can turn our lives bitter. Naomi's life was sweet in comparison to my mama. Mama's was simply bitter from the start. If Naomi had known beforehand how her story would end, she would have considered the journey home to be much sweeter, and she no doubt would have kept her name which means "pleasantness."

Being the creative child that I was, I decided to use my only prized possession—my imagination—to dream up a lovely home for my mama. This imaginary house was filled with gorgeous lace curtains, comfortable beds, a sturdy table with nutritious food, and of course better clothing. Yet by the time mama returned home that evening, I couldn't help but feel disheartened that I couldn't make our home better.

However, my love for her had grown more that day, and I just wanted to grow up and help her live a better life.

The Word of God says we should help and pity the poor. Mama was the first poor person I learned to help and love. "'Honor your father and mother,' which is the first commandment with a promise" (Ephesians 6:2, WEB).

She made it home safely after toiling hard all day long. She rested and then moved on to making our dinner. I tried to help. After dinner, she cleaned herself up and sat alone at the bottom of the bed on the trunk—the same trunk I'd tried and failed miserably to open. That was her place in our small, one-room abode to sit, talk to God (and herself), think, plan, and enjoy her moments of serenity.

The busted water boots she wore dripped from the rain, and so did her feet. She had no choice but to wear her old ones until she was able to purchase another pair in months or years. I watched her wake up that night due to arthritic pain in her knees. Pulling herself towards the bottom of the bed, she reached for the lamp on the table. She screwed off the burner, wet her hand with kerosene from the wick. Then she warmed her hand over the flames and began to rub her knees hoping for relief. I watched her suffer when she had no kerosene in the lamp to use for home remedy, and that happened frequently. What would break my heart is when her whitlow finger would also hurt in the middle of the night. (Whitlow is a painful infection that affect your finger or thumbs).

I stayed up with her even though I couldn't do anything except pray and cry in my heart for my mama's healing. When you're poor, you can't even afford to buy pain meds. To those of you who suffer from chronic pain, I completely understand. I wanted to beat poverty until it was dead.

Have you ever gone to sleep and woken up a completely different person? My prayer to God that night changed me before I emerged out of bed the next morning. Poverty has the propensity to change you, and so does prayer—and I was completely transformed.

It's like I went to sleep as a seven-year-old child, but when I woke up the next morning, I was involuntarily catapulted into my adulthood. You might be wondering if that is even possible. I wondered the same thing, too! It's real as day, because it happened to me. I believe God heard my prayer, and He changed, rewired, and reset my mind while I slept in the wee hours of that morning. It felt as though God literally fast-forwarded my mind into my future and gave me a brand-new hope and vision. I believe this was one of His ways of saving me from my mother's cloak.

After that, whenever I would pray at night, I would always anticipate waking up in the morning. Maybe, just maybe somehow, I would wake up filthy rich like Job.

Yes, it may have seemed that poverty had made its home with my mama and her lineage for generations, but I fought back because I couldn't let it have me or my mind. Some of you right now are under severe attacks because you are breaking generational curses, and you don't even know it! When you refuse to accept the status quo, chains break, and walls come down. If you're wondering, "But Kacey, you were just a little girl; how can you say and know these things?"

First and foremost, nothing about me was normal! I was a spunky and fastidious child. I know it was God who gave me my semblance of normalcy. My normal was different from everyone else's normal. Maybe I was the black sheep of the family: the Joseph, the maverick, the lone wolf, who knows?

I believe the Lord pulled a Philippians 2:5 on me, "Let this mind be in you, which was also in Christ Jesus." And He mixed in a little of Romans 12:2, "And be not conformed to this world: but be ye transformed by the renewing of your mind, that ye may prove what is that good, and acceptable, and perfect, will of God." It was the divine work, divine will, and purpose of God! I was operating from my seven-year-old body, but God had changed my mindset, my thinking, and my thought pattern — my entire perspective on my life had changed. Maybe I should say He literally hijacked my heart, too!

My mother treated me as a child, but it was not who I was. Sure, I was in a child's body, but my spirit was way beyond my years. I know that sounds counterintuitive, but it's not. For example, some people saw my mother's poverty, and they began to believe that all of her children are bound to become just like her. That's how you can be stereotyped and misconstrued because of the home, family, or community you came from, but somehow God had begun the work of setting a new trajectory for my future.

I remember reading in the Gospels of how people criticized Jesus for his hometown. They said, "Can anything good come out of Nazareth?" (John 1:46). But praise be to God that where you come from doesn't define you. Always remember that what you are born to do is so much greater than where you are right now. Just look at Jesus' life.

I want to take this time to encourage you, my sweet readers. To some, you may have come from nothing or nowhere, but with the power of Jesus living inside you, your life can impact your generation and your world. Even at such a tender age, my existence wasn't defined by my mother's poverty nor by my surroundings. The woman God wove inside me saw and knew more.

God, my mother, and I knew that I was different from the children in my community. During this season of my life, I wanted to know everything. So, I questioned God about everything. I know it might sound strange, but I believe God downloaded part of His mind inside of mine. Of course, I know I could never contain all of God's vastness and might, but I know I have His DNA and wits, His tenacity and Spirit; with Him, I was ready to conquer the world and disrupt any mold!

Brewing inside was the passion to recreate my surroundings from within. I was determined not to let the Goliath of poverty defeat me. If you're reading this book and you can't see your way out of your obscurity, if you're suffering or feeling like your circumstance is defeating you, can I encourage you to take on the mind of Jesus Christ? 2 Timothy 1:7 tells us, "For God hath not given us the spirit of fear; but of power, and of love, and of a sound mind." Use your mind and imagination as a weapon to fight back. I did it and won, and so will you.

God gave us our mind to think, serve and be creative with Him, and when we put on the mind of Christ, we possess conquering power over predicaments. The Bible says, "Now to Him who is able to do far more abundantly than all that we ask or think [imagine], according to the power at work within us" (Ephesians 3:20, ESV). I believe what God's Word says, and I decided to immerse myself in it.

Moreover, Paul encouraged us to continuously think this way. "Finally, brethren, whatsoever things are true, whatsoever things are honest, whatsoever things are just, whatsoever things are pure, whatsoever things are lovely, whatsoever things are of good report; if there be any virtue, and if there be any praise, think on these things" (Philippians 4:8).

I purposely and steadfastly rethought my life. I had to rule over this poverty in my mind first, even though the reality of it was so palpable. My plan was to use the Word of God as a weapon to annihilate the curse of poverty. I read in Matthew 4:4 where Jesus uses nothing but the written Word and rejected Satan's idea. I had to use my imagination and faith until the life I deserve became my reality. The Word of God says, "Beloved, I wish above all things that thou mayest prosper and be in health, even as thy soul prospereth" (3 John 1:2). I was determined to prosper, so I wasn't going to let poverty choke out my gifts, my talents, my potential, and my life purpose. I know every one of us is called, and our destinies go way beyond the perpetuity of our current situation or circumstances.

There is a supreme moment of destiny, and it was calling my name, and it's calling your name today. I desired to live a full life of faith, health, and wealth—and not of poverty even though poverty was like a schoolmaster to me. Please tell me that's what you desire as well. A life full of prosperity!

Jesus Christ said to me—to us—in the book of John, "The thief does not come except to steal, and to kill, and to destroy. I have come that they [you and me] may have life and that they may have it more abundantly." (John 10:10, NKJV)

Life more abundantly! Generously, inexhaustibly, richly, sufficiently, affluently, fulsomely, luxuriantly, satisfactorily. This is the Kingdom life God promises us. So I rise to the occasion and take full Kingdom dominion and authority in Jesus' name!

CHAPTER 2

I Didn't Have Any Shoes

If Jesus wore sandals, why didn't I have any shoes? I grew up as the little barefooted girl in the small farming community called Litchfield located in the Parish of Trelawny, country of Jamaica, West Indies. One chilly September morning in 1988, I woke up with my big toe in stinging pain and pounding away like crazy. My head throbbed with pain. I knew exactly what the problem was: The previous day I had gone to school barefooted simply because I was too poor to afford a pair of shoes — and oh boy, I did buck (stub) my big toe severely. The tip was peeling away from the nail.

> *I needed rescuing from what seemed like an eternal pain.*

That Tuesday morning, I sat on my mother's broken-down bed, unable to attend school, thinking of all my friends at school that morning without me. We had no transportation and I couldn't just hop my way to school like a country frog because it was miles away from home.

My toe left me miserable in mind as well as in body. As the morning transitioned into the day, heavy gloominess settled over me—so heavy that it suppressed my agility. I found my body unable to move, so I just sat there, pitied myself, and gave myself permission to cry.

I tilted my head over and looked down at my big toe hanging off the side of the bed. It was wrapped up with a piece of old white sheet my mother had managed to dig out from underneath her decrepit ancient mattress. She didn't have any proper antiseptic to use to wash the wound, so she improvised with a bit of kerosene from her old burnt-out lamp wick. I was happy the bleeding had ceased. However, the pain from my big toe sent shock waves to my brain, and I started behaving eccentrically.

Please don't laugh at me when I tell you, I began to talk to my feet. Oh, wait a minute—you never talk to your feet or any of your other body parts? Come on now. I know I can't be the only one! The dialogue was short. I said, "Foot, if only you were covered with a shoe, whether old or new, you wouldn't have succumbed to this unnecessary injury, and you wouldn't be sitting here today dangling." Oh boy, I am mighty glad that my foot did not respond back to me that day! Ha!

I whined, "If only I had the proper learning materials, I would have been further along. If only I had the proper wardrobe, I could dress stylishly for church or I could be more involved in sports and other activities. If only I had all the things I needed, I would have been at school like everyone else right now." I sighed over and over; my sighing had an attitude. I was so sick and tired of missing out on school, missing out on church activities, and missing out on my life simply because I didn't have the things that I needed to get to the life I wanted. It was a shame.

I wondered long and hard how I could change my narrative. I felt my agitated body begin to convulse. I saw big teardrops trickling and splattering off the side of my face like angry raindrops. If only I could just drown out all my sorrow in them. What was I upset about? I truly wasn't sure. My grief sounded loud! It felt like I was mourning the loss of a loved one.

I muttered something like, "Okay, Sophia, it's only your big toe that's hurt, girl; your life isn't over, you know!"

But it most certainly felt like my life was over at that moment. After all, I was home and I wasn't the mischievous type, so I couldn't generate trouble. My school life was certainly passing me by. Every element of my life seemed to come to a halt that day.

My heart raced faster as I wondered what I was going to do tomorrow. I worried about where my mother would find money to purchase a pair of shoes for my return to school. Would she score a hand-me-down from my sister Shelly, as she did with my little white royal dress? I didn't even have any options. A sea of hopelessness hovered around me. I found it difficult to breathe.

I needed rescuing from what seemed like an eternal pain. I looked down, and my lap was covered in teardrops. I burst out in heavy hysterics at the top of my lungs. The sound came up from the inner recesses of my soul. I didn't care who was inside the tenement yard that might have heard me as I vociferated. I thought, if this is going to be my future, there's no way I can handle it—no way!

With all my might, I cried out to the God of David in my distress—even though I didn't know who He was yet.

If anyone passed by and gave a second thought to the sound that came from our room, one would have thought I had done something terribly wrong, and my mother was whooping the devils out of me. It was the ugliest cry to be heard.

I admit that I was very desperate. I figure the louder the cry then the quicker God might respond. I had gone to Sunday school as often as I could, but I didn't know who God truly was in-depth. All I knew was that I was fed up with the condition of my life. I sat there hammering my head in my palms, thinking, if I could just get a hold of this God that Ms. Clara taught me about in Sunday school, I would tell Him what was wrong, and He would fix my situation. Surely, He would provide shoes for my lowly feet.

Filled with anxiety, I felt the room moving about me. Was I going mad? Then something bubbled up from my unconscious based on all I'd learned about the Queen. I had a love for writing, so I made several attempts in my mind to pen the Queen of England a letter just to ask her to spare a girl a pair of shoes. This was the best I could do since we didn't even have any good writing paper, pencils, or pens with supporting ink.

Like a bird, I just wanted freedom from my gilded cage of poverty. Poverty shackled my shoeless ankles. I wanted shoes. I sobbed at the thought that all I needed was for someone to come into my life and set me free from poverty. I talked with God, and I wept because my young life was full of so many setbacks and obstacles.

Do you ever close your eyes and wish that at the snap of your fingers, you could open your eyes, and what you desire would appear? But then you realize the truth about life, and your inner self begins talking back at you telling you, "Baby girl, life doesn't work that way!" At this point, you realize you'll have to work twice as hard, like Lady Cinderella, and just maybe a Prince or an opportunity will come your way and rescue you.

I laid back on the bed and turned my head up towards our dilapidated ceiling, which was ready to cave in any day now! As I turned up the volume on my crying, I opened my big mouth before God, and I blatantly asked Him:

"Why am I so poor?"

"Why was I born out of wedlock?"

"Why don't I have any clothes?"

"Why don't I have any shoes?"

"Why don't I have a father?"

My younger self had such audacity. Oh, Lord, be merciful unto me even now! I didn't know what type of rescue or response I was going to receive with such vulgarism. The truth is that none of it was ostentatious. I was being real and honest. I didn't know exactly what I was hoping for. It was all ambiguous. I do know, however, that I wanted God to answer me. I was a desperate little girl. I wanted to know that He actually knows my name, address, and the exact position I was in at the moment. If what was happening to me was a life trial, I wanted to know how it would end and if I would have a far better quality of life.

Limitless tears bounced off the sides of my face, fell into my eardrums, and created a stillness. I continued to stare away into the ceiling as if I was staring into the tapestry of the deep white and blue skies of the heavens. As I sobbed uncontrollably, the atmosphere around me began changing. I felt a sudden shift.

I know you might find this odd and hard to believe, and, to be honest, it was mind-boggling for me to believe when it happened. But once I got to know more of God, I soon realized that God was quite capable of pulling off some crazy-out-of-this-world-impossible stuff!

This is noteworthy. I was reading in Exodus 4:4, where God told Moses, "Reach out your hand and take [the snake] by the tail" (NKJV). Every smart shepherd, whether in heaven or on any planet, knows that you never pick up a snake by its tail. Child, you can never expect the ordinary with the Most High God!

Even now, God is looking for any opportunity to awe, amaze, and wow you out of your mind! So just go ahead and let Him. He wants to saturate you with His Word in His world with His love. Don't be afraid. Only trust Him.

His Word is living truth. If you're passing through a difficult season, trials are rising, darkness surrounds you, and everything becomes so dense that you cannot see your way through, God has the power to deliver you! Only believe, my friend. You read of God meeting with Adam, Moses, and the others, right? Why can't He meet with you and me now? Today, even this very moment.

Oh, friend, consider me blessed among women like Mary because He came to me, too—little bitty ole me, and I know He wants to meet with you! You only need to believe. In his book, *The Power of Faith,* Smith Wigglesworth trusted wholeheartedly in the words of Jesus. In almost every chapter, he never ceases to remind us to "Only believe." "All things are possible to him who believes" (Mark 9:23, NKJV), and Mark 9:24, "Lord, I believe; help thou mine unbelief." We only need to trust, obey and believe. Jesus says, "Don't be afraid, only believe" (Mark 5:36, WEB). If you ever had a real-life encounter with the true Holy God of Abraham, Isaac, and Israel, you would believe how very real this experience was for me.

As the presence of God permeated our tiny little room, very quickly, it became hot—hot like the sun. I began to sweat profusely like a wild horse. God showed up inside my room. I smelled the fragrance of His presence. It felt like He was sitting right beside me. By this time, I felt like I was literally on fire. I felt the fumes like smoke exiting my lungs. My heart raced. I panicked. I felt chills shooting up my spine.

Then it grew slightly cool—a cool breeze even. I shut my eyes tightly. Sudden energy coursed through me, seeking release. I felt the gentle Spirit of God move. My body shivered.

The hair on my neck stood tall. My inside churned. Then God spoke. I heard His audible voice for the very first time.

How fortuitous that God showed up immediately and responded to my request—as though He had always been there waiting and ready to answer me. And in a soft whisper, He said my name. "Sophia, Sophia,"—but it really sounded like He was summoning me by my heavenly name—"Open up the headboard."

I was floored. I couldn't believe God was talking to me. He was drawing my diverted attention to Him and His written Word.

With no hesitation, I sprinted towards the headboard. But then, I abruptly stopped. For years—three to be exact—I had tried relentlessly to open that stubborn headboard to no avail. My mother and siblings gave up on it years before I even started. Curiosity nearly killed me. I wondered every single day what was in that headboard.

Mama said that's where our birth certificates were kept. We were much too poor for me to even consider that there might be some paper money stashed away inside. If that had been the case, mama would certainly have made greater effort to open it. She probably would have chopped her way through with her machete. Even just a couple hours before God showed up, I had tried to open the stubborn thing again. But trust me,

God was totally up to something when He said, "Open up the headboard."

I slid my tiny fingers right behind the cracks and yanked it wide open. I was in sweet astonishment that it yielded so quickly! And then, of course, creeping things from Adam with many legs ran and crawled every which way echoing their greetings. And no, this time, I wasn't scared of those vermin—just in case you were wondering. The epic bed trunk moment had prepared me for part two. Besides, you feel no fear when the creator of the universe is inside your room.

There was nothing inside the headboard except for papers and some Bibles, a lot of Bibles. The first thing I reached for was a little green New Testament Bible. Tucked away inside of it was my mother's birth certificate, which had been severely eaten by the vermin—nothing much was left. Later, I discovered that mine was missing and the others were in poorer condition than hers. We all had to apply for new ones at some point.

Again, I heard the audible voice of God say, "Open up the Bible." I immediately obeyed and opened my Bible directly to Psalm 27. Psalm 23 was a staple in our community, school, and Sunday school class; well known by church members and nonchurch goers alike. But I didn't know what Psalm 27 said because I'd never read that chapter before. But as I began to read, my heart melted when I saw verse ten. And then it became difficult for me to breathe.

I couldn't believe what my eyes and heart had seen. "When my father and my mother forsake me, then the LORD will take me up" (Psalm 27:10). I knew my mother hadn't forsaken me in any way, but the feeling of knowing that I have someone like God who was willing to help, that was all I needed. At this point, as the Word of God penetrated my aching heart, I tried to receive and digest the Word. I heard God's audible voice in a soft whisper, saying once more, "I'll be a father to you, my daughter."

My heart lingered and listened to the quiet echo of His voice and then I heard my heart drop to the floor—*bloop*!

I don't know—maybe I died at that moment and came back to life. And when I came back to life, I felt like I had achieved or experienced something pregnant with meaning. It was so surreal. I don't know exactly how to explain or express such an encounter in mere words. But it was the most invigorating move by God yet. I asked Him some questions, and He didn't hesitate to answer me by showing up. God showed up in my room! Crazy, wowzer! He didn't make any mention of my shoe situation, and that was the biggest question brewing, but can I truly tell you how flabbergasted I was! It would take me years before I ever asked God another "why question" after such an encounter.

When God is at work, He will prove Himself mighty. As I mentioned above, I didn't know who God was at the time—so this experience was shocking and nerve-racking! I couldn't believe what I was reading nor what my ears heard. I had a gradient of emotions. My chest tightened. I fell to the floor, sobbing and trembling.

If Yahweh God brings you into oneness and fellowship with Himself, your human nature will tremble in His presence, and you will never be the same. Something spectacular had transpired. The God of heaven made a covenant with me in my room. It was transcendent! The energy that coursed through my anatomy was surreal. All my senses were immediately engaged at the moment. I couldn't believe God came down to me. I couldn't believe He heard my plea. I couldn't believe He told me He would be a father to me—and that He was going to take care of me. As a child in need of help, that's what I needed all along.

I truly believe that God longs to have a deep-seated relationship with us. This intimacy existed between God and Adam, Abraham, Enoch, Seth, and Noah, just to name a few. In Exodus, Moses and God demonstrated that intimacy. God spoke from the pillar of clouds and talked with Moses through the burning bush. God even allowed Moses to see His glory.

I always thought I needed someone to take over from mama and just help a little to take care of me. That truly was my heart's cry and desire. Psalm 37:4 says, "Delight thyself also in the Lord, and He shall give thee the desires of thine heart." At the time of my encounter, I didn't know this verse. However, it was quite fortuitous that whilst I lamented, I had delighted myself in the Lord, even though I was unaware that He took pleasure in me.

As you know, to "delight yourself in the Lord" means to delight in God and to see Him as your ultimate pleasure.

I don't understand it all—I am still learning—but when you delight in God as your intimate savior and friend, when you delight in His care, in His protection, in His love, in His provision, and in His desire to have that kind of intimate personal relationship with you, He will show up, just like He did with me, Enoch, Noah, Seth, Abraham, Moses, Samuel, Joshua, Joseph, Mary, and many others.

When I cried out to Jesus, I was left startled that the God of heaven inclined His ear to my cry (Psalm 40:1). For all I know, I was just frustrated and at my wit's end, and I think I snapped! Have you ever heard of a seven-year-old, who has barely scratched the surface of her life, hitting rock bottom?

Looking back, it seems like that's when I had my first mental breakdown: an hour before I met God. Y'all, I broke down over not having any father or shoes. That's some serious stuff. I can't believe I had to have a mental breakdown for God to come down to my rescue. Ha!

That day is forever etched in my mind. I may see it as a mental breakdown, but God saw all my heart taking delight in Him. He changed my whole heart that day. Dramatic, nerve-racking, and cool describe the way He introduced Himself to me. All I know is that God answered my prayer that day. I prayed one simple prayer, and Jesus heard. And I want to tell you through my story that God still answers prayers today.

Recently, a friend of mine posted a picture of a young man whose shoes didn't fit him anymore, and it caught my attention. In the picture, he wore a pair of shoes that were too small for his feet. He had broken down the back for suitability and room. I was so moved by it, and I broke down in tears. I made inquiries and sought out who the young man was. I wasn't at all surprised when I learned that the shoes belonged to one of his friends who had gotten a new pair and thought it would be kind to hand over the extra pair to his friend.

It didn't matter to him that his shoes couldn't fit. A fire ignited in him—he wanted something more than a pair of shoes. This young man was determined to get an education and whatever else life had to offer him. He got out of bed, got dressed, slid on his shoes, and made his way to school wearing those shoes. I thought, "Even in his state, he was still better off than I was. He had something to wear, and I had nothing to wear."

We had something in common. We shared something far greater than what was happening in our circumstances. Something greater ignited the fire that drives our spirits. It was his dream, his purpose. Shoes are important, but I can't help but think of what Solomon wrote in Ecclesiastes: "For to him that is joined to all the living there is hope: for a living dog is better than a dead lion" (Ecclesiastes 9:4).

Having *life* is better, and a good life at that. It doesn't matter how hard life gets; you can't give up. Shoes or no shoes, keep moving forward. Be grateful for the little you have. Always believe, pray, and hope that one day, your life will improve.

My life did improve, but the truth is that I still had to finish the rest of the school year as "the shoeless" girl. One would think that after God made such a magnificent entrance into our room and my life that day, that He would send down Michael or Gabriel — or anybody, somebody, hello! — the next day or following week to give me a care package including a pair of shoes — but oh no, He didn't. I have learnt with God; everything is a process!

Instead, He gave me Himself. I eventually came to realize that I had successfully *"invoked God's presence"* in my life, and that altered my state of mind and my destiny forever! From poor to rich, coursing with a primal energy that transformed a simple moment in time into an enlightening experience.

The whole thing was a setup! It was never really about the shoes! God orchestrated the plan. Baby, if you should buck your big toe, praise God! Because there's a lesson in it.

He gifted Himself to me. He gave me lesson after lesson in love. He offered me Himself because He's all we really need to survive. I found my love. He became my king, lover, and dear friend. He was so lovely and inviting. When God comes into your life, He will fill you up with Himself. You will find Him to be fulfilling. And trust me, if He said He'll take care of the sparrows, rest assured, my friend, that He's going to take care of you (Matthew 6:26).

He will carry us through the difficult times of the "haves" and the "have-nots." In all of this, He's proven Himself to be true and faithful to me. He said He wouldn't put more on me or you than we can bear. He promised that if we seek Him first, He will provide and add all the other things that we need to have. If there was ever a time when you had no shoes, or maybe you were poor, or maybe you were born out of wedlock, or maybe you were called a bastard, or maybe you have no father but somehow, God showed up and provided for you; you are special and blessed.

If you've overcome the worst, you are indeed blessed. Please stop to think about where you came from. And don't forget to thank the Lord for the things you have now that you once prayed for. Be kind and bless someone else who needs a helping hand. Encourage someone with your story of how you overcame it. You'll never know how far your kindness can reach.

Needless to say, the Lord kept His promise to me. It's been more than thirty years since the Lord made me that promise, and He's still keeping His Word to me. He's the best father I could ever ask for. He gives me what I need daily. So I give back all my life to Him. "By him, therefore, let us offer the sacrifice of praise to God continually, that is, the fruit of our lips giving thanks to his name" (Hebrews 13:15).

CHAPTER 3

The Day I Wore My Mother's Underwear to School

Recently, while organizing my mother-in-law's bedroom, I found a set of brand-new Hanes cotton underwear. She quickly said, "I want you to have them."

I scurried away, but while I was walking, the Lord tickled me and we both started laughing. No kidding! I always knew God had a sense of humor. He reminded me of the day when I had to wear my mother's underwear to school. I giggled so hard. But it was the worst day ever.

> *I searched high and low and couldn't find one decent pair of underwear.*

Unbeknownst to my mother-in-law, the story had triggered a memory in me that brought me to tears. I retreated to my room, closed the door behind me, and wept in deep recollection. Sometimes, when you recognize where the Lord has brought you from, it causes you to weep like Jesus weeping over his friend, Lazarus.

I counted ten pairs of underwear. Mark this, friend, the Lord has been generous to help me prosper with bountiful abundance in the underwear department ever since then. From my retrospection, no one has ever offered me ten brand-new pairs of underwear at once just because.

I know it's not a big deal to some, but maybe it is to others. The memory of something so elementary yet so very humbling would make anyone grateful. Needless to say, I reminisced and wept some more. That day is forever engraved in my memory. Have you ever experienced anything like this in your childhood?

Allow me to take you back a little. I had no shoes, I only had one little white dress, and to make matters worse, I didn't have any underwear.

I remember that bright bleak morning of September 1st, 1986 like it was yesterday. The Saturday morning prior, mama sent me to ask Ms. Henna, our seamstress, for leftover scraps from uniform material. That Sunday evening, my mother, with great pride, sewed me a cloth bag out of the scraps.

Can I tell you the truth? As humble as I was, I was petrified. I thought to myself, "What in the world is mama doing?" Mama had the ability to invent certain things she couldn't afford to buy. I've seen her sew a cloth bag for my sister, Shelly, with her (lefty) left hand. Let me say this in the most modest way. My mama was like the worst shot in the west. Some people with left-handedness can stitch, but my mama, not so much. Deep down, I was praying and wishing to have a regular bag like most kids, but mama kept on knitting away because mama didn't even have two pennies to rub together to purchase school supplies. Things were bad.

For the finishing touch, she stitched my pet name, "Sophia," in a beautiful pale pink hue that looked stunning against my sailor-blue bag. The moment she handed that bag to me, I put it over my shoulder to get a feel — and then I picked it up in my hands to examine my mother's artistry. And that's when I noticed the way she designed my name.

She started out stitching across horizontally. She stitched a super big "SOP" across at the top, and then she ran out of space, and so she had to curve down vertically at the end of the P. She tried her best to stitch a tiny "hia" to finish my name. Mama felt accomplished, but I was terrified. Not only was I taking a cloth bag to school, but my name was stitched crookedly. Today, I think it would make a totally hip handcrafted bag, but back then, I didn't think so.

I was grateful for my cloth bag, but I had mixed emotions over the whole thing. So, I decided the best thing to do was to turn the front part in towards me so that no one would see my name. Sorry, mama!

I wore my old, used uniform from the previous school year since mama couldn't afford to make a new purchase for more uniform material. Trust me when I say God must have favored me, because He caused the same things that happened to the Israelites' clothing to happen to me.

Read the passage for yourself: "Thy raiment waxed not old upon thee, neither did thy foot swell, these forty years" (Deuteronomy 8:4). Except that the color faded a bit, that uniform still fit me well. The only new school items I possessed were my handmade cloth bag, one blue exercise book with the national hummingbird on it, and half of a pencil (my sister got the other half). Hey oh, hey! Poor girl problems!

As I began dressing for the first day of school, I suddenly realized I had no underwear to wear! I searched high and low and couldn't find one decent pair of underwear. Mama was outside in our little dirt kitchen. I dashed outside and ran towards the kitchen, muttering to myself, "Surely mama must have bought us underwear and forgot to tell us or give it to us." I found her singing as she warmed up the overnight rice and peas for our breakfast.

I tried to unburden myself to her about my morning dilemma, but I was so flustered I could hardly get the words out. She moved away from the fireside and kept on singing and beating coffee inside her broken mortar. I said hurriedly, "Mama, I have no underwear to wear to school today."

She responded, "Just wear one of mine."

What did I hear? Was she kidding? For a couple of seconds, I stood dumbfounded. I was tiny and my mother was—well, she was much older and she, by no means, was a woman of small stature.

Eyebrows furrowed, I think I rolled my eyes. Whatever could she possibly mean by just saying, "You can wear one of mine"? She made it sound so easy. But I quickly realized my mama was serious. I had no other choice. I didn't want to be late for school. I ran back inside the house and put on my mother's undies. Lord have mercy! It was more than twice my size, and of course, mama helped me to put a big knot at the waist, so it wouldn't bulge out nor fall off my waist.

But don't you think mama was resourceful? We both laughed so hard, or maybe we cried over my poor girl problems that morning. How very thoughtful of my mother!

I thought, for a moment, that this would be a good secret to keep between mama and I that no one will ever hear about. But it's too good of a secret to keep. Thanks to God and my mother-in-law for bringing out this sweet story out of me!

With great confidence in my mother's idea, off to school I went. I couldn't run and I couldn't walk at my normal pace; I just had to move daintily. But lo and behold, I got to school and went to the latrine to examine the state of my "unfashionable style" and—my, oh my! Nothing was there! It was gone like the wind. Unbeknownst to me, I had walked right out of it. I lost it! I lost my mother's one and only new pair of underwear somewhere along the way.

I bawled a little because underwear was not easy to come by and it was the only good one mama had left.

For the rest of the morning, I found it difficult to concentrate. I wondered if mama would beat me. Mama was left-handed. She couldn't stitch straight, but she could give a good whooping with that lefty. It was no use worrying; I would have to face her.

Fortuitously (I recently learned this cool word from my husband!), I had a sister who was at her relative's house close by the school. She loaned me the only good pair she had, too.

Have you ever experienced anything like this? My life was one bag of upside-down drama! Sounds nothing like a fairytale, right?

To live in poverty is just the worst experience anyone could ever have, I thought! My sister Juju still had to make another knot for me. Talk about a knotted life. I deliberately returned my sister's underwear immediately after school because I didn't want to be responsible for losing two undies in one day. Plus, I was truly hoping I would walk back into mama's pair on my way home.

I know you're probably thinking I'm crazy for walking the street looking for my mother's underwear. This was a well-kept secret. In a sensitive situation like that, you learn to "kibbah yuh mouth" (keep your mouth shut), because you don't want anyone jeering at you, right? I decided to rush out of the schoolyard ahead of all the other students before they start making their way home. I began my search, but there was no sign of the missing garment.

I wonder if maybe someone who had needed it more than I did had found it. I truly didn't know of anyone else who was poorer than us. Once I went to a singles conference in Maryland and heard Sam Emory say that "his family was so 'PO,' they couldn't afford the 'OR.' Truly, he was richer than I! I started thinking that perhaps some of the goats that I had passed on my way to school discovered it and shared it between themselves for lunch. Ha! I looked into every street corner and every bush and nothing! It vanished. It's a mystery.

Breaking the news to my mother was interestingly bittersweet. She wasn't that mad that I lost her underwear; she was more amused by the fact that I walked right out of it and didn't feel a thing. How did I manage to do that? How does anyone walk out of a piece of their undergarment and not feel it? Thirty years later, I'm still puzzled—but I think the answer is: it wasn't my size.

One by one, I'm counting my blessings—counting the smallest blessings. Don't despise small things (Zechariah 4:10). There's no need to complain. When I look around and see what the Lord has done for me, it makes me want to go all the way. In all things, give thanks.

Chapter 4

Poverty Almost Stole My Good Hair

I was most certainly obsessed with long hair, no lie. I simply longed for a head of long, curly-lock goodness! Was that too much to desire?

An old wives' tale claims that if you leave your comb by the riverbank, a mermaid might find it and comb her luxurious hair with it. After you retrieve the comb and use it, they say, your hair will grow as long as the mermaid's hair. So, throughout my childhood, I would pray to find a mermaid with whom to leave my piece of broken comb.

> *When I looked into the piece of broken mirror, all I saw was a picky-picky-head little girl.*

Everything seemed to be broken in my home, including my hair. Since I didn't know exactly where to locate any mermaid, I found myself begging God in my prayers to please make me wake up with long glorious hair. I waited for years and years, and God never did answer me at the time I needed

Him to. I'm still mad (just kidding). Yet, how silly of me to blame God!

For years, we only had a piece of broken mirror, so I couldn't see the full contour of my face. (*Contour* is a word I learned from my husband, Mr. Jacob, when he was trying to woo me. Ha!) I couldn't see my whole head all at once, but I could definitely see the big nose that I inherited from mama along with her big heels.

At some point growing up, mama shared my birth story with me. It left me startled because mama said that when I was born, out of all eight of her babies, I had the most hair. But unbeknownst to mama, her little girl was struggling with the way her hair looked and felt. She had no idea I was going to my bed every night praying and begging God to make my hair grow long and beautiful.

As I got older, I didn't see how what she told me could possibly be true, because, from my perspective, I had hardly any hair on my head to be combed. Regretfully, I have no baby picture for proof (we were too poor to own a camera), so I had to take her word for it, and I believed her every word because she's my mama. I love my mama.

Mama said my hair was beautiful, but when I looked into the piece of broken mirror, all I saw was a picky-picky-head little girl. Of course, when I looked closely enough, I would also see blood-sucking lice crawling around on my head—and a microscopic view would reveal the nits. These vermin would spread all over my little scalp and suck and suck.

Mama was oblivious about the severity of destruction these wingless insects were capable of causing. Our school and home were hardly ever lice-free. No parent nor teacher knew anything about how to prevent the spread of these grotesque parasitic insects. In our community, everybody had lice at some point—it was the norm. The older I got, the more I truly understood the reality of lice when I saw pictures of hairless girls of Sudan and the Congo in Africa. You had to shave all the hair off to combat the spreading.

I look back with one coherent thought. Since I was praying so persuasively for long hair, if mama had the guts to shave off all my little, unromantic, afro kinky coarse glory, maybe I would have struggled to forgive such an inhumane crime against my hair.

Where I came from, cutting off your hair wasn't an option for the women because all women had a desire for long hair. I remember going to bed itching and scratching, and I would wake up itching and scratching from the louse, sucking at my blood and chewing on my scalp. Oh, sweet Jehoshaphat! Every calamity I faced came with an ugly vengeance to destroy me!

Once your hair had just one deggeh louse, it would metastasize in no time. The infestation spread like California wildfires! The lice would crawl everywhere through our clothing and belongings looking for someone to suck. It was violent. Sometimes, mama and I took turns picking out lice from each other's heads like wild cotton. It wasn't at all fun, but we sort of bonded over lice during lice picking season. Ha! Unfortunately — lice are never out of season!

Since they mostly feast at the corner of the hair shaft, my hair hardly had any edges. Today, ladies' edges must be styled, laid and flawless, but nothing about my edges back then were fashionable. For one, my edges were impossible to see, and two, I only had a visible black pepper grain hairline. My hair was constantly dry and loaded with cakes of dandruff. Yet mine was supposed to be the best hair? Mama, what are you talking about?

This claim perplexed me greatly! On the one hand, if I did have "Good Hair," as comedian Chris Rock puts it in the documentary that uncovers some of the truths and myths about black women and their hair, then where did all my good hair go?

On the other hand, according to mama, poverty stole my good hair. Poverty stole what? The audacity! I need to sue Mr. Poverty! Yet truth be told, we never had the proper hair amenities like shampoo and conditioner. We simply couldn't afford it. That was only for the rich folks. So my mother had to use one of the worst-smelling soaps on the Island called "Dutty Gal Soap."

Dutty in patois means dirty, unclean, or unsanitary. *Gal* means *girl,* perhaps in a derogatory way. With that said, "Dutty Gal Soap" can't possibly be good, right? I was once told that "Dutty Gal Soap" was made from other leftover soap substances! It was the poor people's soap, used to get rid of the ugly stains. The smell was odious, but that gal worked her wonders!

We used it to wash our clothes, pots, pans, and whatever else that needed washing. We had no choice but to use it for bathing and for washing our hair as well. It had no label, so we had to use it without directions and without the knowledge and scrutiny of its chemical properties or ingredients. Can you believe that this was our go-to detergent for many years? That's the poverty soap that supposedly stole my good hair along with those ruthless lice.

Of course, many other ingredients and factors contributed to the decline of my good hair. We weren't educated about petroleum jelly's harmful properties, so we often used it. When we ran out of that, my mother used cooking oil. Sweet people of earth—those things were awful for us! Cooking oil, mama? Cooking oil is for cooking, mama! Oh, sweet Moses! No wonder all our hair suffered such harsh persecution and almost died.

Then again, if we didn't have any cooking oil, we'd pull out the lotion. It's not as if we had specific hair lotion and body lotion—it was just plain ordinary lotion. Only God knows what sort of ungodly ingredients were concocted in those overwhelmingly scented lotions. My mama almost killed my good hair beyond repair! But mama, you didn't know any better, so I completely understand, and I forgive you.

One Sunday during in January of 2013, the month of prayer, fasting, and consecration, God showed up at church. He told me, completely out of the blue, that He was sending me my husband. Floored and flabbergasted will only begin to describe my reaction—my mind was blown! The Holy Spirit spoke, and I freaked out! When you decide to ask God to help you choose your spouse, the Holy Spirit becomes the wingman or your Shadchan (matchmaker in Yiddish), and you have to trust that the author, the Creator of all things, knows what's best.

Ladies in waiting, bear in mind that how and when He presents a husband before you might be completely different from what you were expecting. Whoever He gives you will always be a blessing just because you trust Him.

I had no clue what my husband was going to look like. I knew God wasn't going to offer me anything less than the best. You see ladies, God will never prompt you to wait on Him and then hand you trash—no way! I never made a definitive list on exactly what feature, color, race, creed, or ethnicity I wanted my husband to be—I only listed characteristics. In all honesty, I just wanted a husband that came from God. Most assuredly, I had made many wedding lists several times over, but I gave

God the authority to override my will and desires for His—because God always knows what's best.

So, when He said, "I'm sending your husband," my hair suddenly became a major issue in my mind out of nowhere. Because of this prior knowledge, the day that I met Jacob, I knew he was the one God had sent. And wow, God knows how to surprise a waiting girl, because I was totally astounded; I was blown far away! But this book isn't about Jacob, so hold your horses and wait for the book about how we met.

The morning after I met my husband, I made a Leviticus move. I physically and figuratively went down in sackcloth and ashes to pray about my crown and glory. In Bible times, this signified a petition for something important. I'm crazy optimistic! So, what! I've always known that God called me because I'm not normal in any way, shape, or form! And me and God, we talk about everything. We're like two peas in a pod!

I said, "Lord Jesus, you didn't tell me you were sending me a white husband. Oh Lord, with your all-seeing eye, I hope you've known all along that I'm black, black, black. Seriously black! We've been on this friendship journey now for thirty plus years. I know you have 7.5+ billion humans down here on earth. And I'm certain you know my address, too. I'm very black, God…and I have afro kinks!" (Like God needed any help to figure who I am.) "Anyway, God, thanks for sending him. (Goodness, Lord, he's cute. God, you have such good taste. Ha!)"

Then I continued, "Lord, I'm going to need an emergency hair miracle from you right away! Dear God, can you pull the Lazarus miracle with my hair? And please Lord, don't let me have to wait four days. Four days is way too long. Just tell my hair to 'Come forth'! I need you to grow my hair really fast before the wedding because Jacob is going to need long hair to play with. Ha!"

I can't believe I uttered those words. Friend, I don't know what came over me, but suddenly I decided to practice Philippians 4:6b "But in every situation, by prayer and petition, with thanksgiving, present your request to God." (NIV). I use the prayer hotline and telephone the throne room of heaven with my girlish inhibition! (It was all in my head; we hadn't even had our first date yet. I think it was just a single-girl problem!)

I was almost certain I heard silence in heaven that day, and then Jesus and the whole crew started laughing. I couldn't believe my ears. Then all of heaven realized homegirl was serious because I kept on praying persuasively. I let my petition be known that God really needed to help a girl out.

Next thing I know, the Holy Spirit spoke to me and told me exactly what to do to cause my hair to grow. *The Holy Spirit is our helper!* I got up, ran to the store, came back, and did some intensive research. It took me a little while to complete most of my research about my hair.

During my research, God prompted me to read the books of Corinthians along with a few other books. He was intentional in using my hair to show me the headship that I needed to be subjected to. He was very adamant about making me fully aware that I have power on my head because of the angels, according to 1 Corinthians 11:10, "For this cause ought the woman to have power on *her* head because of the angels."

In God's wisdom, He knew exactly why He placed that desire for long uncut hair in my heart, and He was very deliberate about it—though I can't say that He had anything to do with me wanting to have contact with mermaids; that part was all my foolish desire. I believe it's God's will for us women to have long uncut hair. Our hair is our crown and glory that represents and signifies the glory of God. A woman's tresses are the glory of the woman, who is the glory of the man, who is the glory of Christ, who is the glory of God. Thus, by extension, a woman's uncut tresses are the glory of God, whether long or short.

"But I would have you know, that the head of every man is Christ; and the head of the woman *is* the man; and the head of Christ *is* God" (1 Corinthian 11:3). Our crown and glory reflect the very essence of the glory of God. Hair is a glorious, powerful thing.

This is not a book about hair, though when I write my hair book, I will certainly share everything God showed me to use to regrow my hair. In short, I want to emphasize that God wanted me to study the concept of my hair because every strand symbolizes divine authority and power—according to Reverend Lee Stoneking. I believe by the Bible that God still calls for women today to keep her long or uncut hair for their entire lives.

My dear readers, people of God, I live to testify that the Lord God helped me resurrect my "Good Hair," and not just good hair, but a head filled with healthy strands. Is there anything too hard for God? God is so full of wit, humor, and power. God has provided all we need and more. And I've always believed you, mama.

So don't call what's dormant dead. Don't call a temporary situation permanent. Don't call *dead* what God didn't label *dead*! Call out to your dry bones to come alive! God can resurrect your dead situation today. Call out to Him for help and believe!

Bear in mind that God will not do for you what He wants you to do for yourself, like growing and caring for your own hair. That's on you. I believe you can grow your hair just as I grew mine.

By the scent of water shall a tree sprout again (Job 14:9).

My hair in 2016.

My hair in 1999.

CHAPTER 5

I Only Had One Dress

It's not that I'm fashion crazy, oh no! It's simply that I never had much of anything to begin with. I consider myself an incredibly blessed person — not because of anything tangible or concrete, but because I've had so many rich and powerful moments and experiences in life, all because of Jesus Christ. My life has come a mighty long way for a little girl who at one point, had nothing!

> *I didn't mind that it was two sizes too big. I was very happy to finally have a decent frock...*

As I mentioned earlier, my mother rented one of the bedrooms in the tenement yard we shared with some other women. When it rained, my mother worried that the galvanized zinc roofing would blow off, and the dilapidated ceiling would come crashing down on us. On a serious note, that was the least of our problems!

When I was growing up as a little Island girl, Jesus was very much the fabric of my life and home. I remember so vividly my mother kneeling down to pray at night before bed. She would pray first, and then she would tell us what to pray. She would call out to "Massa God" even sometimes in her sleep. "Massa God" was a staple name within the community. Everyone I knew feared and revered God.

My mama loved to sing. She would sing the "spiritual songs of Zion," especially on weekend mornings. Once she was up, she sang. You wouldn't know anything was wrong because she was always singing. She would make her coffee singing; she would sweep the dirt yard with her makeshift broom singing; she would prepare our breakfast singing.

I remember walking around the yard on any ordinary day wearing an oversized shirt. Sometimes, a sleeve would be missing, or a few buttons, or maybe the shirt was torn and holey, and I had to make a big knot somewhere to prevent it from falling off me. What I wore usually belonged either to one of my siblings or my mama! Ninety-five percent of the time, I had no underwear underneath my clothes, and if I did have one on, it was my mother's old ones securely tied in place about my waist in knots.

I remember so vividly how badly I wanted to go to Sabbath or Sunday school, but mama couldn't send me because I had no decent frock to wear. I recall Ms. Clara stopping by sometimes on Saturday evenings to ask mama to get me ready for Sunday school. For a good while, mama wanted her to take me, but I couldn't go because I had nothing proper to wear.

One day out of the blue my bigger sister, Shelly, who wasn't living with us at the time, came to visit and handed down to me this little white dress she had outgrown. I found Ms. Clara's house the very same hour in which I had received my precious little royal dress. I didn't mind that it was two sizes too big. I was very happy to finally have a decent frock—but most importantly, I could at long last go to Sunday school. The joy of waiting for Ms. Clara on Sunday mornings down at the crossroad consumed me and eradicated every other lack I had in my life.

Something was at that church that made me feel happier than anything else in the world. They would sing from a green Pentecostal Hymnal; they clapped and danced for almost every single song. I loved all the songs because I was used to hearing mama's renditions long before I was exposed to the real hymns. The choir always marched up to sit at the podium. I always daydreamed that one day, I too would march up and be in the choir! The entire congregation went forward with their tithes and offering. They played the drums, they had long altar calls, and I watched people receive the gift of the Holy Ghost.

People ran in and around the church while they worshipped sometimes. When the presence of God came down, they knocked many tambourines; they played different types of guitars. I watched as they raised their hands up to the heavens and made joyful melodies unto the Lord. Once service ended, everyone was well spent—from old to young. You never—and I repeat, *never ever*—leave an old-fashioned Apostolic Pentecostal church the same way you've entered. You either leave disheveled, very tired, very sweaty, or soaking wet. You might also leave speaking in unknown tongue or delivered after being baptized in water! I find it so astounding, and I happened to love seeing the move of God after the songs or during the preaching.

As time progressed, I began to realize that something in my spirit was pulling me toward better things. I didn't have any idea what things, but most times, this pull happened at church. It's safe to say that there was also quite a dichotomy between my life at home and my church life. I felt somehow that God was waiting to meet me there. Many, many Sundays, while I was there, all my problems seemed to vanish somehow.

As I've mentioned above, I grew up stricken by poverty. I didn't have any shoes for many years, and to add to that dilemma, I only had that one little white dress. My mother was very diligent in ensuring that I attended Sunday school every single Sunday morning, if possible. To that end, my mother or I washed my little white dress every Friday or Saturday and hung it outside to dry on our little dilapidated clothesline in preparation.

Every Sunday, I was very excited to go to Wait-A-Bit Apostolic Pentecostal Church. It's safe to say that's the church in which I was born and raised. When it was time for church, mama would comb my picky-picky head of hair. She would add whatever products she could find. Whether it was Vaseline, body lotion, ordinary H_2O, or plain ole cooking oil — the object was to make my hair look combed, not necessarily to make it soft or shiny. My job was not to whine or complain about what she was putting in my hair; my job was to hold my head still or else! Since we were poor, whatever was applied to my hair was also used on my face, hands, and ashy feet.

She would divide my hair into six parts and plait it. Most times, the parts weren't straight nor symmetrical like most everything else in the house. The comb only had few teeth sitting on the shaft. There was hardly anything left in the row for pulling through all my hair to untangle or style it — but despite that, you'd best believe mama did her best work when combing my hair. She would smile, feeling accomplished, and then tell me to go and look in the broken mirror. She is left-handed, so combing my hair wasn't smooth or easy.

I didn't have anything fancy to wear, but I loved going to Sunday school. Going to Sunday school was like eating ice cream on Sundays — it just did me good. It was nice to listen to my teachers sharing Bible stories, my pastor's preaching, and the congregation singing. I enjoyed quoting Bible verses and playing with the other children. To be quite honest, I wasn't into playing once I was at church. I was more caught up in learning the song from the Pentecostal Hymnal and the tithing slats on the back wall. I couldn't wait to be able to tithe, but I hardly had much to give from.

Since we didn't have an electric iron, we relied on our little cast iron. Mama normally heated it on the wood fire after we ate breakfast and ironed my little dress if it needed it.

I wore that little white dress with such pride and self-confidence. Frills adorned the dress, and five buttons fastened it in the back. It was skimpy, and it clung to my angular, skinny frame—just as I clung to my own determination to savor the joy of Sunday school, church, and a better life.

I was probably the only little girl without hair ribbons and matching socks. I had no clips, only a hair bobble with the elastic band all stretched out. It wasn't a flight of fancy, but oh boy, I loved my one royal little white dress. I felt so happy each time I wore it.

One morning, I went to Sunday school and rich little Miss Josey, with her gossip-girl comrades, laughed, giggled, and whispered about my one worn-out dress. "Every Sunday, she wears the same dress to church!" said Josey.

I was appalled. Hearing her discriminate against me hurt my little heart.

The tears welled up within me and came running down my face the moment I returned home and reiterated the story to my mama. Mama encouraged my little heart as if she knew something I didn't. She said, "Sophia, one day, Massa God is going to bless you. You won't have enough backs to wear all your clothes." To me, it sounded like a hopeful verse right from the book of Psalms. However, I pondered her words in my heart.

It never occurred to me that I only had "one dress" until Josey pointed it out to me. I was so blinded by my poverty.

You might wonder if that's even possible. But if you've ever experienced the level of poverty that I experienced, then you understand. The reality of my life was that I literally had to wait on hand-me-down clothing or just do without. Hand-me-down was never a guarantee, but the feeling you experience when you finally get some fills you up with sweet, exhilarating joy. You instantly become satisfied because you now have something you needed that you never had.

The fact that I was never even cognizant about having one dress puzzled me. I knew I was poor, but I didn't realize how poor I really was until Josey said so. I was in total ignorance! I wondered about what Jesus had said in the Sermon on the Mount. Was God talking about me when He said, "Blessed are the poor in spirit" (Matthew 5:3)? Because honestly, I didn't want to be either spiritually or physically poor.

But it's like the mean little girl struck a chord in me. The encounter with Josey opened my eyes. After that, I became so conscious to the point where I went to God in prayer and asked for another dress. Before this, most of my prayers were centered on my mother's needs, but there was no way I could circumvent this specific need I now thought I had. So I decided to pray because God promised to be a father unto me, and I needed a new frock—so it was okay for me to ask, right?

"Oh, dear Lord," I said, "I ain't got nothing much to wear, but this one dress; it's my only good dress and I've been wearing it for a few years now! Come to my help, sweet Lord, for I'm in need of a brand-new dress to wear to my Sunday school classes. I'm sure you know how I love going to Sunday school, and you know my size. P.S. Please bless me and silence Josey and her mean friends. This I ask, in Jesus' Name!"

This might seem fortuitous to you, but God orchestrated the whole thing. If God ever made you laugh, you can never be sad. Each time my memory recalls this, I roll over laughing.

Serval weekend following the Sunday of my one dress dilemma, I was carrying water from a street pipe a few miles away from home when I saw one of my Sunday school teachers, Sister Regent, who was also a good friend of my mother's. She had just returned from her vacation in England, and she asked me to come to see her.

I went into her house with the belief she had something for my mama. She handed me a bag and told me to take it home to mama.

When I got home and gave the bag to my mama, she opened it and pulled out this beautiful little plaid dress for me with red, black, and gold embellishments. I was so surprised and overjoyed that I cried profusely. I instantly felt rich, like I had gotten an abundance of dresses. I didn't sleep a wink that night because I was so excited to finally experience the feeling of having a new and fancy dress that was all mine.

Finally, the morning dawned, and it was time to get ready for Sunday school. It was the most beautiful Sunday morning in Trelawny. Summer was awakened. The wild roses bloomed. The birds nested in the thicket. I felt beautiful and pretty like my mother's little flower garden. I cantered from home all the way into my Sunday school class. Man, I was beaming like the sun with pure, authentic happiness! The little princess arrived earlier than everyone else in her brand-new royal dress. (And yes, I'm well aware little real-life princesses never canter.) It was my first ever new dress — since my royal little white dress was a hand-me-down.

I can't begin to tell you the joy that exuded from me that morning. I felt fantastic! If you looked at me, all you would see is my big kind smile with little teeth grinning at you! There were too many butterflies in my stomach. I only wanted to jump, dance, and skip the whole time I was sitting down. I sang a song in my head called, "I'm pretty, I'm pretty," and danced to it. My inner monologue always gets the best of me! Ha! I hardly heard anything Sister Regent said during the Sunday school lesson. Not one thing.

As I'm reflecting, I wonder if this is one reason why God wants us to remain humble, because when we're too lofty, sometimes we can get carried away and miss out on some very important lessons He wants us to learn.

Josey and her gossip girlfriends stared, and yes, I blushed. After church was dismissed, I searched for Sister Regent to tell her many thanks for my new dress. Once I located her, we walked and talked on the way home together. I asked her about the dress, and she told me that the Lord had impressed it on her heart to purchase the dress for me while she was in London. I couldn't believe what my ears had heard.

On that note, I reiterated my story to her about Josey and how she and her friends laughed and ridiculed me over my one little white dress and how it made me feel so cheap and insignificant. Then I repeated to her the simple prayer I had prayed that same Sunday night asking the sweet Lord for a new dress.

At this point in the conversation, I'm bursting with pure exhilarated joy. I wasn't pleased with myself that I had allowed my dress to steal away my attention from my Sunday school lesson and from the sermon. But when she said it was God who had impressed it upon her heart to do something for a poor little country girl, I felt so special. I felt like God was doing something special in my life.

My faith in God was so stimulated. I loved what was happening, and I wanted more. This was too good to be true. It felt like God was on to something.

I said to Sister Regent, "I'm so amazed that God would place the desires of my heart into your heart to buy me a brand-new dress. How's that even possible?"

Suddenly, a flood of emotions came over me. I was even more astonished that she had purchased my exact size without any measurement. The fitting and sizing were so perfect. I took that into consideration because I'm so used to wearing hand-me-downs, which are either too big or too small. I was stunned by God. She told me that prayer was a powerful weapon, and I pondered over that thought. After we parted ways, I turned up the street where I lived, and something unexplainable erupted inside me.

I imagined my guardian angel, whom I named "gentle friend," informing God around the conference table in heaven as to why they can't give me any more new dresses, perhaps not until the next decade—because one dress was too much for me to handle! I admit it made me act a bit eccentric and out of character. This caused me to laugh so hard that it turned into crying.

At the moment, I had this one coherent thought: that my dress was a present from God. I can't express to you how that made me feel. One other thing that materialized at that moment was that God had brought to my remembrance what He had said to me at the beginning when we first met: that He would be a father to me. The feeling of having a father, or someone who truly cares about my smallest needs, felt so good on the inside. And the fact that He was keeping what He promised thwarted every other atrocious feeling I might have had about not having the basic necessities.

Can I just tell you this, if God has ever made you a promise, stand on His Word, baby! Because He's bound by every word He's spoken over your life. Every single one!

One of the main ways God communicated to me back then was via His Word. That evening, He also reminded me of what He said to the disciples in Matthew: "Therefore I say unto you, Take no thought for your life, what ye shall eat, or what ye shall drink; nor yet for your body, what ye shall put on. Is not the life more than meat, and the body than raiment? Behold the fowls of the air: for they sow not, neither do they reap, nor gather into barns; yet your heavenly Father feedeth them. Are ye not much better than they? Which of you by taking thought can add one cubit unto his stature? And why take ye thought for raiment? Consider the lilies of the field, how they grow; they toil not, neither do they spin: and yet I say unto you, That even Solomon in all his glory was not arrayed like one of these.

Wherefore, if God so clothe the grass of the field, which today is, and tomorrow is cast into the oven, *shall he* not much more *clothe* you, O ye of little faith? Therefore take no thought, saying, What shall we eat? or, What shall we drink? or, Wherewithal shall we be clothed? (For after all these things do the Gentiles seek:) for your heavenly Father knoweth that ye have need of all these things. But seek ye first the kingdom of God, and his righteousness; and all these things shall be added unto you. Take therefore no thought for the morrow: for the morrow shall take thought for the things of itself. Sufficient unto the day *is* the evil thereof." (Matthew 6:25-34).

I was just floored. I believe this was the first occasion as a little girl, that prompted me to truly seek the Kingdom continuously—even though my knowledge was limited *about God and his Kingdom*, and still is today. I had just started to develop my relational skills with God, and He took me by surprise and took my breath away!

Due to what Sister Regent had said, I became more and more mesmerized by the power of my prayer. I began to feel God tugging at my heart. There was a deeper calling in my spirit to draw nearer to Him and pray more. I could also sense that God was continuing to work on rewiring my mind and the way that I thought about Him, myself, and my prayers. Just thinking about this is giving me chills up my spine. I must add that prayer became more than just a cliché or passé for me; it became my lifeline.

Once I made it inside my home, I told mama what sister Regent said — and I just cried and cried. I was unable to eat the Sunday dinner that mama had prepared. I started to perceive then with the understanding that I had a Father (God) who truly loves and was looking out for me, and it made my heart full and glad. Oh, sweet friend, if you could ever know His love for you, it would fill every empty space in your life. I was so enamored, so joyful over what God had done for me that I instantaneously began to feel a true sense of security in my life that Sunday. Those of you who have grown up with both parents should know what it feels like to have a secure home. I honestly didn't know what that felt like until I met with God.

Like I mentioned to you so many times — God telling me He would be a father to me was coming to pass in my life. He proved himself to me, and I believed with all my heart what He said in Matthew: "Jesus answered and said unto them, Verily I say unto you, If ye have faith, and doubt not, ye shall not only do this which is done to the fig tree, but also if ye shall say unto this mountain, Be thou removed, and be thou cast into the sea; it shall be done. And all things, whatsoever ye shall ask in prayer, believing, ye shall receive" (Matthew 21:21-22). Whatever you pray and ask God for, just believe Him for it.

Looking back, I knew I was taught to be humble. As I mentioned above, what Josey said puzzled me. She opened up my eyes that Sunday. I thank you, sweet Josey! The memories of this little girl still linger like yesterday. The fact that I wasn't consciously aware that I only had one dress made me question things. Was I perpetuating an emanation from the mentality of slavery? I came to understand that my mama wanted to be emancipated mentally and physically, but she couldn't free herself from the bondage of its grips.

With her mindset and a quiver full of eight fatherless children, it seemed far from possible! Was this behavioral thought pattern handed down to me? "This can't be genetic!" I thought. Was it because of the poverty that was thrust upon her? I couldn't comprehend any of it. Surely, if there was more to be had, I wanted to remain humble, but I didn't want to settle for less, either.

I think all of us need a Josey in our lives to awaken the hidden possibilities of the God-nature in us. I know for a fact that God has more in store for me, for all of us. He's so eager to bless all his children. How many times as children of God do we live life as paupers when He has given us an open invitation to always dine at the King's table?

While I was writing this portion, the Holy Spirit brought to remembrance the story of when King David decided to restore Jonathan's son, Mephibosheth, to his rightful kingly place. According to 2 Samuel chapter 9, Mephibosheth was living life as a pauper in a place called Lodebar—which means *"desolate"* or a *"land of nothing."* Because of his grandfather King Saul's sins, Mephibosheth had lost his kingly heritage.

Therefore, he was living life as a pauper, not realizing that he was still worthy because he was from royal lineage.

To me, David is seen here as a type of Christ coming into the world to restore us back to the Kingdom. In the very same way, King David saw fit to bring Prince Mephibosheth back to his royal palace where he'd always belonged. Amen!

A striking characteristic of Prince Mephibosheth, even though he was so humble, was that he lacked self-confidence and self-worthiness—perhaps because of his handicap. In verse 8, we see that in the presence of King David, the prince saw himself as a dog—and not just a dog but a dead dog. This reminds me of how the enemy today plants seeds of doubts and taunts us about our past. He tries to condemn us because of who we once were; because his goal is to keep us lost and blinded about who we truly are in the Kingdom of God and our true identity in Christ. He does this perpetually to keep us outside of the Kingdom because he knows it belongs to us. He once had access and was cast out, and now he tries to prevent you and me from entering the Kingdom.

1 Peter 2:9 says, "But ye *are* a chosen generation, a royal priesthood, an holy nation, a peculiar people; that ye should shew forth the praises of him who hath called you out of darkness into his marvelous light." We're royalty with Christ. Joint heirs with Him. Just because physical Israel missed the Messiah does not mean that you have to miss spiritual Israel. The Church, the worldwide body of Christ, is spiritual Israel.

But this is a Church you cannot join. You cannot shake a preacher's hand to become a member of this Church. You cannot sign a membership card to get in. The only way you can be royalty with Christ, the only way you can be a joint heir with Him is to be BORN into this Church. You are born into this Church through the new birth process. Paul declares what the Gospel is in 1 Corinthians 15:1-4. It is the death, burial, and resurrection of Jesus Christ. We obey the death by repenting. We obey the burial by being baptized in the Name of Jesus Christ. We obey the resurrection by receiving the wonderful gift of the Holy Ghost. (Acts 2:38)

You will then be a joint heir with Jesus. You will be part of the Kingdom Jesus set up here on earth. "For the kingdom of God is not meat and drink; but righteousness, and peace, and joy in the Holy Ghost." (Romans 14:17) When you are a true child of God, He can use you to do mighty works.

When we are born again of the water and of the Spirit, we possess an everlasting place at the King's table. Jesus is that King who died so that we could be reborn into His Kingdom, but we have allowed the enemy to steal it! If you're reading this book, I want you to know you are more than worthy of it.

It doesn't matter if you find yourself in a state like Prince Mephibosheth or a poorer state like mine. It doesn't matter if you have nothing at all! If all you have or feel is shame, hurt, worthlessness, abandonment, and rejection; if you feel like your life of poverty or the situation you're facing right now in knowledge, I am glad I was poor and only had one dress. Through it all, God was working out His plan and purpose in my life. The fact that I asked, and God provided for me, changed my perspective.

I was more intrigued than ever before, and this was when I believe I fell deeply in love with the Lord God. I just couldn't fathom how I asked Him for a simple dress, and He told my Sunday school teacher miles and miles away across the Atlantic Ocean. She gave me one dress, and God used it to unfold His ultimate plan and destiny for my life. Isn't our God great!? Whatever you want, "come boldly to the throne of grace" (Hebrews 4:16) and ask.

Dear ones, my sweet readers, I wanted to relate this particular childhood story to let you know how much hope I possess inside of me because of this one simple dress.

Trust me when I tell you that I was without hope at times during my childhood. And one day, God resurrected the dead hope buried inside me. You need to know that you always have hope way down deep inside because we are made in His image and likeness. He's the God of our eternal hope. "Now the God of hope fill you with all joy and peace in believing, that ye may abound in hope, through the power of the Holy Ghost" (Romans 15:13). It was my royal white dress of perpetual hope, my faith in God, and one single prayer that inspired this book.

When the curtains of memories are rolled back, I know that at such a tender age, because of that hope, I found the "Pearl of Great Price." I found it in the reading of God's Word and in prayer. The Scripture is where I first learned how to hear God's voice, and how to see Him, how to study and know His mind, will, and character—and mostly how to pray.

For instance, I'm fond of the childhood memory where I wished for a collection of Barbie dolls to play with, but what I ended up with instead was a collection of Scriptures to turn into effective prayers—which, by the way, changed my life. I mean no harm Sista Barbie and I have no regret!

Our prayer is what activates our faith. Can I humbly implore you to pray more? Prayer will activate your faith and release the will of God for your life! Look at prayer this way: we're like a lamp, prayer is the like the cord, and God is like the electric power that it needs to perform its true purpose.

We will only discover what our prayer can manifest when we spend time in prayer and reading of the Word. We can't expect God to pour into our lives if we never seek his face. I'm so glad that I did pray and ask God for help. I'm a living testimony that prayer works and that prayer changes things!

The moral of this story is (and this saying is true): little is much when God is in it. I reasoned this out in my mind, and this is the solemn conclusion I came to. I was so happy to just go to Sunday school that I didn't realize I only had one dress.

To me, it wasn't a big deal, but I was too poor to notice that I was really, really poor! (Just like Prince Mephibosheth—I was too far down in Lo Debar to realize that I belong at the King's table. It's also kind of like the prodigal son in Luke 15:11-32, realizing that he doesn't have to share food with the pigs; he can eat at his father's table where he belongs).

Having just one good dress was such a big blessing to me to the point where I couldn't see past the need to desire more—until Josey, of course. Be grateful for the little things and have a grateful heart. Don't forget where God has brought you from.

"In every thing give thanks: for this is the will of God in Christ Jesus concerning you" (1 Thessalonians 5:18).

The only picture of me as a young girl and wearing the little white dress. Can you guess which one is me?

CHAPTER 6

My Imaginary Closet and My Little Red Sweater

Growing up, I owned very few prized possessions. One of them was my little red sweater with three missing buttons and holes everywhere. My mother reminded me recently about my attachment towards this sweater and how I would wear it everywhere I went. Another was my one little white royal dress.

But my most prized possession was my imagination. I had to imagine up everything because we had nothing much to consider as worthy possessions.

> *It didn't matter which direction I slept in; I had to be ready to encounter those four-legged creatures.*

I hope you all understand that I never mean to be braggadocious. I simply want to share with you all the amazing things God has done in my life to encourage your faith in Him.

Recently, as I strolled inside my walk-in closet, a cheerful feeling spread over me…the kind of feeling that Cinderella experienced once she met her fair prince. Oh, mustard and ketchup! What I'm trying to say is that I felt really good. I know it's just a closet, for crying out loud. But I can't help that it feels like a true luxury experience every time I enter.

I might be making too much of this, but I hope to demonstrate what the hullabaloo is all about with my closet. The truth is growing up, I never had anything that was really nice or of high quality. If you ever had to live in a small one-bedroom house or apartment that could only accommodate two medium beds, one table, a cabinet, and a chair, with a narrow space that only one person can walk through at a time, then, my friend, I know you would understand.

So, there I was getting ready to do some organizing. I sat on the floor on the fuzzy white faux fur rug that I scored at Dillard's on sale…80% off! Hey oh, hey! Who doesn't love a good bargain, right? I started looking around and talking with the Holy Spirit about how I really need to get rid of some stuff — when all of a sudden, the little girl inside me reminded me of the time I had no clothes and no shoes — nothing! Of a truth, the moral is never about the "things" I shared with you that I once lacked but rather the life lessons I learned from the situation — and most importantly how I was able to appreciate and to see God in them!

Let me be honest; this flashback hit me like a ton of bricks. You need not wonder if I cried, because the answer is yes! God is always making me cry. Oh man, I am such a crybaby! But I really think He loves me. So, as I sat there, this little girl rolled back the curtain and took me back to my childhood home once more. I recall wishing we had a closet. Our clothes were always thrown or hung somewhere. I was tired of creeping things crawling all over them.

Since mama had no manpower, she had to make do or do without. My mama intertwined old electrical wires with pieces of cords and strings from old clothes to create a rope. A line stretched horizontally across our little room in the front, another one ran against the wall over the back bed, and another extended horizontally between the beds and the table. Believe it or not, these were our makeshift closets.

On the downside, hanging anything on either of these lines resulted in some serious and lasting rust stains. The centerline hung directly over our bed. It was wild. We would be fast asleep in the middle of the night, and the line would pop all on its own, and everything would come crashing down on us— either the clothing or the creeping things from the book of Genesis.

At times, I used to despise sleeping at night because all the crawling things from Adam came out. It didn't matter which direction I slept in; I had to be ready to encounter those four-legged creatures. I truly believed they were the ones my mother mostly paid the rent for. They benefited the most from eating our food, our clothes, and everything else they could find. It was interesting to me how they would climb from line to line to get from one end of the room to the other—especially at night when their destination was the table.

The clothesline crashing down wasn't the worst part. But I hated it most when the creatures decided to take a shortcut and walk on me or by me. It was my worst fear. I must admit that those creeping, crawling vermin were smart. They carried out their excavating hunt on the table every single night—because we didn't have any refrigerator or anywhere else to stow away any of our food. We never knew anything about Tupperware way back then, and even if we had known, we couldn't afford it. It was life as we knew it. So we had to deal with its distastefulness somehow.

Another reason I never liked sleeping at night in my house was that it felt a bit haunted due to the clotheslines and things hanging on the walls. Since we always used a kerosene oil lamp for lighting, sometimes during the night, it would run out, or mama would put out the wick to save the oil if the moonbeams were especially bright.

One particular night, the moon was at its peak. I looked up and saw that the moonlight was so bright that things outside were casting a shadow through the window. Another downside of hanging stuff on the wall or on a line is that they can appear like people moving around in a semi-dark moonlit room. To make things worse, it was hurricane season, so the nights were very windy, and the breeze would blow through the dilapidated window.

The moonlight created these shadows on the wall in front of the bed I was sleeping on. As I lay there, I began to see all the objects moving against the wall. While everyone was sound asleep, I made a big dramatic scene to make things more interesting. I told you I was the spunky one in the family. A little crazy optimist!

I remember seeing this man with dreadlocks standing there. Suddenly, he moved, and I imagined him grabbing my mother's machete and getting ready to chop up my brother. The more I observed, the more things intensified. At this point, my mother was half awake because I began to verbalize what I imagined I saw.

My mother threatened me with a whooping, so I calmed down a bit. But I couldn't help it since I was distressed and scared out of my wits under the circumstances. I waited a few minutes and went right into scene two. This time, the moving shadow on the wall had doubled, and I got louder.

And I woke the entire house and half the neighbors. I screamed to my brother that the man with the dreadlocks had mama's machete, and he was going to kill him. I made everyone in the room tremble that night—complete silence bathed the room for a few moments.

I was anxious to see what was going to happen next. Nothing happened. But my brother realized what it was, and he nervously got off the bed and showed me that it was just his jacket with a hood that had dreadlocks attached. Let me stress that I was young, really young. I was practically still a baby! Ha!

Oh, but I truly couldn't help the situation. Sometimes, your imagination can run wild. Everyone went back to sleep, and mama promised me a good whooping in the morning for disturbing her rest. What's a girl to do if she happens to have a crazy imagination? It was a wild night, for sure. It sounded like I was directing a horror film. I slept with one eye open the rest of the night. I was watching to see if anything else would move for scene three or four, and I kept watch for mama too, of course.

Morning came around much too quickly. I stared at my brother's jacket hanging on a nail, and I could see from the corner of my eye the banana trees that had reflected the moonlight through the window, moving back and forth with the morning breeze.

Mama quarreled with me about how I woke everyone and made her lose a decent night's rest. I thought for sure I was going to get a good whooping right there and then, but she let me go to school without it. That wasn't very fair, I thought. I was going to miss out on learning since I am too worried about the whooping after school!

Mama never beat me often enough, but when she decided to beat me, she let me know who the boss was. Let's not talk about school since my mother occupied my thoughts most of the day. If I can be honest, let me add that I was a very good child; I only can recall giving good troubles, and only when it was absolutely necessary!

When I returned home from school, I found my mother sitting on the veranda in her usual spot—warming herself in the evening sun. I watched, terrified, as the sun set far away over and beyond the mountains where she gave beauty like strength to the blue Caribbean Sea. I said, "Evening," and she let me pass and enter inside without grabbing me because there's no way I was just going to surrender to a whooping. On my way outside the house, she grabbed me and gave me two licks across my backside before the whip broke, and I pulled away from her.

She quarreled again and sent me to go and pick another whip, and I asked her why. My little girl audacity was wild.

She stormed after me. I knew better than to frustrate my mother. So, I obeyed and got her a second whip, but before I gave it to her, I asked her again why she wanted to beat me.

She said, "You know why!"

I burst out and said, "If we had a closet, none of this would've happened." I went on and on about how it wasn't my fault; it was the fault of the line and the clothes hanging on the wall. Typical Evie blame game style! She stood there speechless, and I think she even had a grin— while all along I was paying keen attention to her left hand and on-my-mark-ready-to-get-set to dash! Gratefully, my speech won her over, and she didn't whoop me anymore.

Mama just looked at me funny and said what she always said when she really doesn't know what to do with me. She shook her head took a long pause and said, "Yuh si yuh sah!" ("You see you.") Some of the things I usually said sounded like nothing she's ever heard before, and it wasn't something a normal child with any regular imagination would say.

I admit that I suffered from the affliction of an overly excessive imagination. That was the day she asked me where I came from. What? What does she mean by "where I came from"?

She looked and acted like some stork had left me on her doorstep, and she was somehow still puzzled by my existence. Then she put the icing on the cake and told me that my mouth was bigger than my body. I was a handful. The daily dialogue between momma and I was the part that made my childhood sort of colorful!

Since mama wasn't mad at me anymore, I told her how I wished we had a closet, and she agreed. Most of the clothes hanging on the lines had belonged to her for decades, even though it wasn't much to begin with. I was little, and I couldn't reach the lines, so I would climb up on to the beds to hang my things. But I'd better not make the mistake of pulling anything too hard, or else the whole line came crashing down. I couldn't deal with the lines, so I ended up settling for any available nails I could find on the wooden beams.

I never liked to hang clothes on the nails, though. They were old and rusty, and when they stained your clothes you still had to wear them. We never had any hangers—every piece of clothing was hung on a nail or thrown over the lines. From this standpoint, I would use my imagination and create a little closet space in my mind. How come I wasn't the one who invented Pinterest? The truth is, when the Lord would provide hand-me-downs, which wasn't often, those were the happiest times in my life. I would hang the garment on the wall and imagine it was hung in my imaginary dream closet.

So as I sat there on the floor getting ready to organize my closet, I picked up a pack of pink velvet hangers and remembered how I had used rusty nails and weak lines made from wires. Those were the good old days, some would say. But I now have shelves, looking mirrors, panels, drawers, rods, baskets, shoe racks, and storage cubes to fold and stow away. The perks are good, don't you think? And did I mention the sliding closet doors? It doesn't get any better than that. It's like a piece of heaven in there. A whole different world. A place of serenity for me. Who would have thought that one day, I would own a walk-in closet?

I felt so blessed and overjoyed because I see how God doubled the space of my "childhood imaginary closet" and caused my dreams to come true. Like me, if you've lived your whole life in a box or a cube, let me warn you never to put God in a one. He can fulfill your wildest, weirdest, most outlandish daydreams. I know this seems minute, but it is a huge deal to me. It's amazing how God can bless you above and beyond what you can think, ask, or even imagine.

Never stop dreaming. Never stop believing and hoping in God that things will change even if it seems too impossible. Still dream and believe God, even when you really don't understand how. The impossible is possible with Him. Dreams do come true. You might not have anything tangible in front of you to work with, but don't forget you have your imagination. It's God's gift to you. Use it wisely. "Now unto him that is able to do exceeding abundantly above all that we ask or think, according to the power that worketh in us" (Ephesians 3:20).

CHAPTER 7

My Bed Was Broken

Each time I passed our linen closet in our new home, my heart skipped a beat. One day as I prepared to wash some laundry, I stripped the sheets off our bed and entered the linen closet. I walked inside, all the way inside. It hadn't occurred to me that we had so much space inside.

I paused a moment, admiring the shelving with all the fluffy towels, lovely sheets, comforters, and spreads we had received as wedding gifts. I decided to finally use the queen-sized one-thousand-thread-count Egyptian cotton sheets. The grade was luxurious, and the feel was flat-out amazing! (By no means am I boasting in material goods—be it far from me. Instead, if I should take thought of them, I direct my praise and thanks to God, who provided them.)

> *Wires ran through and poked out every which way.*

My sister Shelly and I spent countless hours reflecting on how poor we were in our childhood days and how God brought us through those tough times. We had no towels, no good sheets, and no decent washcloths to bathe with. She recollected that, "Even though all our sheets were raggedy, torn, and had holes, we found the parts that could cover us — and it really kept us warm somehow."

Back in our bedroom, as I began making our bed, I was so tickled by the fact that I finally have nice sheets that I started laughing to myself like Sarah in Genesis 18:12. Gratefulness bubbled and overflowed within me. You can't imagine how much God has changed the entire trajectory of my life! I know it's just linens but it's the simple things in life that have the biggest impact on you.

Honestly, when I think back to those years as a little girl, I used to sleep on a broken-down wire Kaya Mattress bed with wires running through and poking out every which way (I still have scars for proof). My mother would use old clothing for mattress padding and cardboard boxes to add support because the sponge was rotten. Nevertheless, I always woke up with my body in a sinkhole.

Every single sheet had a hole somewhere — in fact, the only possession that wasn't worn out was some of mama's so-called china. In our extreme poverty, we sat on the floor and ate *so-so food*. Rats and roaches celebrated their victory dances over our leftovers at night. Yet, we were happy somehow!

Our pit toilet (outhouse) was rotten and it boasted unsafe conditions. I don't know how God kept us from not falling in, but He kept us safe. To this day, when I look back over my life, I'm amazed because I know it was God's hands that kept me and led us through.

It wasn't long before my laughter turned into joyful crying. Jacob passed by and saw me lying prostrate across our bed sobbing, and he inquired after my disposition. And once again, I went back in time to unfold from memory my story to Jacob. I went back to the day Jesus came through Litchfield and visited the place where I was born. My Litchfield, but in my full recollection, I call that place my Samaria.

I said to Jacob, "You should have met me before the God of heaven came and found me." This one encounter that took place one lonely Tuesday morning changed the course of my life. I was only seven, when I sat down on my mama's broken-down bed, crying out and praying to the God of Abraham, Isaac, and Jacob. The God who heard me.

Can I reiterate that He heard me? Child of God, you must not be afraid to cry out to our God, because He's always listening. He hears and will answer (1 Kings 8:28)! It was like God and all the host of heaven stopped by for me that day.

I know that nothing about my life seems to correlate with the woman at the well in any fashion. But we were both desperate for a change, and we needed Jesus. Jesus came down and visited me just like He visited her at that well. On both occasions, His visit was deliberate. John records that "When He left Judaea and departed again into Galilee," He told his disciples, "I must needs go through Samaria" (John 4:3-4). This was how He decided to visit me. He must have said to the host of heaven, "Today, I must needs go through Litchfield—my daughter Sophia needs me."

Can you imagine how the splendor of heaven came to meet with me in my humble little abode? Oh, glory! I read in the Gospels where Jesus, who is God in the flesh, visited Zacchaeus, Simon the leper, and many others. In my home in Litchfield, He came down and visited me. There's nothing too hard for God to do (Luke 19:1-10).

I can't get over how He sat with me on my mama's broken-down bed and talked with me like friend with friend. Imagine if I had known ahead of time that He was coming. It would have been difficult for me to find anything fancy to set up to accommodate His presence—remember how Mary and Martha cooked and entertained Him? (Luke 10:38-42).

But oh, how richly I felt his presence! The hair on my neck stood up dancing. Illuminating heat enveloped my soul. Jeremiah, the prophet said it best! His Word felt like fire shut up in his bones, and I felt that fire! To me, His presence and His Word are the same (Jeremiah 20:9).

The Shekinah glory and Splendor of God wrapped me that day from head to toe. He changed my whole life. Before proceeding any further, I want you to know that God always desires to fellowship with mankind. That's the reason He created us.

In Genesis, we see Him in a deep relationship with Adam in the garden. The Bible says He came down in the cool of the day to talk with Adam (Genesis 3:8). We see Him with Moses on Mount Sinai. David spent every day with God while he attended to the sheep in the desert place. God wants to have a divine fellowship with us. According to the book of Revelation, "Thou art worthy, O Lord, to receive glory and honor and power: for thou hast created all things, and for thy pleasure, they and were created." (Revelation 4:11). We are created for God's pleasure. Our age and status don't matter; He's always interested in meeting and communing with us.

After the woman at the well encountered the God of her father Abraham, something transpired inside her. John says she left her water pots and went into the city to tell everyone (John 4:20-30). With my encounter, I was captured and captivated by His aura. I had this fire burning inside me, and as you can see, that fire is still burning, because I can't keep quiet about Him.

That day, He set me free from my fear of growing up fatherless. It's like He came down to decide my case. The verdict was in on my life. Can anything good come from

Litchfield? He walked in as my mercy. He edited and changed the script. The sentence of poverty that was handed down to me was thrown out! It was broken! Jesus *overturned* my sentence. He spoke life over my begrimed life. He declared His Word over me. He said I belong to Him. He reassured me that He had paid all my debts in full. His hands and feet bear the evidence! I was overjoyed that He came. Thrilled to know that where and how I was born couldn't dictate my future. Blessed to know I would not die in poverty because I am redeemed by the blood of Jesus! So, please, don't mind if I testify about this man from Galilee, for He has done so very much for me. You see, He took me from a "horrible pit" condition.

My home wasn't the nicest place for the God of heaven to visit. I understand better why He would decide to enter the world through a lowly manger. The state in which He found me was bad. (I promise you the rats, roaches, and lice owned our little room. My mother paid the little rent she could afford for those four-legged things!) But nonetheless, God came down and filled my heart with His love right there.

That visit changed my whole life. God chose to bless me and give me the good desires of my heart. So I didn't mind crying into my new sheets and pouring out to my husband my heart of gratitude for how much God has blessed and transformed my whole life. He has provided all my needs according to His riches in glory!

I beg of you: never complain. Look back and be grateful! The good days always by far outweigh the bad ones. Thankfulness attracts God's blessings. I pray that Jesus of Nazareth will make His abode with you today! I pray that He will stop by your well and change your circumstances!

"And my God will supply every need of yours according to his riches in glory in Christ Jesus!" Amen (Philippians 4:19, ESV).

CHAPTER 8

We Only Had One Door

Three doors directly in front of me caught my attention. I sat in the middle of our bed, reflecting on God's goodness when all of a sudden, I glanced up to the presence of these doors that focused my consciousness. Something stirred inside of me. I leaped off the bed and started counting one, two, three, four, five, six, seven. The happy feelings of a carefree little girl welled within me. I didn't realize we had so many doors! Who in their right mind walks around their house counting doors? It's not like I'm a shepherd who counts sheep!

> *...and don't forget the plus-sized rats and roaches and other creeping things with four legs that lived with us.*

Downstairs, I continued my count, and I counted sixteen doors. Of course, Jacob was busy working, but I had to get his attention. I asked him to recount all the doors to make sure it was sixteen. He had this "Is my wife going through a mid-life crisis" look on his face.

Then I burst out crying in front of him as I remembered the dream the Lord gave me as a child. In the dream, I stood inside of a house that has many doors and one huge crystal chandelier.

Guilt assailed me at interrupting Jacob's work hour, but I had to tell him again about growing up without a proper place to live—this time it was about our little dilapidated door.

We occupied one of the middle rooms in a five-bedroom tenement house. It had to do. Mama did her best. Everything my mama owned fit inside that tiny little matchbox: eight children (oh my, that's more than a handful!), two beds, one table, a cabinet, and a trunk... and don't forget the plus-sized rats and roaches and other creeping things with four legs that lived with us. I was more than grateful for the day when it was time to move from that place.

The state of the two windows and the one door worried my little mind. The door had a bolt on the inside, but we were never able to lock it on the outside because the lock was broken. Over time, the weak little bolt fell off, and we had to use a nail for security. A nail—and it's not like we lived on the secure streets of heaven!

Did I mention how scared to death I would be at nighttime? (I was chiefly afraid of what they called a "duppy" or "ghost." When I was a child, I spoke as a child and understood childish things...that's Scriptural!) I can never forget the night a man broke in. At first, I thought I was dreaming, or my crazy imagination was running wild with me again. We thought it was a real ghost and not a real man. But it was a real man. He broke in on mama because the door security was weak, or so I thought.

I was sleeping behind mama that night and heard her ask this man who he was and what he wanted. Of course, we couldn't switch the lights on because all we had was a little wick lamp, and the stranger had put out the lamp when he came in.

Mama was terrified. I could feel her fears and we all shook like leaves. I was softly praying for Massa God's help. After a while, the man left without hurting any of us. Fear and worry kept us all awake for the rest of the night. Morning couldn't come too soon. I was happy to see the light of day and feel the sun.

That day marked the first time I prayed all day long—asking God if He could let the sun stand still as He did for Joshua. Scared out of my wits, I didn't want to see another night like that—or any night at all. I wondered if he would come back the following night because we didn't have a properly secured door to keep him out. Mama said all our lives flashed before her eyes that night, and it was only Massa God's mercies that kept us.

If God hadn't kept us, we wouldn't be here today. Unless the Lord God watch the house, the keeper watches in vain (Psalm 127). The door was broken, and our security was up to the mercies of God.

If we slammed the door too hard, it could have fallen off the hinges. Did I mention the holes and cracks? We weren't properly protected from the outside elements. But it was my home—my Samaria, the broken place where I first met my LORD God and King, the Savior and Redeemer of the whole world, the Good Shepherd, the Lord Jesus Christ!

Jacob returned to work, and I continued to talk with God. He reminded me that He's the only door to life more abundant and that protection is found only in and through Him. He led me to Revelation: "I know thy works: behold, I have set before thee an open door, and no man can shut it: for thou hast a little strength, and hast kept my word, and hast not denied my name" (Revelation 3:8). I'm still pondering this, and I encourage you to meditate on this passage as well.

Stay humble and let God be the keeper of your one door. Know also that when He chooses to open up another door for you, many, many more doors will swing wide open for you just like that.

A visiting preacher at our church recently centered his sermon around *The Importance of a Door* and reiterated how Jesus is the only door to eternal life. In the midst of his discourse, he threw out an attention-grabbing question to the congregation, invoking a conversation. He asked, "Has anyone here ever counted the doors in your house?"

My mouth dropped. I was so astonished at the question, and of course, Jacob brought attention to me by saying, "My wife has."

It turned out I was the only crazy door-counting Christian weirdo in the congregation. But the real question is, did God send him to confirm my insanity?

CHAPTER 9

From Going in the Bushes to Having Three Toilets

I begin in Jamaican patois: Unnu evah jus luk bac ova unnu life ah wata jus drop outta unnu eye? Mi sah, mi staat fi halla ah bawl becaz mi cyah believe seh mi finally hav sinting becuz wen mi luk bac, mi life di suh haad ah full ah lack. (Have you ever just looked over your life and cried because you finally have something you never had before because your life was so hard?)

Recently, the Lord blessed us with a house. The simple act of taking out the toilet bowl cleaners prompted tears to roll down my cheeks. God's gratefulness and goodness flooded my little heart. I lay flat on the floor in my bathroom and worshipped God because there was no way I could repay Him. I could only fall on my knees and praise because of grace. Grace and love lifted me.

> *Many people fell into their latrines and died there before anyone could find them...*

Growing up in the Caribbean, we headed into the bushes to answer the call of nature. People, I had to pick leaves from bushes (thank you, God, for nature) or use an old faded book page we might have laying around. We couldn't afford newspaper nor toilet paper, we never had any plumbing, and as I mentioned above, the outhouse toilet was broken down and rotten.

My mother woke up late at night to relieve herself when sweet nanny goat did run her belly (upset tummy). Ah, poor little me couldn't sleep a wink until I heard the door open, signaling her return. If time passed and she didn't return, my heart would sink as I started to wonder if she fell in. I would walk in the moonlight towards the toilet. When one lives in the countryside without electricity, the moonlight at night is like precious gold. When you look into the galaxy and stare at the heavens…God's bright and enormous handmade sky-jewelry; the moon and stars just glisten in all their splendor. However, happiness always filled me when I heard her voice answering to my call. Still, sometimes, I was scared to death of where she might be answering from until I saw her!

Many people fell into their latrines and died there before anyone could find them — so my worry was justified. I love my mama. But trust me, it's only Massa God who prevented us from falling in that dark hole. The wood was old and rotten — deterioration everywhere — and we were too poor to do any better.

Realizing how I grew up and that I now have not one but *three* toilet bowls to clean gives me tumultuous joy! I love, love, *love* my bathrooms. I now have a real toilet paper: Cottonelle, Charmin, and Bounty. Lawd mi happy yuh si. Mama, oh, I have three toilets now, you can use anyone you want. God is just too good to be true! Blows my poor little mind every day!

Oh Lord, I can't forget how you brought me out. Lord, I can't forget what you've done for us. Lord, I want to publicly thank you for providing me with three toilet bowls to clean.

God will bless you with bigger things when you appreciate the smaller things. "Do not despise these small beginnings, for the Lord rejoices to see the work begin, to see the plumb line in Zerubbabel's hand" (Zechariah 4:10, NLT). Believe that you're coming *out* of poverty, and you shall!

Chapter 10

I Went to School Barefoot

One day, shortly after we got married, I treated my husband's feet to a much-needed massage. When I got to the soles of his feet, they were so unbelievably soft and smooth. My heart throbbed violently with anxiety because my own heels were rough—very rough, to be quite honest. At that moment, the roughness of my feet caused my mind to wander back to the days when my mother used to dry cow's skin in order to preserve it. After several days of drying the skin in the hot sun, it would become firm and inflexible. That's how hard and calloused my heels had become.

> Sometimes, it's a good thing to take people to see the journey of your scars.

Running around outside barefooted for years had hardened the soles of my feet like leather shoes. Jacob noticed my slight smirk, and when it was time to massage my feet, he had much to say. He couldn't help his curiosity. He asked me why I had so many black spots on my heels. Where did all the scattered scars on my heels come from?

Have you ever had to give an answer for your scars? I must admit that I resisted slightly. I wanted to fly away like a falcon and avoid the answers about why my heels were ugly instead of cute and soft. It was bittersweet to return to that chapter in my childhood, but nonetheless, I was willing to take my husband there to revisit the roads his wife had walked as a little girl—a road that had caused her heels to be dark and calloused. I'm not at all ashamed of where I came from, so let me escort you there, too.

I hated walking around barefooted as a little girl. There wasn't anything romantic about any of it…unless you consider walking on a beach or riverbanks barefooted. Walking around for years and years was not much of an adventure for me—not like people of today think it can be. I didn't do it for the health benefits nor for fun. And no, I didn't do it because it brings me closer to nature, though that is cool and wholesome!

How many of you ever had to go barefooted? I went barefooted due to poverty. Where I grew up, it was a social norm for most young children to play outside barefooted. Most parents would encourage this to preserve the lifespan of the shoes.

Playing barefooted in a culture like mine was the natural thing to do. From what I recall, ninety percent of children who played barefooted had at least one pair of "good shoes" for school, church, and special occasions, but I didn't have any at all, and the knowledge of this always bothered my mama and I.

My Neighbor's Shoes

No part of going to school barefooted year after year was easy. Basic school, all-age school, and then came high school in 1994…and home girl went down in sackcloth and ashes like Mordecai and Esther. I petitioned the sweet God of heaven not to allow this shoeless curse to follow me into high school. Let me ask you this, can having no shoes be considered a curse? According to John the Baptist, it might be—because even the humble man Jesus had a worthy pair of sandals! So this girl wanted shoes, too!

Thankfully, for high school, my neighbor and friend, Sheryl, had a pair of school shoes she hated. I hated them, too! But she was so happy to part ways with her ugly shoes, and shoeless me was more than glad to take them off her hands. And just in time, before my high school life commenced.

Of course, they didn't come free nor cheap. My payment for them was carrying buckets of water on my head from the local standpipe. I had to help fill up her drum. I won't lie; I was very happy to comply despite the difficulty of the task for a pair of shoes I so desperately needed.

It was worth every drop in my bucket. I dreamed of wearing those ugly shoes for days before they were in my possession. In my mind's eye, I had created a mental picture of how fabulous they would look on my cute little shoeless feet. With that picture, they became as pretty as Cinderella's beloved glass slippers. When you are born in poverty, despicable things can appear golden. There's an old cliché: "one man's trash is another man's treasure!"

The day came, and Sheryl finally handed over the shoes, and…it was the ugliest pair of shoes I ever did see! There was no attraction there! And no turning back, for I had labored like a slave for them. What I had conjured up inside my mental psyche was the furthest thing from the obvious truth. They were quite hideous and ugly! They looked like shoes the mother superiors would wear inside a hidden convent. The heels were two and a half inches thick. It was ludicrous.

Somehow, overnight, they slightly grew on me—in my sleep, perhaps, out of sheer need. The black shiny authentic leather was very well made. Sheryl didn't know their worth, and neither did I. Her father had sent them to her from America.

Neither of us could break those ugly brutes. It seemed the absurdly hideous shoes were made to last. My only downer was that the shoes were size seven and half, but I wore size eight at the time.

When you're poorer than a church mouse, you see life differently. I had asked God to provide my school fee for high school, and He did. By faith, I had enough to stretch things out as far as the east is from the west to make ends meet. I paid all the fees and bought all the school supplies I could afford except for a pair of shoes—because I had gotten the ugly pair from Sheryl. I thought that since I had a sturdy pair of shoes, I could use the little leftover money from my school fee for transportation.

I eventually ended up calling the shoes "Miss Myrtle" after a stern lady I knew. When I consider all the shoes put my feet through…the pair resembled her character.

I knew the shoes were a bit smaller than my feet, but my mama and I both concluded that my feet would break them in. What a surprise—we were wrong! Still, I would rather have money to travel to school than a nice pair of well-fitting shoes. But I simply had no idea what I was up against. Miss Myrtle was out to get me.

Looking back, I still cringe. It was a horrendous ordeal that I wouldn't want for my worst enemy! She was ruthless to my toes and soles! She committed murder against my feet five days a week. She was merciless; she didn't show my toes an ounce of kindness! Jesus lived at my house because if He didn't, the rest of me might have died along with my feet!

This happened for almost seven hours every day! I never lingered anywhere after school. I was always so happy to head home to have a foot encounter with Jesus. For a whole year, to be frank, I had the resurrection and the life living with me. My toes, my feet, came alive like brother Lazarus once I took off my shoes, and they felt the presence and resurrection power of Jesus!

Miss Myrtle ruined my manners. In our culture, having manners is everything! That one year I wore Miss Myrtle, I learned how to masquerade. I pretended in public, but once I was alone, my face looked like someone baptized me in lime juice—my shoes made my life miserable!

Let me explain the atrocity my toes and feet experienced. I read that the slaves going through the Middle Passage on the Atlantic slave ships had absolutely no room to move around—none whatsoever! That's the kind of cramped-up agony my feet endured. They experienced slavery for a whole year—every toe thirsting for freedom to experience a brand-new pair of shoes!

Mama grew somewhat agitated with me over my manners several times. I had to walk daintily to and from school every day like I was walking on broken glass. I literally had to walk on the side of my heels; I couldn't walk straight on my soles for a whole year. No wonder all the young men had their eyes on me! Little did they know that I walked that way because Miss Myrtle was down there trying to snatch my dear life from me through my toes.

Poverty is terrible, y'all. It almost killed my feet! Almost killed me! Talk about severe numbness! No longer could I greet my loving mama properly after school. One evening, after leaving school, my feet hurt so badly that I snapped—my toes and feet were completely numb—which rendered me speechless. Mama had to wait until I sat down, untied my laces, removed Myrtle, and waited for life, consciousness, and soundness to re-enter my feet. Once I was calm and my feet experienced restored peace because Jesus had revived them, I could finally extend pleasantries to mama. Of course, once mama realized the situation, she pardoned me because she understood the foot pain. For decades, she had worn shoes that hurt like shackles on her feet!

I was delighted when the agonizing school year ended. The heels were worn out on each side because of the pressure from my inability to walk properly in the shoes. Yet I held on to them until I received another pair. I was grateful she carried me through, but one day, I suddenly felt this intrinsic desire to distance myself from Myrtle—so I gave them to a little girl who could use them.

I still can't believe Jesus lived with me all that time and let me wait a whole year before considering to providing me with another pair of shoes. I can't believe Him! What was He thinking? Was He trying to get me killed just to use His resurrection power on me? I don't know! Was He trying to get this moment of time has handicapped you: please know that you are not your past. You're not what's been done to you. You're not your struggles nor mistakes. You're a child of God and you are loved. You and I are offered an eternal inheritance of true royalty and all you have to do is invite Jesus in and let Him lead you to your place at the King's table.

The truth might be that in my subconscious mind, I had somehow come to accept this one good dress as everything! I told myself it was all I needed to go to Sunday school, and nothing else seemed to matter when all along God had a closet filled with more pretty royal dresses — in my exact size because I am the King's daughter.

I was taught to be grateful and humble, and with that in mind, I was satisfied with nothing! I didn't realize I could ask God for more and just get it. (Hey, oh, hey, you can actually ask.)

My mother, on the other hand, was our sole provider, and I didn't bother to ask many times for what I thought I needed — because it was too obvious from the rampant instability in our lives that this woman was too poor. And for the most part, I didn't really understand the nature of God at the time, so I was stuck to the narrative I knew.

In retrospect, not having enough ended up becoming the greatest catalyst for me to access God — and access from God for all of what His Kingdom had to offer to me. With this humor out of me, or was He trying to teach my feet a life lesson? Still puzzled.

Barefoot Gal

It's never easy living without shoes in a tropical climate. One minute, it's super-hot, and the next minute, it's hurricane season: cold and raining like crazy. When the temperature tops a hundred degrees, the cement and tar radiate unbearable heat. Then the tar starts bubbling and melting on the road! No footwear means no protection from burns. Our feet were always exposed to the elements. Having no clothes was bad but having to walk miles and miles in the heat without shoes was evil, pure evil. Some days, I used to wish I had falcon power to fly away! This is one painful part of my childhood that I don't think I would want to relive.

Mama didn't have a good pair of shoes for herself for a long time either. I remember her wearing her worn-out busted-up galoshes to her bush and to the shops many times. I remember how she wanted to go to church, but her shoes weren't sufficient.

Back in what we called all-age school (middle school), my mother acquired a hand-me-down, North Star Sneakers— which was a bit dry-rotted—but nonetheless, I would pray at nights that my feet would grow by morning so that I could wear them to school and church. How ridiculous! I don't know who in their right mind would pray to have big feet. Only a country girl would pray such a foolish and incongruous prayer!

To me, having a pair of functional shoes was a big deal in more ways than one. I'm not refuting the health benefits of going barefooted, but as a little girl, I wasn't consciously aware of that. I just wanted a decent pair of shoes that fit on my feet properly.

At times, I wondered if I would grow up completely shoeless. I would see us going years and years without one pair, and the poverty level never declined, but rather increased around us. Man, it was rough sometimes! It seemed that the older I got, the more colossal our needs became. The one coherent fact was that I knew mama couldn't supply them all.

I didn't even want two pairs, I only wanted one that belonged to me—one that I broke in myself. Having no shoes when I walked back and forth from school meant I was at risk of stepping on rocks, puncturing my heels, bucking my toes, cuts, thorn pricks, bruises, abrasions, wounds from glass, splinters, exposure to rusty nails or zinc, and parasites such as ringworm, hookworm, and fungus. Whatever anyone says, it's a blessing to have shoes.

The distance from home to my all-age (middle) school varied between fun, tricky, and tedious, depending on the weather. I had to walk over an hour to and from school five days each week, rain or shine. Some days, going to school terrified me. Yet, no matter what the weather might be, I had no choice. As a child, I had to understand that if I went to school barefooted, I could learn how to read and write and someday, I could get a decent job—so I would be able to buy shoes for me, my mother, and my siblings!

I must admit that going barefooted long term can hurt your feet, but I would be remiss if I didn't mention the enjoyable side of going barefooted. Certain games required me to be barefooted in order to win: like Jamaican Chinese skipping, jump rope, hopscotch, track and field, and many more. I also loved racing to climb trees to pick seasonal fruits, because the person without any shoes would always be the first up the tree and the first to pick the best fruits at the top.

Have you ever dreamed of a certain type of shoes you wanted and perhaps even the backpack to match? You dreamed of it all summer long, night and day, and you imagine how awesome it would feel to look like the coolest kid on the block. In what I remember as the summer of 1988, I prayed and longed for a pair of shoes before returning to school for the first morning in September. Truth be told, in my reality I wasn't a "cool kid." I didn't care about being a part of the "in-crowd," even though it wouldn't hurt. The truth is, it didn't matter if my full dream didn't come true. I was getting older and I just wanted to have a pair of shoes this time around for the first day of school.

Yet I didn't receive any, not even a hand-me-down—and mama didn't have any money to purchase any. When she told me a few days before school opened, I cried.

She tried to cheer me up. "Go try on my shoes to see if they fit," she said.

The funny thing is, I did, even while my weeping intensified. I got me some old book leaves and began stuffing away like I was stuffing an unromantic turkey for Thanksgiving!

Simply because I was so very daring and optimistic. I prayed the night before school and asked God to add a couple of inches to my feet by morning. I woke up in great expectation. When I looked down, my feet weren't as big as mama's. Pouting, I was sort of mad at God. He knew how my heart desired for my feet to be properly covered in shoes! I'm still working on forgiving God. Just kidding! I love how ridiculously awesome God is!

I was happy, and I was sad simultaneously. Did I want to go to school that morning? I can recount every unpleasant and happy step I took! Let me not pretend. I wasn't at all happy. The ground I walked on that morning bore witness of my unhappy feet! *I had to go barefoot again*! I was walking to school that morning with my feet all covered in Vaseline! Thank you, Jesus, for providing Vaseline for my ashy feet.

Walking in the cold dampness caused by intermittent rain had me wishing I was still a baby — that way, I could stay home or be carried! — or wishing I was grown so I could afford to buy some decent shoes.

I started praying to God, with teary eyes, that He would allow me to find a pair of shoes on the way. Maybe a lost pair from a student heading to school, I didn't care — anything would do. I would wear it and then return it if I found out who they belonged to! You can't find a stranger creature than me!

I know I sound like a paranoid fool — if I said I literally looked up to the skies on a regular basis, you'd best believe I did. I was hoping to see if God would throw me a pair of shoes, a nicer backpack, or a new dress. Poor girl problems! As a child, I literally believed God had piles and piles of stuff locked up in heaven for His children. I don't even know where this scary nonsensical notion came from.

Several years after this dreary day, I prayed, fasted, and asked God to provide my school fee, and He did. The story is in chapter fourteen. I love God and what He can do. I read how Joshua told the sun to stand still and, man, I seriously believed my prayer caused God to drop the money from heaven. When no one claimed it, I thought it fell from the skies for real, for real! Rumor in my head said that it came straight from the bank of heaven — signed and delivered! God might even be laughing at me right now!

Immediately following this experience, I believed that if I didn't literally see my husband walking straight out of heaven, there's no way I would marry him—how fatuous! I was a strange creature, unlike any other! Have you ever become so desperate about a need in your life that you think and act unconventionally, nonsensically, and eccentrically?

September morning was when all the little children who seemed to have hibernated all summer long became awake, loud, and braggadocious! Everyone looks at you that morning to see what you're wearing. Good thing I trekked to school like an aged turtle because I didn't have a thing to show off. By the time I arrived, all the classes had marched in grade by grade.

That morning, I was the only one who marched into my class without a pair of shoes…and I was utterly mortified. I'm sure other barefooted pupils attended school that day, but it would be one percent. Since it was the very first day of the school term, every parent made the extra effort—but mama had no money to match all her efforts and wishes for us with her big heart.

I wanted to hide my feet or fly away to the heavens like a little eagle to get a pair of Clarks. Why hadn't God endowed me with shoes from on high yet? Was this a test of my feet and my faith? I was growing older and becoming more self-aware—or maybe I was obsessed with shoes.

Every Sunday morning, I headed off to Sunday school, barefooted or not, and it didn't bother me one tiny bit. But as soon as I prepared for school, my feet would quarrel with each other because they didn't want to go barefoot. Perhaps the distance agitated them? To this day, I don't understand the difference!

Imagine how you would feel to be the only barefooted pupil in your class today. I was terrified. I struggled with my reality that morning and the mornings that followed. I would have to attend another school year without shoes. Internally, I rolled over in my mind like a puppy dog and pouted to myself. Why must this be?

Have you ever heard this saying, "Wherever there's a barefooted girl, there's a bully lurking"? I dealt with a lot of discrimination because I was poor. Some bully always lurked in a corner to call me names like "barefoot gal," "barefoot Dassa," "dried head gal," "picky-picky head gal," or "maggah barefoot gal." But that's a story for another book. It's sad to know that discrimination follows those in poverty. Have you ever had to deal with discrimination while growing up or even today?

Having a pair of shoes back then was a big deal to everyone I knew. Some parents sacrificed a great deal for their children to have a decent pair of shoes and a backpack or other school-related supplies, only because they didn't want them to walk to school barefooted nor suffer humiliation.

Even though the privilege of having an education was huge, dealing with the severity of poverty along the way can often shift the focus and even thwart growth. I know this affected my learning efficacy to some degree.

Having shoes, to most people, was a huge sign that they had overcome the struggles of poverty that slavery had incited. In our community and school, the different classes of people were easily distinguishable by their shoes. When someone was extremely poor, the evidence showed in their bare feet and torn or worn-out clothing.

Walking barefooted was not something I can admit I enjoyed doing back then. It was more of an involuntary lifestyle thrust upon us. If you should ask me if I would go completely barefooted again long term, my answer would be yes and no. Recently, I returned home from church. As I sat on the stairs untying my shoelaces, the Lord brought me back to the days when I had no shoes. He asked me, "Would you go to church barefooted again if you didn't have any shoes?"

My response was a resounding "Yes!" Even though I now have lots of shoes, that hasn't changed my heart from who He created me to be.

During our foot massage, what my hubby noticed in me at first was intimidation. My heels have been a secret place, I've never allowed anyone to see or touch. But as I took him back with me into the history of the soles of my ugly feet, it began to create deeper intimacy between us. I was able to find deeper healing and let go of some insecurities. I was able to fully enjoy and take pleasure in the pleasure he was taking by rubbing into my once-painful scars and calloused heels. I'm so glad for such a modest and humbling experience that taught me how to trust God and how to never forget the days of humble beginnings!

Sometimes, it's a good thing to take people to see the journey of your scars. It was a long and tedious road, but I learned a lot. As he lovingly dug into my callouses, I remarked, "I'm so glad that I chose to have an education over shoes, because I probably would have spent too much time looking down at my feet and might have even missed the road forward to my future. How thankful I am to God that He answered my prayers and provided shoes for me! It's just shoes, but I am beyond happy that my heels don't hurt anymore."

If you're reading this and you don't have any shoes, I pray that God will provide for your needs or that I may be able to bless you with a pair. I know that shoes and clothes don't define us as humans—it is our character and humility that speak—but it's a blessing to be able to afford and enjoy these basic human needs.

And lastly, your scars aren't bad! Don't let your scars define you; don't let them hold you back from your future. Use your scars as a catalyst instead of a crutch. Use them as a weapon and as armor to fight! You can be healed without your scars becoming a roadblock for you. Embrace your scars, tell your story, and strengthen others whether you had shoes or not!

God did answer the desperate prayer of the little barefooted girl and grew my feet. Today, mama and I are the only ones out of all her children who wear the same exact size. God is so amazing! Thank you, Jesus, for being my great provider!

"But if we have food and clothing, with these we will be content" (1 Timothy 6:8, ESV).

CHAPTER 11

Thank You, Mass Charlie

Not so long ago, I entered my walk-in closet, and my half-finished shoe rack was pining for my attention. Right away, I huddled over to get to work, and suddenly, I started to reminisce. I remembered what kindness Mass Charlie, the shoemaker who lived near my church in Wait-A-Bit, had shown me. The thought of him took my mind back to one unforgettable Sunday morning in 1989, when my only pair of shoes gave way right from underneath me.

> *I started walking barefoot to prolong the shoes' life and would put them on once I got nearer to the church.*

I will never be quiet about the Lord Jesus Christ! Truly, if any of you knew what my life was like before the Savior found me, you'd understand why I love Him. You heard me say it: I had only one dress, I went to school barefooted, my bed was broken, and I didn't have any shoes. After going barefooted for a year, I obtained a pair of white shoes as payment after doing some domestic work. These were my only shoes for church. I wore them every Sunday and for any other church-related events—until one Sunday morning, one of the shoe heels popped off right before I reached the church.

If you are an Apostolic Pentecostal like me, then you would only assume that the devil was preventing me from going because he knows I'm bound to receive more Holy Ghost power, and God had an extra blessing with my name on it! But truth be told, my shoes were old and dry rotted. When I realized what happened, I freaked out! I said, "Oh gracious Lord, no, you can't let this happen to me!"

Thankfully, Mass Charlie's shoe shop stood nearby. I went knocking, even though I knew Mass Charlie didn't fix shoes on Sundays—he probably would praise Chick-fil-A today. I guess I had too much faith. Of course, he didn't answer my knock because he was at the church too.

There's no way I was going to turn back. I ended up hopping to Sunday school that morning. But who cares when you love Jesus, and you're already used to going to school, church, and everywhere else barefooted!

On my way home from school the next day, I stopped to see Mass Charlie and presented my case of the broken heel. He said, "I can fix it. Pick it up by Saturday."

"How much will it cost to fix the shoes?" I asked him.

He said $4.00, and I started to sweat. I didn't have any money to pay Mass Charlie, but I said okay for Saturday.

The whole week I prayed and fretted over my shoes and how I was going to pay Mass Charlie by Saturday. Poverty stings! Man, it really does! Those who feels it know!

When I returned to pick up my shoes, I gave him a dollar and owed him the rest. At that moment, I felt like my mother. I love my mama. Trust me when I tell you mama knows how to make a dollar stretch from A to Z, but when she had no money, she would trust (take things on credit). She sent me to every shop in Litchfield who would trust her flour, sugar, milk, salt, bulla cake, tin mackerel, sardines, kerosene oil, toothpaste, cooking oil, dutty gal soap, butter, chicken back (we couldn't afford chicken)—you name it, we trusted everything! Now, I had to trust tacks and glue from Mass Charlie because I had no money. This is what you call calamity!

Did I mention I had to go down some hills before I reached church? Please, don't ask me about the roads, because they were "so-so potholed" (full of potholes). My poor feet and shoes couldn't manage the hardship and pressure.

Mass Charlie and I became friends overnight because almost every Monday, I had to drop my shoes off. Sometimes, I sat and watched him apply the tacks and glue and we would have meaningful conversations about God and the good old days. He worked with such pride. I, too, took pride in my one little pair of white shoes.

For about two years, I gave my shoes to Mass Charlie to fix. He never collected any more money from me because it took me such a long, long time to pay off the three-dollar balance. I paid him in six installments for the first fix, but he never charged me for the rest.

I told God I didn't want to end up trusting from people like my mama since she was poor and had no other option. I told God I wanted to be rich and well off just like Him. God nuh beg nor borrow from nobody, so why should I, hey oh hey!

One day while Mass Charlie was adding more tacks to one of my shoes, I counted the tacks in the other shoe. I counted close to forty little baby tacks inside and outside before I lost count!

I would leave the house extra early for Sunday school because I had to walk like a turtle to prevent my shoes from falling apart. I started walking barefoot to prolong the shoes' life and would put them on once I got nearer to the church. I was seriously happy to have a pair of shoes; it didn't matter that they were broken; as long as I could fix them and wear them, all was well. I often prayed over them and thanked God for them.

One Sunday, it rained while I was heading home. I took my shoes off, but they still got soaked. The following Sunday, when I put them on for Church, they felt a little wobbly, as usual. But as soon as church was dismissed and I headed out of the churchyard, both heels gave way under me. I cried, "Jesus! Yuh couldah wait till mi reach innah di shortcut waah nuh bady cyah see mi!" (Jesus, couldn't you wait until I was in the shortcut where nobody can't see me?)

I panicked, lo and behold, my two shoe-heels lay there as still as the sun. They retired right in the churchyard. I froze for a moment, and then, I proudly picked up my heels and marched home sobbing to mama. Mama said, "Sophia, mi tink dem dun now brah. You betta tank Massa God fi spearing dem dat long." (Sophia, I think they are done now. You better thank God for sparing them that long.)

I replied, "Mama, Mass Charlie can fix them; I'm very sure he can."

Monday evening couldn't come fast enough. I wanted to save my shoes so badly — so I galloped like a donkey to Mass Charlie's shop. I ran in, out of breath. I asked, "Mass Charlie, mass Charlie, can these shoes live? If they're as dead as my mother claimed, can you make them live, good sir?"

As a child, I thought Mass Charlie was called to fix shoes. He was so good at fixing shoes, you could call him the shoe doctor. I hoped he could resurrect my shoes like Jesus resurrected Lazarus. I'm not kidding! Mass Charlie examined them and took a deep breath, shook his head, and responded to me like a doctor to a patient: "No, my dear, there's no hope here. I have nowhere else to apply glue or tacks. Sorry, my dear, I'm afraid your mama is right. These shoes are dead."

When he broke the news to me that my shoes could no longer hold up, it dealt a serious blow to my fainting heart. Tears welled up in my eyes, and my heart sang, "It's me, it's me, oh Lord, standing in need of a pair of church shoes." I couldn't believe my shoes were dead. I tried to convince the shoemaker that they could be fixed to no avail.

That evening, I returned home heartbroken because I had no other shoes for church. My mama rehearsed the same line she did during my one white dress dilemma: "One day Massa God will provide shoes for you, and you won't have feet enough to wear them."

I wanted that "one day" to be instant. I didn't want to wait any longer.

On my way home from school the following day, Mass Charlie watched for me. When I stopped in, he gave me a bag and told me to open it when I got home. I knew it was shoes, and I took that bag and rushed home in a flash. I was the happiest barefooted girl that day. I didn't know where he got them, but they were mine. I thank you, Jesus, for manifesting yourself to me through Mass Charlie.

Don't ever forget the smallest things God has done or has provided for you. In my smallest blessings, I see the greatness of a mighty God. Remember when you prayed for what you have now? Don't forget where He's brought you from. I only had one pair of shoes, and this is my incredible story of how they got replaced. I hope this blessed you.

I remember when the Lord showed me this unfailing promise at seven: "I have been young, and now am old; yet have I not seen the righteous forsaken, nor his seed begging bread" (Psalm 37:25).

CHAPTER 12

Growing Up Fatherless

My home suffered from fatherlessness and brokenness. None of the eight of us had a father to protect, provide, or give us any validation. No father figure was present to cover us and be the head of the household as God originally ordained. We had no male role model. I didn't know what love or a godly relationship should look like.

> *I went to his house for the very first time to make my first appearance in his world.*

I grew up desperately in need of fathering. The little girl in me desperately thirsted for his presence and to dialogue with him. The ominous absence was felt every single day! I wish I had had these four Ps during my childhood:

- I wish I had Protection.
- I wish I had Provision.
- I wish I had Presence.
- I wish I had his Praise.

Some of my childhood friends had fathers who would visit them intermittently, and this stirred up something in my soul. "Where is my father?" I pondered. The absence of my father combined with my dysfunctional home, made me question my very existence. Things in this fatherless home looked dismal and grim every day. I was always worried about my tomorrow because my mother was too poor, and I didn't have a father nor anyone else to help me. At one point, I felt like something was wrong with me because some of my friends had fathers, and I didn't have one.

Since I had no relatives to talk to other than my siblings, I decided to become a thorn in my mama's side. I intended to badger her — since I wanted to know who I was, where I came from, and where my life was going. I always had questions for mama, but she was busy most days with her farming life, trying to keep food on the table.

I was spunky and vivacious, full of life and childhood vigor. According to mama, I used to talk way too much, like a Quaker parakeet! I remember her saying, "Gal mek yuh chat suh much lakka parakeet." (Girl why you talk so much like a parakeet!)

But how could I have kept silent when I had so many questions? I made it my mission to question any oversized human who towered over me.

I was very persuasive, so I would press into her every single day until she got frustrated with me. Later on in life, she confessed to me, "I used to wonder if you were the bad apple, the black sheep, or the misfit in the family. You never operated 'normally' like all my other children."

She said this with the best of intentions. She said I would drill her like I knew more than she did, and sometimes, she wondered if I was sent into her life deliberately to torment her. But, hey, what do you do when you have so many unanswered questions?

I was her little problem child, it seems. The truth is I was never comfortable with my environment or the way things were, so I had to disrupt the soil. Sometimes, you have to disrupt the mold to get the outcome you are looking for. Mama wasn't happy about having a little firecracker to contend with every single day, but I was all for it.

Unsurprisingly, it didn't take her too long to concede to my bothering. Then again, it wasn't too much of a bother to get an audience of one with her—but it was because she was carrying a heavy load and wearing the hats of father and mother.

Carrying the burden for all of us exhausted her mentally, emotionally, and physically. When she was in good spirits, I often tried to seek her out. Some days, life beat down hard upon her like the hot sun. Her infectious smile would draw me to her. There, I would see a reflection of a single woman who was bent and broken from life's toils and snares, yet still very strong!

One Sunday evening, I returned from church, determined to ask my mama about the absence of my father. I often heard her speak of my siblings' fathers. She would murmur about how they left her alone and never gave her a shilling or a penny to help. Her disappointed look and the harsh reality of her struggles indicated that life had dealt her a terrible hand. To add insult to injury, from my point of view, she had met some of the worst men on planet Earth. She's not a perfect mother, but she didn't deserve what these men did to her by denying her children a decent life.

What puzzled me is that she rarely mentioned my father. When I learned the whole story later in my life, the truth bit me sharply.

She finished making our dinner and prepared to grind her coffee in her dilapidated mortar. As soon as she tossed the coffee beans to grind them, I gathered up the courage and asked her, "Who is my father?"

While I anticipated her answer, my beating heart seemed to synchronize with the strength of my mama beating her coffee beans. As she continued to grind, she stopped abruptly, took a long deep breath, looked at me dejectedly, and then sighed.

I tried to make eye contact with her, and it was as though I could see the pain in her soul through her eyes. Then suddenly, she fully stopped, straightened up, looked at me again, and said his name. Her voice was charged with emotions as she expressed what had transpired between her and this man, seven years prior. For my understanding, she recapitulated how Massa God helped her when I was born and how, if it wasn't for Massa God, she didn't know what would have happened to her and me.

She said that the very moment she informed my father she was pregnant with me, he angrily denied that the pregnancy was his. This man blatantly told the woman he slept with that he wanted nothing to do with either her or the pregnancy. (Up until to this day, I still don't understand how a man can sleep with a woman in that way and deny the possibility of procreation.) From the time she told him about the pregnancy around April of 1981, he never spoke to her again until I was two years old.

Hearing what she said made my heart bleed. Tears began welling in my soul for both of us. She had stowed this away in the crevices of her soul, and now, it was being unearthed. It was painful to watch her conveying this message from her soul to mine. I felt the pain of her being forced to endure her pregnancy alone.

Have you ever felt like the truth that was supposed to set you free left you more wounded? Can you imagine how hard it was for me to learn these things as a child? But finding out about my father wasn't the hardest thing that happened to me that Sunday. Meeting him for the first time was even worse.

After my mother revealed my father's identity, she said to me despairingly, "School is about to reopen in two weeks, and I don't have a red cent to my name to send you back. You might have to go to him, or otherwise, I don't know how you're going to go back."

Hearing this made my heart sink further into despair. Out of desperation, she wanted me to go before a man I didn't know and ask for help. Have you ever experienced any type of poverty that caused you to do desperate things? I thought to myself, "But surely, if I could find the courage to approach and ask mama who he was, I can find the courage to approach him, too."

It was my first opportunity to meet my father, and I was sore afraid — afraid to approach this human I had never met. I didn't want to go, and my mother was hesitant as well. It was a big risk, but we had no choice. It was time to meet this man, and besides, I had nothing to allow me to return to school for the new school year, so I could use whatever help I could get. I felt like I was between a rock and a very hard place! I felt like the four lepers, risking all by entering the camp of the Syrians with the inclination that they're going to die either way (2 Kings 7). So why not? I told myself I didn't know him, and he doesn't know me. So, what did I have to lose?

I went to his house for the very first time to make my first appearance in his world. It was only a short walking distance—a few minutes, actually—but it was the longest walk of my life. It felt like an eternity! I shyly approached his house and met a woman who was sitting on the veranda. I expressed pleasantry and said to her, "I am looking for my father."

"Who are you?" she asked.

"My name is Sophia," I replied. This lady, who I didn't know at the time, said he wasn't home and bid me to wait for a little while. I waited in great agony like Jesus. I cried out to God in silence, "Oh, Lord, this cross is too hard to bear." I was terrified. I honestly didn't feel a sense of belonging. It seemed the longest wait of my life, but it was only about twenty minutes.

Upon having those ugly thoughts, I heard voices whispering through the walls behind me: "She's a jacket; she's a jacket. She's not Daddy's pickney (daughter)."

I pondered the word jacket. The thought crossed my mind that I'd heard the word used a lot in my community, but I never took any time to study the meaning or its association. I wondered, "What is a jacket, and what does that have to do with me?" It didn't sound good to me, and my heart sank for the third time that Sunday. I stood in grave despair. My heart was already filled with my tears for my mother, and now, more tears leaked over into my soul.

Another one of my ugly thoughts got the better of me again. I prayed verbatim, "Dear Lord, please, split this veranda like the Red Sea and take me in. I feel like Pharaoh and his whole army is behind me. Please, deliver me from this place."

At that moment, I opened my eyes, held up my head, and saw this man who resembled my image walking down towards the veranda. Though I was shy, I looked upon the full contour of his face with fresh tears filling up my eyes. I noticed he had a straight face, a medium brown-skinned complexion, and short curly hair. I steered towards him and then lowered my gaze again into the red concrete tiles once he fully approached the veranda.

I then heard the lady telling this man I was his daughter. He didn't recognize me, nor did he know my name. It was a shame. It was obvious to me—to the whole world—that I bore his full resemblance. How could he not know my name?

Nothing had prepared my heart for this moment in my life. He cussed and quarreled with the lady, then he denied me all over again—and said I was not his, right in front of me. My heart raced. The hair on the back of my neck danced to the beats of my hurting heart. I felt the fumes exiting my nostrils; the exhaustion of it all left my body immobile. I had one coherent thought: this surely can't be the father figure I was missing and longing for. But I soon realized I wasn't missing anything because the ideal dream I had of my father in my head was completely different from the truth of my reality right in front of me.

He was upset at my presence, yet he chose to unleash most of his displeasure on the woman instead. The woman, whose name and identity I didn't know at the time, defended my cause as though she knew something I didn't. She asked me to come again the following week. I was so distraught—such an ungracious and unrewarding visit, I thought! I remember feeling numb and lacking the ability to maneuver—as though someone had shot me in my heart and the bullet lodged in my feet. That Sunday evening, I believe that God turned my body, beckoned it to run, and He ran through me.

If that had been a marathon, I won! It was the quickest I've ever sprung up over any hill. That was certainly the work of God or the angels. Before I knew it, I stood in front of my mother. But before I could get closer to her, I floated in the reservoir of tears that exploded inside me. Sunday evenings are usually happy times, but that was the saddest one I had ever experienced. My tears could have filled the Nile River.

My mama knew the moment she saw the tears falling that it hadn't gone well. Her posture changed instantaneously, and unbeknownst to me, a wound reopened inside her. (Chapter 15 recounts what happened.) She said, "Just know now that you have no father."

She disappeared by herself, and I heard her cry. The outcome did not sit well with me. I went inside our one room, inundated with tears. I asked God, "Why don't I have a father?" Somehow at that moment, I understood her years of silence. Maybe she was trying to protect me.

Not having a father and the whole "jacket" thing plagued my mind. I finally bothered my mama once more. I straight-up asked her if I was a jacket and she said yes. But she never fully explained how I came about. She added that she was also a jacket, and it became objectively clear that both of us were illegitimate children. With sadness, she admitted that she grew up fatherless, too. Something in what she said resonated with my soul. This was our reality, but I wish it was a fairytale. My mother and I suffered together. I wondered how my life would turn out without a father in it.

I ended up going back to school with a hole in my heart. I wore whatever hand-me-down I was able to salvage from my sister, Shelly. The next week arrived, but mama never let me go back to see him. This third rejection hurt. It pained my heart to see my mother struggle alone to be a mother and a father to us.

At times, I prayed and wished that one day, my mother would wake up and tell me she gave me the wrong name—that my father was someone else or somewhere else. My life was out of congruence with the order God had designed for it. I knew God created me to have a thriving relationship with my father. I knew I would need someone to fight for me and protect me from terrible men like those my mother had met. I wanted my father to place me on his lap and tell me he loved me and that I was going to grow up into a beautiful woman.

I craved for my father because my identity was insecure. I didn't know how to identify my gifts, talents, and strengths.

Some days, I wanted to wake up from this nightmare and truly meet my father. My desire for him throbbed in my soul daily. I felt lost without my father in my life, especially at school. His help with my homework, his praise, his validation, his notice of and help with the changes I was going through, his help with making life-healthy decisions, and his direction for good boundaries: I needed him.

As I got older, the sting of fatherlessness became harder to bear. As I was entering puberty, I was faced with different changes in my life that horrified me. Before this moment, no one had sat me down and educated me about my body and what to expect. The talk of femininity was entirely a taboo. I had peeked in a book the day before, while I was at Sister P's house, and I barely glanced over how a girl becomes a woman. That was the only knowledge I had. When I told my mother about the very personal changes that were happening in my life, she decided to educate me with everything she knew: "Nuh yuh cyaan git pregnant." "Now you can get pregnant," she muttered. And that's all it was, end of the story.

Experiencing adolescence at this juncture in my life was extremely difficult. First, all girls require sanitary necessities, and we were too poor to afford them. After I told my mother, she immediately sent me to purchase a pack at Mass Sam's shop. I had to use it sparingly since the pack only had ten. Every woman learns you need more than ten. Out of love, my mother checked underneath her mattress for old cloth that she deemed suitable to use. During the months ahead, when she couldn't come up with a single ten-dollar bill, she would wash and make homemade items for my use. My mother was resourceful in many areas. Cutting up old sheets to make these items was one of the skills in her repertoire because she, too, had to endure the same thing.

She did this just to keep me in school. Wearing these items to school affected me severely every single time, and that mental effect lingers even today. Imagine going to school and losing your protection on the school compound because you don't have the proper undergarment to keep things discreet. (And oh, this was bad, since I have the tendency to walk right out things unaware!). I was always afraid of mishaps during these times because you only have one uniform to last you for the school year.

I could go on and on about how dreadful those days were in my young life. I know this should be a bonding time between mother and daughter, and it was, but I wish I'd had my father in my life at this time! I wish he had been there to expound on what my mother had said about getting pregnant. I wish he could have supplied me with sanitary necessities on the days my mother couldn't. It would have made my life that much easier.

To make matters worse, I became so completely afraid of men to the point where I would literally run away from them, whether I felt threatened or not. I wished my father was there to protect me from this fear. A girl needs her father, especially when she enters young adulthood.

I am sad to say that for the majority of the crucial development of my youth, I had no father figure in my life. Learning my predicament wasn't pretty, and I didn't know what to make of it. I have great respect for single moms. And I have an abundance of love for my mother. I give her all the credit for raising me on her own as a single parent. However, this also meant that my mother would have to continue to raise me all on her own, just like she did with my other siblings.

As we all know, growing up in a single-parent household means that children can also live close to the poverty line. In fact, studies from Fathers.com and KIDS COUNT Data Center show that 41% of kids who live in fatherless homes will end up poor. These children are four times more likely to grow up in poverty and nine times more likely to drop out of high school. Close to 81% of teen pregnancies come from a fatherless home.

Imagine all of my daily fears! I knew we fell way below the poverty line in our little farming community. I know my mother's presence was a blessing to me, but it would be greater with my father's presence too! There are certain things that a father can bring to bear upon his children that a mother can't. There is a certain affirmation and significance that only a father can provide.

Even Jesus' life indicates the importance of a father's presence and validation. Matthew recorded that a voice affirmed who Jesus was: "and lo a voice from heaven, saying, This is my beloved Son, in whom I am well pleased." (Matthew 3:17). That was confirmation from the Father, letting Jesus know He was pleased.

The impact on the development of little girls and boys dealing with the absence of their father is real and can be generational. The absence of fathers knows no gender, geographic, or socioeconomic boundaries. It exists in urban, suburban, and rural communities all around the world. It's a real problem!

Upon exploring and examining the poverty of my childhood on a daily basis, I realized that the word "poor" is an understatement. We were perpetually deprived. I felt like the pressure from its sting was going to destroy me. This sprung me into early childhood depression (ECD). Yes, I know some of you never heard of ECD. Laugh a little. I made up the acronym!

But the truth is, that was my condition and reality. I was well aware of the fact that I was held back because I didn't have the same advantages as other children. My destitution and lack of privileges created a tight restriction upon many opportunities in my young life. This knowledge caused distress that coerced me to grow up much faster.

All this misfortune came with acute physical and mental suffering. I crossed over into the world of adulthood way too soon. I missed out on some things. On the whole, I enjoyed my childhood as a little girl, but it's sad to say that I didn't enjoy any part of my fatherlessness.

As old as I am today, I still inherently experience childhood desires. I often find myself beckoning to my husband — asking him to play hide and go seek with me or desiring him to speak to me in ways that I desired from my father. As weird as it sounds, that's one of the ripple effects. Poor girl problems! It's unbelievably uncanny that the rifts and wounds caused by absent fathers are so prevalent today in the lives of millions of children. Freedom from "childhood poverty" is always tied up in the presence of good fathers.

The normal thoughts of fatherless children became my thoughts. I wondered *why*. Why didn't he want anything to do with me? Calling someone Daddy, Dad, or Dadda is so neat, and I wished I could have done it. It would have been a privilege to say "dad" to the man whose loins I was woven from. I often wished I had been kissed on the forehead before

I left for school and again upon my return. It would have been lovely to be kissed good night! I wanted to hear "I love you, Sophia" — and I would have happily returned the sentiment.

Numerous studies have shown that fatherlessness has a lasting negative impact on a young girl's self-esteem. An unhealthy or non-existent relationship with her father can diminish her self-worth and self-confidence. Due to this she sometimes lacks the ability to fully function and prosper in society. Low self-esteem can affect all areas: such as her professional, physical, emotional, personal, social, and romantic life. The fatherless daughters are prone to suffer from depression, divorce, eating disorders, self-mutilation, promiscuity, social anxiety, and substance abuse. Most importantly, they will struggle the hardest to build healthy relationships.

My father's rejection brought shame and sadness. He never loved me, and that festered something inside of me — I am so glad it wasn't anything dark. I never struggled with low self-esteem issues on the level others do, but I must admit I may have been depressed a few times over the matter. According to Dr. Alice M. Millsap, the author of *Disinherited! Daddy How Could You?* Said she was "wounded and bruised from years of abandonment, frustration, emotional abuse, and a broken heart." Her childhood relationship between her and her father caused her marriage to decline and eventually fail. I was never a daddy's little girl, so what was going to happen to me, I wondered! Girls look for their identity in their fathers.

If he had been there, I probably wouldn't have had to worry so much about my tomorrows and my future. I would have had peace of mind. I would have been protected from the young men who ridiculed me because I wasn't an easy catch. I probably wouldn't have been so hungry in school. If he had been there, I might not have had to leave my mom at fifteen years old. Maybe I wouldn't have been verbally abused by people who didn't know how to love me and tried to marginalize my worth.

On the other hand, I can't say I have too many regrets over the fact that he wasn't there, because look at how well and strong I turned out. God crafted me into a strong woman even though there were times as an adult, I felt vulnerable and cried because of a desire for an earthly, fatherly presence. But God, in His sovereignty, has made up the difference for all I lacked.

When all is said and done, maybe my life would have been a little bit better if he were there. For the record, I'm very thankful for the father figures He placed later on in my life.

There is a great price to pay for the absence of fathers. I share my personal story, not for pity, but to empathize with those who still struggle—because I know that fatherless wounds run deep. This was, by far, one of the most painful chapters I had to pen.

If God hadn't come to my rescue and saved me when I cried out to Him, I'm not sure what my fate would have been. If He hadn't fostered, nurtured, and cared for me, I wouldn't be writing my story. It was during this period of my life that I encountered God, and He gave me Psalm 27:10. He made a solemn covenant to me to be a father to me, and He kept His promise. I never gave up on myself. I never accepted the fact that I would have to grow up without a father. I believed with all my heart that I wasn't just an unplanned child or my mother's misfortune.

Instead, I saw myself unequivocally as:

- Purposed
- Potential
- Promised
- Planned

So, yes, all of the poverty, pain, lack, and dysfunction that so uninvitedly overflow our lives serve as an apparatus to truly prepare and fill our lives with endless possibilities! If you are fatherless or have fatherless children, please know that the sovereign God will not leave you an orphan. He will be a father to you like He is to me.

To that single mom or that single dad, your children will make it through their fatherlessness or motherlessness somehow. First and foremost, teach them the way of God. If you ever have any doubts, reread this book over and over so that I can be a voice or a good reminder that God is well able to protect, provide, keep, and deliver from the captivity of poverty and fatherlessness. I pray that you find healing and hope in God through every page. God the good, good Father loves you best!

"A father to the fatherless, a defender of widows, is God in His holy dwelling" (Psalm 68:5, NIV).

CHAPTER 13

God Baptized Me with the Holy Ghost and Fire!

From age seven to eleven, God possessed me with a mighty zeal and a burning desire to know Him more intimately. All I did was study and read the Word of God consistently because I was so hungry for God. Day by day, I felt God tugging at my heart. I went on daily adventures within the lines of the Bible. This became a secure place for me. Every day, my whole body overran with the consciousness of God's presence—a consciousness that has remained with me today. At some point, I discovered this verse in Jeremiah, "You will seek me and find me when you search for me with all your heart" (Jeremiah 29:13, NASB).

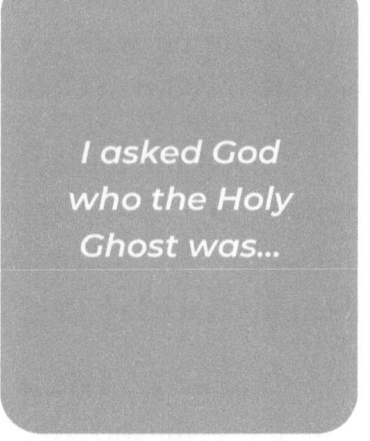

I asked God who the Holy Ghost was...

I love the Word of God. Not to be braggadocious, but God causes me to be always praying and seeking after Him somehow. None of us can be strong in God unless we are diligently seeking and constantly hearkening to God's voice to us through His Word. You cannot know the power, character and the nature of God unless you partake of His anointed Word.

Like the Psalmist David, I found life through the written Word. He said that he hid God's Word in his heart that he might not sin against Him (Psalm 119:11). The more of God's Word you hide in your heart, the easier it is to live a holy life. David also testified that God's Word led and quickened him — God's Word was a lamp unto his feet and light to his path. As you receive God's Word into yourself, your whole physical being will be quickened, and you will be empowered! Faith will spring up within you as you receive with meekness the engrafted Word of God.

I lived life through the Word, but now I could feel God drawing me closer unto Himself. "No one can come to me unless the Father who sent me draws them, and I will raise them up at the last day" (John 6:44, NIV).

October 27, 1992 was the three hundred first day of the year. It was the forty-third Tuesday of that year, and it was also my eleventh birthday. I reminded my mother it was my birthday. When you have eight fatherless children and you're severely impoverished, it's rather difficult to keep tabs on your quiver full. However, I vividly remember my mother's reply. She said, "I know it's your birthday and I have nothing to give you. Even if I had some flour, I couldn't afford to use it to flour you because I don't even have a red cent to my name to buy any more."

Where I grew up, there is a tradition of dumping flour on the unsuspecting birthday person. We both laughed, and I pondered in my heart all night long how it happened that I was eleven, and I had never received a wrapped birthday present with my name on it.

I didn't feel too bad, because none of my siblings got anything either. At least mama wanted to celebrate me if she could. It's the thought that counts, right!? I sure love my mama!

When it finally got to Sunday, I went to church as usual. Pastor Stanley Watson announced that there would be a Holy Ghost revival service and crusade. He started preaching from the book of Acts and I heard him say, "When you have the baptism of the Holy Ghost and you are baptized in the name of the Lord Jesus Christ, you have the power to pray and ask God for anything in His name and you'll receive it."

Something stirred in me when I heard those words, "Holy Ghost" and "anything!" It bothered me when I thought about how my birthday came and went through the door—and I didn't receive anything, nor could I ask for what I desired because I had no one to ask.

That sweet word "anything" was just what I needed to hear. I wished somehow I had heard this before my birthday. I'll be honest with you: I did not hear anything else my pastor preached after that sentence. I felt like an old lady who took her medicine and went to church to get one word from the Lord — she got it and then fell asleep the rest of the service! The word "anything" struck a chord and consumed my mind. The whole time I sat there engrossed in my thoughts, musing over how getting the Holy Ghost was going to solve all of my problems — if not all, then some!

With long, deep breaths, I pondered deep down how this would be the answer to all my prayers. This would surely eradicate my poverty and change my whole life. I had a long list drafted in my mind with "Urgent things I need to ask God for" as the header. This meant I was in imperative need of this Holy Ghost more than anything you can fathom — this was a real emergency!

I left church ecstatic that Sunday evening. During the sermon, I had lost my appetite for the delicious and modest dinner I anticipated my mother was preparing. There could be nothing I needed more than this Holy Ghost!

Bear in mind that I have been sitting in the Pentecostal pew all my young years, but the Gospel message of the Kingdom hadn't fully penetrated my heart yet. I felt like I was about to hit the jackpot, and all I needed to cash in for gold was this Holy Ghost. Man, was I pumped! When I left my home for church that morning, I didn't desire the Holy Ghost so strongly, but on my way home, it was a burning passion inside me. I wanted something greater than myself, my family, and my community. I needed a miraculous rescue. I needed God to govern my life.

On the way home, I took a shortcut and stopped to reason—or more like bargain—with the Lord. First, I reminded Him that I was a very poor little country girl (as if he didn't already know that). I told Him about my family being dysfunctional. I let Him in on the fact that I wasn't getting the best educational opportunities. And of course, I had to tell him again that I was disinherited by my father. I talked to Him about my clothes, which tickled me. Seriously, who talks to God about clothes? But how can we forget that he designed and made the first pieces of clothing Adam and Eve wore? I had to inform Him I relied on hand-me-down clothes and shoes from my sisters—and I wasn't complaining; I was just giving valuable information that I thought He might need in order to have urgent sympathy for me. (He must be missing the yearly memos: that I would prefer brand new clothes and shoes, not that I don't appreciate hand-me-downs.) I told him I was requesting some new things along with a birthday cake for my next birthday.

For a moment, I thought I heard God laugh. Haha! I made myself very clear, trying to convince God that I was the perfect candidate for the gift of the Holy Ghost—all done in innocence and ignorance because I didn't have a full understanding of what the Holy Ghost is—nor did I fully comprehend the prerequisites.

Of course, the Holy Ghost had already been given as a gift—but I was spiritually blind to the message of the Cross, Pentecost, and the Kingdom of God. No wonder I thought I heard God laugh when I begin to bargain my way to earn salvation.

Once I made it home, I forced the door open, but mama was still inside in the dirt kitchen, cooking our Sunday dinner. I quickly greeted her, and I shared the only thing I took hold of from the sermon. I told her I wanted to get baptized right away and that I wanted the gift of the Holy Ghost. She asked me what I would get baptized in and I told her God would provide. She was concerned because getting baptized in white was the tradition and she knew I had outgrown my one little white dress.

Eleven-year-old girls usually play Chinese skipping or hopscotch on Sundays after church. Instead of the mundane Sunday evening routine, I decided to search out the scriptures about what Pastor had said. I needed some things from God—and I was more curious than ever to learn about the Holy Ghost. I began reading through the Gospels. In Matthew, where John spoke of the Holy Ghost: "I indeed baptize you with water unto repentance: but he that cometh after me is mightier than I, whose shoes I am not worthy to bear: He shall baptize you with the Holy Ghost, and with fire" (Matthew 3:11).

"Fire," I reasoned in myself. "What fire is John referring to here?"

I digested all I could from my short read since I was so eager to enter the book of Acts. As I read Acts chapter one, I realized that before Jesus ascended into heaven, Jesus told all His disciples to wait in Jerusalem.

"And, being assembled together with them, commanded them that they should not depart from Jerusalem, but wait for the promise of the Father, which, saith he, ye have heard of me. For John truly baptized with water, but ye shall be baptized with the Holy Ghost not many days hence" (Acts 1:4-5).

I moved on to Acts chapter two. "And when the day of Pentecost was fully come, they were all with one accord in one place. And suddenly there came a sound from heaven as of a rushing mighty wind, and it filled all the house where they were sitting. And there appeared unto them cloven tongues like as of fire" — there it is again, that fire John spoke of — "and it sat upon each of them. And they were all filled with the Holy Ghost and began to speak with other tongues, as the Spirit gave them utterance."

Super excited, I read on and on until I got to Act 2:38. "Then Peter said unto them, Repent, and be baptized every one of you in the name of Jesus Christ for the remission of sins, and ye shall receive the gift of the Holy Ghost. For the promise is unto you, and to your children, and to all that are afar off, even as many as the Lord our God shall call."

I was happy to learn how to receive the Holy Spirit, even though I truly didn't understand it all. Now, my little heart yearned for more of God. I continued to read the entire book of Acts trying to find the scripture my pastor had mentioned about asking God for "anything" and receiving it.

Several days later, I discovered it in 1 John: "And this is the confidence that we have toward him, that if we ask anything according to his will, He hears us. And we know that He hears us in whatever we ask, we know that we have the requests that we have asked of Him" (1 John 5:14-15, ESV). Oh boy, oh boy, was I ecstatic!

It was nearing the end of December, and the Holy Ghost crusade — which was tied in with consecration service — was right around the corner. I decided to prepare myself to receive the baptism of the Holy Spirit by giving myself to studying the Word, fasting, and much prayer. I asked God who the Holy Ghost was — and He caused me to understand that He would be the Holy Spirit living fully inside me. I wanted Him more than anything else, considering I truly had nothing and no one.

The Holy Spirit, first and foremost, is God's personal presence that permeates your life or your walk with Him. The

Holy Spirit is beautiful and powerful and is necessary for life. The Holy Spirit is God indwelling the believer!

Throughout the Bible, we see the Holy Spirit's power used to empower individuals for specific tasks. We see this in Genesis in the story of Joseph; "And Pharaoh said unto his servants, Can we find such a one as this is, a man in whom the Spirit of God is?" (Genesis 41:38). By God's Spirit, Joseph is empowered to understand and interpret dreams.

Then there is the artist named Bezaleel in Exodus:

"And the LORD spake unto Moses, saying, See, I have called by name Bezaleel, the son of Uri, the son of Hur, of the tribe of Judah: And I have filled him with the spirit of God, in wisdom, and in understanding, and in knowledge, and in all manner of workmanship to devise cunning works, to work in gold, and in silver, and in brass, and in cutting of stones, to set them, and in carving of timber, to work in all manner of workmanship" (Exodus 31:1-5).

Like Joseph, Bezaleel was empowered to create beautiful things for the tabernacle.

The Holy Spirit empowered prophets of old to bring messages from God to the people of Israel and to see what was happening from God's point of view. In the New Testament in Acts 6, two ordinary young men, Phillip and Stephen, were chosen and greatly empowered by the Spirit of God. This infilling always lifts a plain man above the ordinary. What God requires is a yielded, consecrated, and clean vessel. He can baptize you with the Holy Ghost anywhere, at any time, and can make your life such a flame of fire! When you are filled with the power of the Holy Ghost, God will wonderfully work through you wherever you go!

My first encounter with God at age seven sets the center stage for what I'm about to share with you. I believe that God breathed His Spirit upon me like He breathed His Spirit into Adam in Genesis and into the apostles in the book of John. "And when he had said this, He breathed on them, and said unto them, Receive ye the Holy Ghost" (John 20:22). He had breathed newness of life into me aforehand because I experienced a new and changed mindset, but I felt He had more in store for me. Even though God was with me all along my journey, I felt that this time would be different. I believed this experience would somehow change my life forever!

On Sunday, January 3, Pastor Watson commenced the week of services. I anticipated receiving the baptism of the Holy Spirit by any means necessary. But when the time came for the altar call that night, I was a bit scared to go. John said Jesus was going to baptize the believers with Holy Ghost and fire—and the book of Acts states that when the day of Pentecost was fully come, they were in one place, in one accord, and the Holy Ghost descended upon everyone like cloven tongues as of fire. As a child, I attended Sunday school and midday service every week. As far as my recollection took me, I had seen countless people receiving this gift of the Holy Ghost, but I had never seen any cloven tongue of fire sitting anywhere like in Acts 2:3. (Yes, I was weird and ignant—yes, I said ignant not ignorant.) I stood in the pew watching people receiving the Holy Ghost while I told God that I didn't want that Holy Ghost, I wanted the real one, like the one that came down on the day of Pentecost with the cloven tongues like fire.

Looking back, I can just imagine the host in heaven laughing at me—for I had such a childlike spirit. I've always been a visual thinker, and by the time I reached home that night, I realized that the "cloven tongue like as of fire" was meant to be a metaphoric symbol and not literal. Duh! I was eleven, and maybe I literally thought he was referring to a real fire.

You can laugh now. But you must understand how I came to where I am in God. You don't have to come from a lineage of Apostolic Pentecostals for God to fill you and use you; you just have to believe and avail yourself of His gift. The prophet Joel prophesied "And it shall come to pass afterward, *that* I will pour out my spirit upon all flesh; and your sons and your daughters shall prophesy, your old men shall dream dreams, your young men shall see visions:" (Joel 2:28). We are living in that day. "I am first generation Apostolic Pentecostal. No one in my home knew anything of the Holy Ghost at that time. My mother, brother, and sisters received it years later. So I thank God for teaching me about Himself.

By Wednesday night, the revival service was in full swing, and the local churches were rolling in. Believers from the Battersea, Albert Town, Staten, and Ulster Spring were present. Again, many people received the Holy Ghost and were baptized, but still, I was afraid to go up for the altar call.

However, on Friday night, January 8, 1993, after the Word was preached, I came under heavy conviction. I was pricked in my little heart. As I stood in my pew, tears spilled down my cheeks. I was desperate. I didn't know what to do, but I knew I wanted the Holy Ghost — I wanted more of this God. I could sense the atmosphere changing around me. The voice from the sermon echoed in my ears again — of how Jesus came and died to redeem my life from sins and the grave. I pondered the thought: Christ died for me while I was yet a sinner? These words penetrated deeper into the recesses of my heart. I found myself sobbing and crying out loud, repenting of my sins. I had managed, somehow, to learn what repentance was from God, my ultimate life teacher. I thanked God for coming — and for dying on the cross for my sins.

I felt a stirring deep down and reached out and asked Him to wash me and forgive my sins — and I asked Him to fill me, fill me up with the baptism of the Holy Ghost. I felt a prompting and, my heart pounding; I walked down to the Pentecostal altar in faith. I lifted my hands up to heaven in repentance according to Acts 2:38. I heard a woman's voice saying, "Receive ye the Holy Ghost! Just let go and let God fill you up with the Holy Ghost!" And as she prayed with me, I also began to pray—and that tug came to my tongue and I began to lose control of what I was saying. I just yielded my tongue to the anointed presence of God that was upon me—and God got a hold of me—and within minutes, the Lord poured out upon me the baptism of the Holy Ghost and Fire. I began to speak with other tongues, unknown tongues as the Spirit gave the utterance—just like on the day of Pentecost!

"And they were all filled with the Holy Ghost, and began to speak with other tongues, as the Spirit gave them utterance" (Acts 2:4).

I spoke and spoke until I felt like my body was in space, floating on the clouds.

I felt so happy and free, so good, so great, so magnificent!

It felt like God's love was literally infused inside of me.

I felt like someone had poured a bucket of joy mixed with the sweetest sugar all over me.

It felt like I was with God, speaking to Him in a heavenly language. I was so happy I just wanted to stay there.

I felt I could fly freely up to the heavens like an eagle.

It felt like fire was shut up in my bones; Jeremiah was right!

It's the greatest experience a mortal can ever experience.

I was shaking and dazed under the power of the Holy Ghost.

As the God of heaven drew near to me, He poured himself into me with His Spirit. Two ladies held on to me and rejoiced with me as the anointing of God flowed down and I was soaked in His presence. I did not want to leave the altar because I wanted this feeling of holiness, mercy and truth, power, and affections of his infinite beauty to last forever!

I felt born again. Converted. Changed! I experienced my personal Pentecost. I must have heard many, many times that Jesus died for our sins. But I simply did not see it the way God intended. I was spiritually blind. Once I received the baptism of the Holy Ghost, He stirred up in me the true conception and nature of his divine image. My eyes were opened, and I understood more about the cross and the Gospel of the Kingdom. I was totally amazed by the depth of Jesus' love that enveloped me during this second encounter.

After I received the Holy Ghost, I was on cloud nine—and I'm still there, praise God! Of a surety, receiving the Holy Ghost was much more than I had bargained for. My needs were still there, but I had Jesus and He met my needs one by one! I had the God of the universe indwelling my mortal being—I was filled with the greatest miracle! Like Hannah, I relinquished and surrendered the rights to what I truly wanted—to be free from my state of poverty. I was no longer over-worried about all the things I thought I needed. God got a hold of my heart, and my heart was satisfied and exalted in the God of my salvation (1 Samuel 2:1). When God becomes all you need, you will give Him anything when you believe He's everything!

Walking home in the Holy Ghost that night was surreal. I spoke in tongues the whole journey home. I was astonished without measure. I spoke in new tongues until I fell asleep in the wee hours of the morning—and even spoke them in my sleep, it seems. Mama shook me several times and asked if I was okay.

I woke up late in the morning still speaking in tongues. My mama did not quite understand the drastic change in me. I tried to explain to her that I received the baptism of the Holy Ghost—when all of a sudden, He came upon me and I began speaking out in tongues again.

I told mama I was getting baptized come Sunday morning. To my joy she was very elated to help me get everything I needed for my baptism. Noonday on Saturday she made sure all the buttons on the back of my dress were secured. She also tried to stitch together the lace that was falling apart around the waistline. I was eleven, and I had been wearing my little white royal dress for a number of years. It wasn't supposed to fit me at all—but since I was full of the Holy Ghost's power and was feeling optimistic like Superwoman, I thought I'd just pray over it and ask God to cause it to fit me again.

On Sunday, January 10, I woke up to the clear, grey sky; the sun moving quickly away from the horizon. Our little community was far from quiet. All the little children were getting ready for their Sunday school morning rituals. The sounds of birds chirping, dogs barking, and the neighbor's rooster crowing echoed in the distance. I couldn't wait to get to the church and get baptized. It was time to get ready, and mama helped me get into my little dress. My little bang belly protruded through it—but somehow, it still fit, and I was surprised and glad.

That morning, I let everyone who passed my house know I was getting baptized! I didn't walk to church; I ran! I arrived before everyone else. At close to ten o'clock, people started coming in. Once Sunday school started, I wanted it to end so that I could head inside to the midday service for my baptism.

The morning passed very quickly. The choir sang, "Pentecostal Fire is Falling" from the Pentecostal Hymnal. Soon afterward, the church erupted in worship, and the Holy Ghost came down—and Pentecost repeated itself all over again! I remember Sister P singing a solo, "What will it be when we get over yonder," while they were getting the baptistry ready and that song broke me into tears.

They called out my name, and I walked happily and nervously towards the baptistry with the other candidates. I walked inside the big pool of water and they baptized me by immersion upon the confession of my faith in the name of the Lord Jesus Christ—according to Acts 2:38. I'm glad I obeyed the Apostolic Doctrine: "Then Peter said unto them, Repent, and be baptized every one of you in the name of Jesus Christ for the remission of sins, and ye shall receive the gift of the Holy Ghost."

All of a sudden, this little girl who was poor and didn't have anything going for her possessed the greatest gift—the gift of the Holy Ghost; the Spirit of the living God! This was now the only credential that I had to get through life. Jesus had come fully into my life. I was now a new creature in Christ Jesus. (2 Corinthians 5:17) The new birth experience was amazing!

I was born again, just like Jesus said, of the Spirit and water. Jesus told Nicodemus in John, "Verily, verily, I say unto thee, Except a man be born of water and *of* the Spirit, he cannot enter into the kingdom of God." (John 3:5).

In short, this refers to the relationship that Adam had in the beginning, but because of sin, he was separated from God. Jesus came and died to restore the relationship once more to enter the Kingdom through the blood—the infilling of His Holy Spirit and baptism by immersion in the name of the Lord Jesus Christ!

I felt light, brand new. I now identified with Jesus Christ, according to Romans 6:4: "Therefore we are buried with him by baptism into death: that like as Christ was raised up from the dead by the glory of the Father, even so, we also should walk in newness of life."

I can't explain fully how I truly felt that Sunday. It was pure romance, I tell you—Jesus became my ultimate love. I would talk to God about everything. He was in me and all over me. I was wrapped up and tangled up in Him. I was literally lost in his Love. He filled me up, and I started to abide daily in God. He said, "Abide in me, and I in you. As the branch cannot bear fruit by itself, unless it abides in the vine, neither can you, unless you abide in me" (John 15:4, ESV). I would have daily encounters with this God I came to love and trust. This one true God the Father became the answer to all my problems.

I don't say this to sound braggadocious in any way, but you can now understand why I'm always testifying and making mention that His Name is exalted. I spent my teenage years praying, fasting, studying the Bible, and boasting in the Lord Jesus! My relationship with Jesus is the most experiential spiritual reality I ever encountered. He's actually alive and truly wants to engage with us on a personal level. Oh, how He loves you and me! Wouldn't you agree?

It was during this season that God cultivated my mind. Philippians says, "Let this mind be in you, which was also in Christ Jesus" (Philippians 2:5). I didn't think like many of my teenage friends. My attitude and approach differed in all areas. I gave my life and body completely over to the leading of the Holy Spirit, and I did nothing without first consulting with the Holy Spirit. He led and guided me all day long. I learned to walk with God out of love and not out of expectation.

If you haven't received this promised gift yet, I would love to stir your soul. I want to encourage your heart, as I feel the power of the Holy Spirit still coursing through me. If you feel like something is missing in your life, this Holy Spirit is what can fill that void. I hope you'll receive Him and get into a deeper relationship walk with Him and His Word before the end of this book.

Can I just be a little theological right here and interject how wonderful it is to be Apostolic in lifestyle and in doctrine? Pentecost is an experience that dates back to the "Day of Pentecost" over two thousand years ago. The Holy Ghost came down on that day and was freely given to us as a gift from God. It's not something that you earn. You can't buy it; it is a wonderful gift of God. I had the opportunity to experience my personal Pentecost, and directly afterward, I was immediately immersed in water baptism in the name of the Lord Jesus Christ! Just like the biblical apostles were and taught. This Acts 2:38 experience changed the course of my entire life.

Apostolic, however, is a much broader word than *Pentecost*. As I mentioned above, Pentecost is an experience, not a denomination, as some may think. The apostolic experience encompasses teaching, doctrine, lifestyle, power, and principles. This is where my relationship with the Lord Jesus Christ intensified, developed, and grew real and personal. And so I am thrilled to be a Kingdom Apostolic Pentecostal. This is the belief that governs my walk, talk, deeds, and—most importantly—my faith in the Lord Jesus Christ.

As you read further along, you will understand how the Holy Spirit took over my entire life once I gave Him permission to do so. He's my teacher, advocate, guide, counselor, healer, and the transformer of my life.

I didn't have anyone besides my mother and Jesus, and Jesus became my whole life; my very best friend! I was so captivated by the whole experience that I tried spending all my time with God. He became everything to me. Sometimes, it takes living a life of not having anything at all for Christ to become all and everything to you! This experience took root in my soul. Since then, it's become the most powerful driving force in my life.

CHAPTER 14

Miracle Money

I don't know if you'll get the chance to go to high school — because I don't have the money to send you, and besides, remember you have no father." My mother approached me before she took off to her farm and said these words.

Even though I wasn't expecting to hear that, at that moment, I felt something rising up inside me that was stronger than my fears, so I didn't flinch. When I gazed up at her, I could see the tears welling up in her eyes. She quickly turned away.

> *God, you can't let what happened to mama happen to me. No, no!*

I felt perplexity. It was a hot day in June, and heat leaped off my skin. It felt like I was breathing in fire — I couldn't see it, but I felt it. My head spun, my heart burned, my stomach churned — it was as if my soul was about to explode inside me like a volcanic eruption!

Her words burned through my soul, and I didn't know if I should cry, run, or sit down. I didn't know how to handle what seemed like cognitive dissonance. But something else erupted inside me at that moment—maybe it was courage, or maybe it was faith. I had one coherent thought. I uttered it in a soft, languid tone: "Mama, have faith in God! He shall provide!"

I had no idea what I was saying, but I believed in the Holy Spirit Power that still resides within. I hadn't been in this position before. I was only thirteen years old. I had been filled with the Holy Ghost for only two years, so I was still learning and discovering what my faith in God could do. I didn't even completely know what faith was, but, somehow, I believed in faith.

Scripture states, "So then faith comes by hearing, and hearing by the word of God" (Romans 10:17, NKJV). I read it, but I didn't quite understand the dynamics of having faith. I listened attentively as Pastor Stanley Watson preached from the pulpit Sunday after Sunday. I listened to what he had to say on the subject of faith. One Sunday, he made a statement on faith: "Have faith in God," He proclaimed!

I cogitate on those words in my heart. I became quite fascinated with studying and learning the Word of God. So I asked the Holy Spirit to teach me about faith, and He did.

You will soon discover my entire life is contingent on one significant word: FAITH! Why? Because "...without faith *it is* impossible to please *him:* for he that cometh to God must believe that he is, and *that* he is a rewarder of them that diligently seek him" (Hebrews 11:6).

Just like most people, dealing with the problems of life doesn't exactly bring me great joy. In the modern world, we face a variety of dilemmas—so many more than anyone would want—and all the fears that come along with them. But like all problems, no matter how big, elusive, or frightening they are, there is always a solution.

For instance, take the fact that I was born poverty-stricken; how do I raise myself out of this obscure and bitter condition? Exactly how will I beat the odds? The answer for most people is education.

On this particular day, my opportunity for an education was put to the ultimate test, along with my faith—faith that I didn't even know I possessed. Did you know that God has given all of us a measure of faith? "For I say, through the grace given unto me, to every man that is among you, not to think *of himself* more highly than he ought to think; but to think soberly, according as God hath dealt to every man the measure of faith" (Romans 12:3).

When I was certain my mother had left that morning, I felt an urgency in my spirit to fast and pray. As I knelt by her bedside—I remembered seeing her kneeling there countless times. A well of emotion erupted. Things I never felt before started coming up from the very bottom of my soul. What was I going to do? What was going to happen to me? I didn't know how to pray. I was confused. I started panicking like the prophet Elijah did after Jezebel handed him a letter. He felt like it was a death sentence, and his life was about to be over. I can't lie: when the reality of what my mother said settled in, I felt like she had just handed me a death sentence too. Even though I told her to have faith in God, I truly had no idea what was going to happen. Hey, I'm no Abraham, so what do I know?

I cried, "Lord, Lord, you know education is the only way out of this community." With my heart beating out of my chest, I wept. I cried out again, "Lord, Lord, I must go to school; Lord, I must go to school!"

Her words echoed over and over in my ears. I began to think about all the women and teenagers my age in the community who were home, giving suck to their babies and trying to take care of houses full of little children with no fathers. And I cried out louder to God again to spare my life. I said, "God, I don't want children out of wedlock. God, if you don't help me to go to school, I'm probably going to stay here and push out children men don't even want."

I reflected on my mother's life and her quiver full of children with no fathers. I cried even louder, "Lord, you can't let this happen to me. God, you can't let what happened to mama happen to me. No, no!" I bawled. "Please, Lord, save me and spare me."

Yes, what my mother said was the "truth," but it was only her perspective. I refused to accept the status quo! The odds were stacked up against me. First, she couldn't afford the fees for extra evening classes that came with sitting the Common Entrance Exams—so I wasn't able to sit them. I had to settle for taking the entry-level exam in order to enter my high school instead—which I'm eternally very grateful for, by the way. But I had a purpose in my heart that I never wanted to settle again. The Holy Spirit helped me to pass my entry level exams with flying colors! In fact, the compelling story I wrote for my essay left the teachers who graded my work in tears.

At this point, I was still a babe in Christ. The only thing I knew how to do was try to pray the Word and read my Bible. Reading the Word of God set me free, gave meaning to my life, and transformed my pattern of thinking.

That morning after I panicked, I reached out for my Bible and asked the Holy Spirit to guide me through as I buried my eyes, ears, and heart in reading.

The first thing the Holy Spirit did was calm my nerves. Boy, I was a hot mess. He prompted me to sing to encourage my heart. I remembered reading, "This poor man cried, and the LORD heard *him* and saved him out of all his troubles" (Psalm 34:6). I began to cry out to the Lord again like I was this poor man until my voice was hoarse. Then the Holy Spirit guided my full attention to Hebrews. I began reading in chapter one and found a gem in chapter eleven. "Now faith is the substance of things hoped for, the evidence of things not seen." (Hebrews 11:1).

I read it over and over but just couldn't comprehend it, yet I was so intrigued. I was truly a faith novice. I kept reading to verse 6: "But without faith, *it is* impossible to please *him*: for he that cometh to God must believe that He is, and *that* He is a rewarder of them that diligently seek him" (Hebrews 11:6). By the time I was done reading through the thirteen chapters of Hebrews, something astoundingly fierce had happened in my spirit. I was blown away! I was floored by all the hardships those heroes of our faith had encountered and yet they endured for the cause.

I looked at my future, and I said, "Unless I do something and get as radical as these heroes of our faith, my life is going to be an uglier journey, or maybe there won't be any journey at all." I remember agonizing and praying again earnestly to the Lord, "Lord Jesus, I believe in you with all my heart, but please, help my unbelief. Show me and teach me how to exercise my faith in you. You are the hope and help of my countenance." (Psalm 42:11). Next thing I knew, the Holy Ghost began to lead me through his Word again. I came across something very profound that Jesus said. "Because of your unbelief: for verily I say unto you, If ye have faith as a grain of mustard seed, ye shall say unto this mountain, Remove hence to yonder place; and it shall remove; and nothing shall be impossible unto you. Howbeit this kind goeth not out but by prayer and fasting." (Matthew 17:20-21). He also led me to the book of John: "If ye shall ask anything in my name, I will do *it*." (John 14:14).

This Scripture was pivotal. The Spirit bade me fast, and I decided to fast for the very first time ever. I had always prayed, but I had never attempted to fast until now. As I mentioned before, the only way I knew how to pray was to pray God's Word. So, as I attempted to fast, I started to worship and magnify God. I began to pray his Word over my situation.

My first prayer:

"Dear Jesus, I know that You are God and that You are well able to do anything, even the impossible things—according to all that Your Word quoted in Matthew 17:20: 'And nothing shall be impossible unto me.' Loving Father, remember how You promised me that You were going to be a father unto me when I was seven, and You quoted from Your Word in Psalm 27, 'When my father forsakes me, then You, Lord, will take me up.' Well, You heard what my mother just said to me (I hope You were listening? Ha!). Anyway, I can reiterate it again. She said that I might not get the chance to attend my high school because she has no money, and besides, I have no father."

"Dear Jesus, I do believe all Your Word and believe like the Psalmist David: 'I have been young, and now am old, yet I have not seen the righteous forsaken, nor his seed begging bread' (Psalm 37:25). He said You provided for him all his days—from the time he was young until he was old—so, Lord, I believe You can make a way for me, somehow. I'm only thirteen, and according to the prophet Jeremiah, You knew me way before I was even conceived in my mother's womb. I wish to know everything about You, but I don't know it yet—but it's my heartfelt desire. I don't even understand what it is to have faith in You, but I extend my faith to You this day. Whatever little faith you find in me, dear Lord—I use it to believe You with all my heart. I believe that you are well able to open up a door and provide all the money I need for my school registration. For your Scriptures said, in Isaiah 43:19; Micah 7:8; John 10:9; Isaiah 35:6; Isaiah 43:20; Psalm 27:10; Deuteronomy 8:10; Mark 11:22-24, that you God will make a way where there seems to be no way. I ask all of this in Jesus' Name. Amen."

Tears streamed like an overflowing fountain. I began to thank the Lord in advance.

I pause here to say that God has provided everything you need to win. ALL THINGS PERTAIN TO LIFE. The most amazing thing you possess in the Kingdom of God is His Holy Spirit. When you are filled with the Spirit, you carry the very being, character, and nature of Almighty God in your temple

When you are in trouble, the Holy Spirit will assist you. Jesus declared this in John 14:14-18:

"If ye shall ask anything in my name, I will do *it*. If ye love me, keep my commandments. And I will ask the Father, and he will give you another advocate to help you and be with you forever…I will not leave you as orphans; I will come to you" (NIV).

Having the Spirit of God gives you direct access to all of God's Kingdom Power and Authority. We have six powerful weapons from God to help us be victorious.

The first weapon is the Word of God. "For the word of God *is* quick, and powerful, and sharper than any two-edged sword, piercing even to the dividing asunder of soul and spirit, and of the joints and marrow, and *is* a discerner of the thoughts and intents of the heart" (Hebrews 4:12).

I've come to understand that God has already given me in His Word the answers of how to combat any situation or tactic of the enemy. All I had to pray is the Word with the authority of God in the Spirit. When we pray God's Word in the Spirit, the Spirit goes to work and war on our behalf.

Often times, when I pray the Word, I receive instant results. When you pray, you are making a direct declaration of what God said about you—you are making a direct connection with God because the Word is God. "In the beginning was the

Word, and the Word was with God, and the Word was God... And the Word was made flesh, and dwelt among us, (and we beheld his glory, the glory as of the only begotten of the Father,) full of grace and truth." (John 1:1, 14).

Praying the Word takes you into the spirit realm. When you pray the Word, you call forth the promises God says you have in Him, and then you praise Him for the answers. Remember how in Genesis, God used His own Word and said, "Let there be..." and it was. Likewise, we have the same Kingdom authority over the enemy.

The second weapon we have is prayer. Prayer invites God into the situation. It's an open dialogue between you and God. Praying releases angelic interference. Prayer opens doors. Prayer pulls down strongholds. As you read the following chapters, you will see me testifying to the power of prayer.

The third weapon is fasting. Fasting is a very powerful weapon. What fasting is not: it is not used to twist God's arm into submission to answer a prayer. We do not force God to do anything because we fast. What fasting is: it is a weapon against OUR flesh. Our flesh gets in the way of our faith. When we fast (enough), we break down the barriers our flesh puts up so when we, for example, pray against the strongholds of the enemy, the faith necessary for that is released. Fasting breaks down strongholds in our flesh and activates the supernatural flow of abundance in your life. When your flesh is out of the way, then the supernatural can flow. It's like opening a valve when we fast (enough for the situation).

Fasting is a sacrifice. When you fast, you deny the flesh. Fasting creates the ability to experience supernatural breakthroughs and unblock whatever is hindering you from your destiny in God. Fasting empowers you to live above the flesh and keeps you sharp and more alert in the spirit. Fasting delivers you from what Jesus called "this kind" of circumstance, situation, and demons you can't fight on your own. "And he said unto them, This kind can come forth by nothing, but by prayer and fasting." (Mark 9:29).

The fourth weapon is obedience. Obedience is always better than any sacrifice. We saw the huge difference between how King Saul and King David walked before God. God showed favor and delighted in David because he was so willing to walk in complete obedience. When we walk in obedience before God, it attracts His blessings. "And Samuel said, Hath the LORD *as great* delight in burnt offerings and sacrifices, as in obeying the voice of the LORD? Behold, to obey *is* better than sacrifice, *and* to hearken than the fat of rams" (I Samuel 15:22).

The fifth weapon is praise. Praise and worship are similar but different. Praise is: Lord, I praise you for answering that prayer. Or I praise you for saving me. (See Psalm 150). David was a great worshipper, and he said that God inhabits the praise of his saints. "But thou *art* holy, O *thou* that inhabitest the praises of Israel." (Psalm 22:3). We praise God for who He is, what He has done, and what He can do. When we praise God—no matter what's happening in our lives—our praise has the ability to work miracles and deliver us from troubles. In the book of Acts, we read that at midnight, when Paul and Silas decided to have a praise and worship service in jail, God showed up and showed off. "And at midnight, Paul and Silas prayed, and sang praises unto God: and the prisoners heard them. And suddenly there was a great earthquake so that the foundations of the prison were shaken: and immediately all the doors were opened, and every one's bands were loosed." (Acts 16:25-26)

The sixth weapon is worship. Worship is: Lord, I worship you for who you are and what you are to me.

Worship is divine. Worship is yielding our will, heart, mind, and body. "And be not conformed to this world, but be transformed by the renewing of your mind, that you may prove what is that good, and acceptable, and perfect will of God" (Romans 12:2). Worship is surrendering all of ourselves wholly on the altar as a complete sacrifice. "I beseech you therefore, brethren, by the mercies of God, that ye present your bodies a living sacrifice, holy, acceptable unto God, which is your reasonable service [spiritual worship]" (Romans 12:1). Worship is submission to the Lordship of Christ by the complete leading of His Holy Spirit. "God *is* a Spirit: and they that worship him must worship *him* in spirit and in truth" (John 4:24).

Worship and praise are two great weapons. Whenever David entered into praise and worship with God, we see the results of how God fought on his behalf against his enemy.

I was determined to grasp hold of God, and I decided to persevere in prayer. Around 11:00 a.m., I entered into the second round of intensive prayer. As I knelt beside my mother's bedside, I read and declared God's Word over my life verbatim. When I was reading Psalm 23, my faith was stirred. I reminded God of what His word said.

My second prayer:

"Dear Lord, I thank You that the weapons of my warfare *are* not carnal, but mighty through God to the pulling down of strongholds (2 Corinthians 10:4). I have no father, for he has disowned me. But You said You're a Father to the fatherless (Psalm 68:5). I feel disinherited! I have no help but You. But You said in Your Word that when I call upon You that You will hear and answer me (Psalm 91:15). You said when my father forsakes me; then You will take me up (Psalm 27:10). Lord Jesus, you're my Jehovah-jireh! You're a father to the fatherless, and I'm fatherless (Psalm 68:5)! Hearken unto me. I extend my faith to Thee; I believe in Your Words. I declare Your Words over my life. I declare that Your Word becomes active and alive in my life. I put my trust in You, Lord. I am victorious through the blood of Jesus (1 Corinthians 15:57). Please give me peace. I declare that where the Spirit of the Lord is, there is liberty (2 Corinthians 3:17). I ask You to provide all my needs according to Your riches in glory, in Christ Jesus, according to Philippians 4:19. Lord, I will praise You with my whole heart. I worship You in spirit and truth. I bow before You in obedience and righteousness in Jesus' Name!"

With tears streaming like a river down my face, with my knees against the cold floor, I began to worship and invoke his name with praise, adoration, and thanksgiving. According to Philippians 4:6, "Do not be anxious about anything, but in every situation, by prayer and petition, with thanksgiving, present your requests to God" (NIV).

After a while, I felt a sudden change in the atmosphere around me. I felt this energy. The presence of the Lord came down so richly. There was stillness. And all of a sudden, around 1:00 p.m., I heard the audible still voice of God. He spoke to me clearly and said, "Get up and go down the street now to see Ms. Theresa!"

My knees knocked together, and my teeth chattered together. I got goose bumps all over me. I looked around, and I knew it was God because I heard His voice before. I was a bit startled as to why He wanted me to go down the street at that particular time of day.

I lived on a hill and I was scheduled to cornrow Ms. Theresa's hair at around 5 p.m. that day. So, it wasn't time yet. I got up without hesitation! I felt a bit lightheaded and weak because I'd had nothing to eat all morning, but I acted in obedience and cantered down the street.

But then my eyes detected something in the distance. As I hurried closer to the object, I realized it was a tiny little purse. I looked up, down, and across the street, and no one was in sight. I picked it up, put it in my pocket, and ran off to my appointment. But I couldn't keep still for two reasons. First, it was a purse, and I felt it had something to do with my fasting and prayer. Secondly, when you're poor, you can't afford a fancy vintage purse, and if you find one, it's a big deal. All I ever saw my mother use was a cloth thread bag she sewed by hand; I'd never seen her with an actual purse.

The thought of what was inside the purse distracted my mind. It was hard to stay still and focus on the hair job that was going to earn me about ten dollars or some other type of payment.

Finally, I excused myself and escaped to the outhouse to check. I opened it and, lo and behold, it contained money — lots of money! At that moment, I believe I suffered temporary amnesia, as I completely forgot what I was doing and where I was. I dashed home like a lightning bolt to go tell my mother up yonder! I totally forgot about the lady's hair. I went back a few days later to finish her cornrow! Haha!

When I reached the yard, mama was just arriving home from her farm. I tried to tell her, but I was out of breath, and I was overcome with tumultuous joy! I gushed out with stammering lips. I felt like I was getting the Holy Ghost all over again! I began to sing my words. I said, "Mama, mama, mama, oh, mama! Mama, mama, luk wah mi fine, mi fine wah purseeeeee!" (Mama, I found a purse.)

My mother reacted with astonishment! She was very God-fearing and didn't ever encourage wrongdoing. She asked, "Wah yuh get dis ah purse from?" (Where did you get this purse from?)

Finally, I caught my breath and gave her a succinct account of the whole day. She was so God-fearing that she drilled me with question after question just to make sure. "Did you see anyone?" she asked verbatim.

I said, "No, mama." I reiterated to her, that I took a leap of faith and that I really prayed and fasted all morning long. Mama had this incredulous look on her face. She looked frightened like she had seen a duppy (ghost). And I made it very clear to my mother that no one would be claiming the purse because I believed God with all my heart and I'd prayed and fasted for God to open a door for me. I prayed and fasted for five straight hours, but it felt like I had fasted for five days! She took the purse and said, "We'll wait to see who will claim it."

What God did for me yesteryear; he can absolutely do for you right now! You might feel hopeless, but have faith in God! Don't allow hard times and poverty to annihilate your faith. I know life is hard, but our God is *Mighty*! Remember, we will encounter difficulties in living for God. Living for God doesn't insulate or isolate us from hard times and troubles. But He promised you and me that He would keep us through them. "Be strong and courageous. Do not be afraid or terrified because of them, for the LORD your God goes with you; he will never leave you nor forsake you." (Deuteronomy 31:6, NIV).

Praying God's Word was commonplace for me but not fasting. When you learn how to seek God through prayer and fasting, you will see Him move mountains in your life. Faith can turn impossible situations around. It is so easy for you and me to see what seems impossible and get frustrated to the point where we lose our faith and fears take grip. No one likes things that are impossible, but God does! He's the God of the impossible. Genesis 18:14.

Believe that God is still able. Nothing is too hard for Him. I encourage you to activate your faith, or if your faith lies dormant, reactivate it now! Sometimes we need to look back over our lives; see the situations or circumstances the Lord has brought us through before, and learn to hope and trust Him again. He will honor our faith when we direct it towards His purpose and plans for our lives. I dare you to step out in faith today. I dare you to believe God.

CHAPTER 15

The Death of My Sister Restarted the Struggle

My first school year of high school ended, and so did my miracle money. Starting the second year proved to be the same struggle, but with help from my sisters, Juju and Shelly, I was making it through.

But in April of 1997, news came that my sister, Juju—who was trying to help me financially as best as she could—had suddenly passed away.

> God showed me the black hole she had fallen into.

Our world turned upside down. I didn't understand why she had to go so soon. I watched my mother mourn her death for weeks, and then the weeks turned into months. Grief is so lonely. It hurts to live after someone you love so much has died. It just does. I was very close to Juju and my mama, so I took on their pain. I was hurting. "Did my future die, too?" I pondered.

My sister had been my only way out for that season. Juju helped me with my bus fare when she could. If it hadn't been for her, along with my other sisters, Joan and Shelly, pitching in here and there, I wouldn't have had lunch nor transportation money most days. Juju's efforts alleviated the stress from my mother for the first quarter of my second year. When I said my mother was poorer than a church mouse, I wasn't joking. My mother had no set income, and I had no father. My little life was encompassed with great poverty.

I had to wing it when it came to finishing that year of school. No lie, I had a lot of faith, but I was sick and tired of my story. I worried about how I was going to get to school the next day, and the next day after that.

About one month after my sister's passing, I came home from school and found my mother sitting on a stone inside our dirt kitchen sobbing. We were still mourning Juju's untimely death. Mama's grief engulfed something in my soul. I somehow mustered up the courage and asked mama about my father again. It had been about eight years since the last conversation about him. I had to know if I had any hope with him or if my life was just doomed to fatherlessness. I asked her how she met him, and she shared her story of all our births from her very first pregnancy down to her pregnancy with me and my little sister Marcia. While she shared her story, a vision from God transpired simultaneously right in front of me. God showed me the black hole she had fallen into.

She refreshed my memory regarding the day she swallowed her pride and had to send me to my father's house. She tearfully explained how terrible it made her feel. She said things had gotten so bad, and she needed some help for me. She reminded me how he hadn't given her anything while she was carrying me, nor after I was born. In fact, he broke off contact with her the same day she told him she was expecting me. When I was two years old, she decided to take him to court, and the judge ordered him to pay her two hundred dollars. It seems two hundred was all I was worth—I assumed it was one hundred for each year missed.

However, she said he stopped at her house on his way home from the courthouse and threatened her life. He never handed over a penny to her. Mama remembered, "He said if I ever took him back to court, he was going to kill me."

I guess he didn't feel that way while he slept with her. (Just saying.) She implied that she was alone and afraid, and so she had no choice but to leave him alone entirely and shoulder the responsibility to raise me on her own.

When she said this to me, it crushed my spirit. These details forever burned in my mind. Meanwhile, as she continued to share her story about our births, I saw the big, black hole my mother fell in—not once but eight times. My mama was pregnant for 81 months and roughly 2,470 days, plus she lost a baby. God didn't intend for women to go through their pregnancies alone and then turn around and raise their children alone. I still tear up over this at times, because she had to endure every single labor by herself with whatever responsible children and midwives she had by her side. Can you imagine that *none* of these men ever loved her enough to marry her, nor had the heart to help her with their offspring? Can you imagine yourself in her shoes? It was quite the calamity for this poor woman.

I have nothing against her. I'm glad she defied the horrible odds and gave birth to the lights of God in the world—because that's what all my siblings are, and that's what you are...Salt & Light! We are the salt and light of the earth. (Matthew 5:13). If you ever get to thinking that your life was a mistake, please, believe me when I say you're no mistake. God has a glorious plan to redeem and use your life for His glory. My mama is a beautiful, strong, black woman, but was she naïve? What was it? Was she tricked? Did these men manipulate her? I cried for my mama so many times trying to comprehend what happened to her.

Out of this realization, I made a declaration over myself: that I would not raise my children by myself. I said, "Not so, Lord Jesus! This shall not be my lot."

I could hear God's audible voice saying, "No, my child, this shall not be your life." In the vision, I could see that with each pregnancy, the hole had grown much bigger. The blackness that I saw represented all the heartaches, sorrows, and troubles she had to face alone.

As she continued talking, I looked again, and I saw myself standing at the edge of this pit. I heard the Lord say, "You have to jump over it as high as you can."

It was a huge hole. It looked impossible to jump over. But the Lord told me, "You can do it."

In the vision, I saw myself taking a long jump right in front of my mama. The jump was symbolic of the leap of faith I was going to take with God. I barely made it across; I saw myself dangling on edge, and then I saw the hand of God reaching for me.

At that moment, I suddenly felt the burden of teenage pregnancy lifted off my shoulders. I glanced at her and saw her drying her tears. I then looked her straight in the eyes and said with full assurance, "Mama, I just saw the black hole you fell in, and God just helped me to jump straight across. Mama, I'm so sorry for your hardship and the sufferings you faced as a single mother, but what has happened to you cannot repeat itself in my life. God has helped me, and somehow, I'm going to try to help you." That was me speaking out by faith.

She didn't fully understand, and neither did I, but she came into agreement with me.

Juju and I shared a very close bond. When she died, I felt a part of me had died, too. It was so painful because I'd truly loved her. During this time, I felt my mother's cloak of poverty trying to choke every ounce of hope from out of me. It was trying to choke me out of school before the school year ended. Money was hard to come by, and even though the Lord had shown me that I had overcome teenage pregnancy, the notion of this happening to me still lingered. I didn't want to become a part of the statistics; because not only was I going to grow up fatherless, but I was probably going to raise a child or children who were also going to grow up fatherless. When I saw how poverty had robbed my sister of her life by her untimely death, it shifted something in me. I saw what it did to my mama, and her mother, and many other mothers within my community, even some of my peers. I got sick of it!

Due to my love for God, His strength in me had grown. My sister's untimely death fostered in me greater desperation for more of God. I cried out to Him for days and began to pray and fast for God's divine intervention in my life. During this time, the Holy Spirit showed up and began His work in my life. Even though I was only fifteen years old, at that moment, I realized I belonged to God and God alone. I was woven into a family I didn't choose. I didn't choose the chromosomes nor the genetic material that brought me into existence. This loving and holy God had loved me enough to nurture and prepare me for the day my mother revealed the full story of my birth. I'm not sure how well I would have received this news if God hadn't intercepted my mind earlier on. I knew the Lord had a plan, and I knew He wanted me to defeat my poverty-stricken life. I knew He had chosen me.

That day, all kinds of thoughts went through my mind. But in God's Word, I found comfort. "In the multitude of thoughts within me, thy comforts delight my soul" (Psalm 94:19). I came to the full conclusion that if God's hands wove and fashioned me inside my mother's womb, then those same hands that pulled me across that pit will keep and preserve my life. There I stood in confidence upon his Word. I believed God's plan, and I believed He wanted me here today.

Maybe this story reflects something about your life. One day, you will look back over your life and see that every seemingly insignificant thing was a part of something that was much bigger than you. Perhaps that "one day" could be today.

Even now, while you read my story, may you learn to see God in all the little things and in all-new ways. You may not be happy with the family you were born in, or maybe you are as poor today as I was back then. I hope I can help you understand that God has a good plan, and He will put all the puzzle pieces together for you to see one day. "Before I formed you in the womb, I knew you, before you were born, I set you apart; I appointed you as a prophet to the nations" (Jeremiah 1:5, NIV).

CHAPTER 16

God Sent Me to Listen to the Radio

After my sister's passing, I didn't know how to pick up the pieces of my life and keep moving forward. I probably wouldn't have started that school term in the first place if God hadn't made a way for me. Now how would I finish?

End-of-term exams were right around the corner, which meant I needed to be in school every day to study all I could. Keeping up with my studies seemed futile, especially since we had no electricity. I had to rely on whatever kerosene we had, and because money was scarce, kerosene was hard to come by. At times, I struggled to keep keenly focused on my studies, so I would just cry and wish for my life to improve. Worst of all, worry kept me awake at night. Frankly, I didn't realize at the time that worry is a great sin—until the Holy Spirit pointed it out to me one day.

> *We were too poor to afford a radio, and we had no electric power...*

One Wednesday, after I returned from one of my exams, mama told me that she only had ten dollars to her name. Two more exams loomed that week, and my bus fare cost fifteen dollars both ways. Knowing I had no steady money to travel to the school to sit my final exams depressed me. I didn't worry too much about lunch—sometimes, I would fast, and sometimes, my sister Shelly would bring me a little butter dish filled with white rice and curry chicken back.

Since I only had one ten-dollar bill promised, I had to hustle. While everyone else was still at work or at school and wouldn't see me, I searched the neighboring yards for D&G soda bottles to recycle—a scary task, since most people owned watchdogs. My mother helped wash the bottles so I could resell them to the local shops.

I couldn't keep doing this long term, but I was able to come up with the money for Thursday. I earned a few extra dollars for Friday, and my sister, Shelly, helped cover the rest.

Over the weekend, I shouldered some domestic work; washing laundry, carrying water, and cleaning. I earned enough to cover me for few more days for the week ahead. Since my exams were almost over, attendance every day wasn't mandatory by this time. On Sunday, when I went to church, I started crying out at the altar to God for help, and I heard the Lord say, "Don't worry, child."

I pondered this in my heart, and I tried so hard not to worry anymore. If one could get rich from worry, I would be a millionaire!

I was so skinny. Ever since I fasted for my school fee and God provided it, I took fasting to the next level. Since I attended a shift school, it was easier for me to fast all day or part of the day. I decided that since I didn't have much going on, I was going to go on an extended fast and seek God for divine help. In Matthew, Jesus said I should seek Him. "But seek ye first the kingdom of God, and his righteousness; and all these things shall be added unto you" (Matthew 6:33).

One afternoon after school in May 1997, the Holy Spirit prompted me to fast. So I began to seek diligently after the Lord in prayer and fasting. While I was praying, the Holy Spirit led me to the book of Psalms: "Delight thyself also in the LORD, and he shall give thee the desires of thine heart. Commit thy way unto the LORD; trust also in him, and he shall bring *it* to pass" (Psalm 37:4-5).

I didn't know what to pray for specifically, but I began to pray in my spirit with the understanding that God is mighty and that He's able to help me again. As I delighted myself in Him, I shared my personal desires with Him and asked Him, "What are Your desires for me?"

At that moment, the Holy Spirit overshadowed me profusely and began to pray through me, according to Romans

8:26. "Likewise the Spirit also helpeth our infirmities: for we know not what we should pray for as we ought: but the Spirit itself maketh intercession for us with groanings which cannot be uttered."

After the Holy Spirit finished praying through me, the desire entered my heart to pray specifically for a family to help me. I didn't quite comprehend any of it, but I prayed according to the leading of the Spirit.

After a while, the Holy Spirit nudged me to go visit Sister P's house and listen to her radio. It was quite odd, but I obeyed God's audible voice. I ran the few miles that separated our new home from hers as quickly as I could. I visited without a good reason to be there other than to listen to the radio. It made me feel a bit awkward.

We were too poor to afford a radio, and we had no electric power — so thank you, God, for Sister P! When I got there the radio was already playing, so I nervously listened in. Right away, a woman came over the airwaves on Love 101 FM Radio. This is a religious radio station located in Kingston. I believe her name was either Colleen or Nadine. She announced, "That a lady needed a young girl from the country to be a part of her family."

I was floored. "No way! God, are you mad?" I muttered underneath my breath. (Lord, please forgive me — You aren't mad; I'm the one who's crazy!) I could not believe my ears. The

Holy Spirit nudged me again to write down the woman's number. I scurried around to find a pen and wrote down the number during the second announcement. Since no one knew why I was there. I muttered again silently. "God, you have got to be kidding me, right!? God, you want me to call a total stranger?"

God replied, "Yes."

I said, "God, you really want me to leave my mother and go and live with a total stranger all the way in Kingston?" Kingston is Jamaica's equivalent to the United States' New York City.

He responded, "Yes!"

Can I tell you how baffled I was? Then I heard God saying, "I'm not sure why you are acting so surprised when you've asked me for help."

If that wasn't enough to shut me up! He shut me up like He shut Job's mouth. No lie!

This is why without faith it's impossible to please God because what He's asking you to do most time is unconventional. (Hebrews 11:6).

CHAPTER 17

I Had to Leave My Mother

As I walked frantically back to my house, my eyes fixated on the phone number written on the palm of my sweaty hand. Surprise and bewilderment overcame me. I tried long and hard to comprehend what had just transpired. This was a bit of an anomaly! Inside my chest, my heart galloped up and down like a racehorse as I now cantered down the hill home. *What in the world just happened to me?* I cogitated.

A thought leaped out at me, and I cringed, wondering what I was supposed to really do with this number for real, for real, even though my heart were filled with yearning for a better life! The thought of leaving my mother gripped my heart with pain, squeezing it tightly, causing me to hyperventilate. I'd never been without her. "God, I'm fifteen," I said. "I can't go to Kingston. I can't leave mama. She's like my best friend. We've grown a lot closer since Juju's

> *I began to weep for her because I knew she needed me around as much I needed her...*

death, and she's more open and unassuming towards me now. God. Are you mad? I can't go."

She was the only one I knew who genuinely loved and cared for me. She never verbal expressed her love in words but she expressed though her affections. I couldn't bear the agonizing grief of leaving mama. A ton of sadness swept over me as I ran the few miles home thinking about the future.

Plague by amorphous anxieties, I began to weep for her because I knew she needed me around as much I needed her — but it was inevitable, considering I had no one else to provide the help. I so desperately needed to finish my high school education. Fatherless, impoverished, disinherited, without inheritance, heirlooms or wealth, and with no extended family that I knew of — what choice did I have? What would you have done differently?

I possessed a keen awareness of all these reasons. After much surveying of my environment, calculating, and evaluating my life's dilemmas, I realized I had to go because my life lacked every sweet essence of privilege and opportunity a young girl should have. We could hardly afford the bare minimum or simple necessities. This was not the life I longingly daydreamed about. The burden of my mother's cloak of poverty always hovered over me like gloomy clouds. I knew I had to leave her and could in no wise escape this persuasive appeal or call.

God is wise. Consequently, He prompted me to pray for a family who can help me, and then He sent me to get the number. What a God! Oh, but the idea of leaving my poor mama killed me! Bear in mind that God's will is perfect but never easy. My unsteady thoughts traveling back and forth in my head like a ping pong ball, kept me up several nights in a row.

Most nights, I brooded and brooded until I began to aimlessly count the flicker of flames from our kerosene lamp reflected against the wall like stars. I prayed and cried for days, wondering why God couldn't use someone closer to sponsor and help me right there at home.

I tried to slink away from the thought of leaving mama. I tried praying away the situation, and the agony in my prayer grew immensely. I contemplated how I couldn't become like mama. I wrestled with my thoughts. The inner voice in my head affirmed verbatim that I just couldn't become like mama, yet I wished to someday acquire mama's strength. She was a beautiful, soft, brave, and strong black woman.

I might sound more like a hypocrite rather than an enthusiast for only desiring her strength and rebuffing her weaknesses. Surely, a girl like me could never endure the pain and shame she had succumbed to for having all of us way-out-of-wedlock. (That sounds like a curse — doesn't it? But it's not! I am not a curse, and neither are you if you were also born out of wedlock.) However, somewhere in the armory of my mind,

I forged many weapons with my imagination, and one was determination! I was determined to fight against my mother's woes, so they would never become mine. I weaponized my thoughts with tools of hope, courage, faith, endurance, and strength. I wanted better. I wanted to build wealth and have riches enough to get me to where I needed to go and plenty to spare for helping others.

I made up my mind and refused to be poor. I wanted to be prosperous in all my endeavors, so, indeed, I must go! At that moment, I didn't even know what the Word of God said in 3 John 1:2, "Beloved, I wish above all things that thou mayest prosper and be in health, even as thy soul prospereth." The word prosper is the Greek word euporiá or euperoé, which means to have a prosperous, successful life journey, a life thriving as the person God created us to be. I also believe true prosperity goes deeper beyond riches and wealth—and that's to experience the manifestation of God's full blessing here on earth: in mind, body, soul, and spirit. The desire for a better life was innate within the inner recesses of my soul. This was when I realized that this was more than a mere phone number; it was my ticket to destiny!

This was a paradigm shift for me. A call of destiny beckoned my name and I felt God calling me away from under mama's cloak. I knew that somehow, I had to make use of this number and opportunity. I continued to talk with God through

She was wavering, but I was optimistic in waiting for the most favorable outcome because of my faith.

Two weeks passed. During those two weeks, I postulated on what I believed God for by faith. Plans were made. I looked over my school supplies list, and I went on my school orientations. I got my book lists and bank slips. I really wanted to go to high school, so I decided to exercise my faith by stepping out! Faith without works is dead, dead, dead! (James 2:14-26)

No one reported a missing purse to the police station. The sum of money was $3,800, more than enough to cover my school fee and book rental and to buy fabric to construct my uniform. I even had enough left over to cover my transportation costs for an entire year!

Try to tell me that faith in God and His Word can't move mountains! Not only did God provide, but He gave me a bonus. This reminded me of what He placed in Boaz's heart to give to Ruth. "And let fall also some of the 'handfuls of purpose' [extra] for her, and leave them, that she may glean them, and rebuke her not" (Ruth 2:16). Talk about favor!

Some of you today are faced with uncertainties—situations so rough, circumstances so ugly and terrifying that your life feels stifled. Please, let this testimony encourage you to put your faith in God! Stretch your faith to the same degree that your life and circumstances are stretching right now!

much prayer, fasting, and reading of the Word for direction. This was the only life I knew.

When I fasted and asked God for divine help, I hadn't thought that far ahead. I didn't think I would have to leave my mama — but I couldn't just sit and watch my future so full of uncertainties — where was I going to climb to? I was enthusiastic and sad simultaneously as the time drew nigh. One might question as to how can this be God's will, accompanied by such inundated sorrows? When the Word of God said in Proverbs 10:22, "The **blessing of the LORD**, it maketh rich, and he addeth no sorrow with it." But leaving mama was an arduous undertaking for my young soul.

Have your emotions ever driven you up the wall? Mama had just lost my sister, Juju, and now, I was planning to leave her too. My mind was a royal mess. It was the worst feeling and timing in the world, I thought. But God's timing is always perfect and right! The end of May fast approached, and I manage to saved fifty cents to make that dreadful phone call to this stranger lady.

I had thought about Love 101 FM and that lady every single day since. It had been fourteen days since I wrote down her number in utter panic. The day came, and the Holy Spirit prompted me that it was time. With my body shivering and my heart racing, floods of emotion coursed through me as I started out on my journey. It was a warm spring evening. The beautiful Caribbean sun still cascaded her tropical light across the sky. I cantered a bit while. I walked. It seemed like the bushes and trees were dancing and clapping for me—and if you listen quietly, you could hear them hum and sing sweetly.

New flowers and new blossoms bloomed everywhere. I sniffed in the wind the aroma of rotten guava, rotten mangoes, rotten Soursop, and naseberry getting ready to deliquesce their sweetness back into the roots of nature. I gazed away into some of the biggest beautiful trees, wondering which one I would climb to the very top to conquer and devour its fruits.

I walked for several miles to the phone box at the local police station, directly around the corner from my old school. Every mile closer, my heart flip-flopped like a fish out of water on a riverbank.

Even though I had mixed emotions, I suddenly began to dream. I tried to see past the phone call into what my new life might look like. I dreamed of what my new high school would be like. What color uniform would I wear? Would I get a new pair of shoes along with a cool backpack and all the fancy school supplies? Would I have my own room and a good place to sleep and study with electric light? Who would my new friends be—would I even have new friends? Who would give me enough money for school? Would I be hungry or full all the time? Would I finally be able to concentrate on my schoolwork without any worry?

This would be my first real phone call since I knew no one who had a telephone at that time. I also kept thinking that God was mad and that I was way too crazy to listen, follow, and believe Him. I was praying and rehearsing what to say to this stranger lady and also what to convey to my mama upon my return home. My mother had always thought I was her strangest child, and now, I would give her all the ammunition to make her think she was right all along. I was a bit cuckoo in the head.

Finally, I made it to the phone booth. Standing alone in that phone box was one of the most nerve-racking moments of my teenage life! But I felt excited, too! I stood there, shaking like a leaf as my gut roiled inside me. The thoughts that had run up and down in my mind for weeks were about to become my reality. I had thought long and hard about what possibility and opportunity would exist for my new life with this stranger if she said yes. I could join her family!

I wondered what she would say on the other end of the phone to me. Would she really open up her home to a stranger and accommodate my needs? I wonder if she would truly love and care for me as a mother should. I had to wonder, because I was still just a young girl who had never left home, nor had I ever met anyone who had embarked on such an ambitious and ambiguous life journey before — other than what I learned and believed about Abraham in the Bible.

With shaking hands and sweaty palms, I picked up the phone and dialed the number. It rang and rang again. She picked up the phone and said hello. I heard her voice, and I was so nervous that my heart leaped into the back of my throat. I almost forgot to keep breathing. We extended pleasantries, then I gathered my composure and jumped right into the reason for the call. I told her I got her number off the Love 101 FM Christian radio station. A feeling of self-pity hovered over me, and I felt as though I was about to drown in the tears so involuntarily running down my face. I strained to maintain good composure and be professional. My voice cracked a little when I told her, "I'd like to be a part of your family, and I was wondering if you could help me to finish up high school."

She said yes, with no hesitation. The moment I heard that, I saw for the first time in months a shimmering mirage of hope standing before me.

She asked about my parents. I stuttered in my response as my mind clutched on to her "yes" like the rest of my life depended on that one word. I told her I only had a mother and one minute remaining before the call would end.

She then asked me, "When would you like to join my family?"

I hurriedly answered, "Once I'm done with the school semester."

She said okay, and the call ended. I stood there dumbfounded; my body continued shivering in shock. I was floored, speechless, and breathless. I stood there crying, paralyzed by the great happiness and the power of a fifty-cent phone call. I felt so empowered by the believable voice of a stranger woman, who supposedly just changed my life's fate over the phone forever!

Sharing this is bittersweet, but I want you to understand why I love to testify about God and why my faith in God is so unflinching. It's bedrock. It's the blueprint for my life. My faith is of utmost importance to me. It's the catalyst for my existence. None of us should take the journey of life without it.

What was so crazy about this phone call is that I waited exactly two weeks before I finally made the call after I heard the announcement. Once the lady heard my voice, she sounded happy, as though she had been waiting to hear from me specifically. I was flummoxed, I am not going to lie to you! That's the part that had me scratching my head for days.

The fact that no one other than me had called her within that time frame didn't go over my head too easily. How serendipitous! I kept thinking to myself that God is surely mad, and that made me crazy, too. Ha! I am serving a very mad God! The things He tells me to do are just crazy! Nothing is normal with Him, absolutely nothing! This was quite a phenomenon!

Since I'm always using the Bible as God's blueprint for my life, I wonder if the Lord had sought an occasion for me as He did with Samson and Philistines (Judges 14:4). Baby, expect God to do the great anomaly in your life! God will put you where He wants you even if no one thinks you deserve the position.

Let's pause to put things in perspective and see how crazy-mad all of this sounds! For fourteen days, no one else called her other than me...hmm? I'm no detective, but doesn't this look crazy to you? The following chapters reveal more about how crazy and amazing God can be when you trust Him. Oh boy, oh boy, I'm so excited about what God is going to do in your life once you put all your trust in Him too!

One of the police officers heard me sobbing and walked over courteously to see if I was fine. And of course, my face leaked fluid from my eyes, nose, and mouth. I was a hot fudge sundae of a mess, I tell you! Walking home, I was too baffled, nervous, and overly excited to be scared. I thought that God was so cool, mad, and awesome at the same time—I didn't fully comprehend what He was doing in my life, but yet I somehow fully trusted Him.

As I pondered the crazy idea of leaving my mother and the even more crazy idea of leaving her to carry on the rest of my life with a complete stranger, I decided I would take refuge in His word: "And we know that all things work together for good to them that love God, to them who are the called according to his purpose" (Romans 8:28). I didn't know how this was going to work, but I trusted God.

As I walked home, the strangeness of my experience caused me to halt several times because I was thinking deeply about what had happened. One moment, this new hope had given me wings to soar about the skies like an eagle, and then, the next thing I knew, I was shaking in fright.

With heavy tears cascading down my neck, I wondered, "How can I face my mama? What in God's name will I tell her? I can't just go off on my own — I'm just a girl, not yet a woman." Ugh! Oh, my sweet Jehoshaphat! I felt terrified, like a little baby fawn who had lost its mother.

At that moment, my adrenaline rush ignited an emotional burst that left me stunned by the event that just happened. The thought rendered my frail little body motionless. My mind wandered, and I wondered what it had been like for Abraham to answer the call to leave home — but I was not Abraham. I had lots of God-confidence, but I was worried sick, as to what I was going to say to my poor mama. Maybe Abraham had anxiety like I did because God called him alone, but he decided to take his nephew Lot along on the journey. He probably couldn't stand leaving him behind.

Deep in my thoughts, I remember trying to breathe, gasping for air, but I was inundated by too much grief. "Who do I think I am? Where am I going? I am only fifteen! Fifteen! How am I going to travel close to a hundred miles away from home on my own?" I was happy yet nervous to the point where I could have collapsed! How could these two emotions coexist in me at the same time?

Ask me if I was afraid and the answer is yes! The little girl inside was super psyched while the older me was tumbling over in fright! Like Christian on his journey to the Celestial City in *Pilgrim's Progress*, I had extreme apprehension. But no reluctance came from my optimistic spirit. None! I gained unwelcome companions who lingered around me day and night—such as Fearful, Doubtful, and Much Afraid; but Faithful and Hopeful helped me to silence them!

I knew I would have to navigate to this stranger's home alone, but I was never truly alone because the Holy Spirit was with me. Plus, all along, I had this innate feeling that I was being called towards something so much greater than myself.

How crazy is all of this! All I had was a phone number and a tiny mustard seed of faith. I was reminded that having faith is believing God for the things I do not yet see. "Now faith is the substance of things hoped for, the evidence of things not seen" (Hebrews 11:1). I knew the story of Abraham well, and I partially knew how to live for God—and that was going to take all my faith. We are required to have absolute faith. Paul said, "For e walk by faith, not by sight" (2 Corinthians 5:7).

I had always been fascinated with Abraham's spirit, boldness, and faith. I had the inkling that, just like him, I was now going to tread upon unknown borders and territory. I didn't know to whom I was going, and I didn't know where I was going. All I knew is that I wanted to finish my high school education and help my mama. I hoped I had enough faith in God that He could help me get there, according to Romans 12:3. "For I say, through the grace given unto me, to every man that is among you, not to think *of himself* more highly than he ought to think; but to think soberly, according as God hath dealt to every man the measure of faith."

I believed God. I believed in the written Word of God with all my heart. I believed that He can make a way out of no way. "For I, the LORD your God, hold your right hand; it is I who say to you, 'Fear not, I am the one who helps you'" (Isaiah 41:13, ESV). So I decided to take the journey of faith to find out my fate. You'd best believe that in my humanity, I was terrified like Christ before his passion. He prayed, "O my Father, if it be possible, let this cup pass from me: nevertheless not as I will, but as thou *wilt.*" (Matthew 26:39). In my spirit, I was a bold and determined fifteen-year-old girl with a vision. I didn't entirely know what I was doing, but I felt the anointing of God over my life.

When Samuel had anointed the boy David, the Spirit of God instantaneously came upon him. When King Saul, who wasn't named among the prophets, began to prophesy, it was because the Spirit of God came upon him. When David killed the bear and the lion with his bare hands, that same Spirit of God gave him the strength to do so. (1 Samuel 17:34).

I didn't know where my steps would lead, but I felt the Holy Spirit helping me and leading me. Jesus promised He would order my steps, and I believe sincerely that "The steps of a *good* man are ordered by the LORD: and He delights in his way" (Psalm 37:23). After a while, I began to feel a peace and a calmness in my spirit and my faith in me rose to the occasion.

If you're at a crossroads in your life right now and you have to make a hard-to-believe outlandish decision like I did — I promise you, you can trust God to get you through all of it, even if you can't see exactly how it's going to unfold. When you put all your faith, trust, and confidence in Him, He will work it out for your good and God's glory.

"And we know that all things work together for good to those who love God, to them who are the called according to *his* purpose." (Romans 8:28).

Chapter 18

My Journey to Kingston

Once I finally made it home, I found mama sitting serenely inside our dirt-floored kitchen on her favorite rock. The wood fire had burnt out, but the embers still glowed. I decided to try to warm some water for my evening wash since the late evening breeze sent off a chill.

Between the phone call and the long journey home, I felt drained, so I retired for the night. Since I had school in the morning, it seemed like a good idea. I decided I would pray and wait on the Holy Spirit to nudge me when it was an opportune time to have a dialogue with my mother about my departure. I found rest in my spirit, but my body was restless, so I didn't sleep much that night. I suffered much tossing and turning, overly concerned about how to tell mama and what her reaction would be.

> *I can never forget that look as long as I live.*

By morning, this weight had lifted off my shoulders. Throughout the day at school, I sang praises in my heart while

I reminisced about how loving and holy God is. He had loved and nurtured me and prepared me for what was ahead. I felt like God somehow had a purpose for my life. I believed I existed in the mind of God from creation and He needed a womb to carry me, so He chose my mother and my father. The book of Ephesians explains, "Just as [in His love] He chose us in Christ [actually selected us for Himself as His own] before the foundation of the world so that we would be holy [that is, consecrated, set apart for Him, purpose-driven] and blameless in His sight in love" (Ephesians 1:4, AMP). This promise gave me so much unexplainable assurance.

It was God's hands that wove and fashioned me inside my mother's womb. Some folks thought I was pretty, and some say I was ugly, but all I thought of was how I belong to God. His hands pulled me across that pit and those same hands will hold all the facets of my life together. This gave me boldness, and I was able to walk home after school to my mother with this confidence. "In whom we have boldness and confident access through faith in Him." (Ephesians 3:12, NASB).

I believed what prophet Jeremiah said: "Before I formed you in the womb, I knew you, before you were born, I set you apart; I appointed you as a prophet" (Jeremiah 1:5, NIV). I'm no prophet, but I could feel His hands leading and guiding me towards my future and the curveball called life. I knew the Lord had a plan, and I knew He wanted me to defeat poverty, and I totally agreed with Him. I came to the full conclusion that

God meant what He said when I was seven. He was going to be a father to me, and that gave me security.

I had my final exams to sit, and oh boy, I had the most difficult time staying focused—I was overly encumbered by the weight of my passage. I asked the Holy Spirit for help, and He helped me, and when it was time, He gave me the signal and the courage to tell my mama.

This was two weeks after I had called the lady. I didn't beat around the bush about it; I humbly took my future into my own hands and conveyed the news. Would it be good or bad news for her?

I delicately approached her, and at first, I thought of reiterating verbatim what the Holy Spirit had instructed me to do about the radio—then I thought, "Nah, nah!" Telling her that God sent me to listen to the radio would sound like a duppy or anancy story to her. Plus, she already thought I was the crazy nutcase child with the loose screws in the family. No sah! I'm not going down in mama's history book like that. So I didn't. I let that thought stay right there in my mind.

I simply said, "Mama, a lady came on the radio while I was at Sister P's house the other day. And all of a sudden, she announced that she was looking for a young girl from the country to join her family. I wrote down her number, and God told me to call her up, so I did." I sighed deeply.

She stopped me once I mentioned God. She said, "God told you to do what?"

I said, "God told me to call her, and I did."

I still remember the look of surprise, mingled with consternation, that sprang into mama's eyes. Astounded, she sat there, speechless. I continued. "I found a family in Kingston who is willing to accommodate and help me finish up high school—since you're not able to help me. And besides, I have no father nor any other relative to help me."

She didn't say yes, and she didn't say no. She just had this look on her face as though she subliminally knew what was going on. I can never forget that look as long as I live. It was a look of permission and a look of uncertainties! She quietly said, "Massa God knows that I'm not able to help you," and the tears welled up in her eyes and mine. She continued, "If you said Massa God told you to go, who am I to stop you."

And the conflict and tug of war between my heart and soul froze. That war was over and a new one inaugurates.

To prevent her and myself from crying, I refrained from talking. I prayed again and asked God to tell me when it was time to depart. In the meantime, I had to figure out how to pay my passage to Kingston—and I was concerned that I didn't have a decent traveling bag nor very many decent clothes. I did some domestic work so I could earn an honest fare.

As the time drew nearer, the Holy Spirit nudged me that it was time to call the lady again to notify her of my departure.

On the last Friday in May, I made that nerve-racking journey to the phone box once again. This time around was a bit different. Much of my fear had subsided. I dialed the lady and informed her of my departure itinerary so that she could make preparation for me.

On Sunday, June 22, I made a final attempt to gather up my few little belongings — which wasn't much of anything for starting out on a new journey of life.

My mother was very melancholic during the weeks remaining, and I was inundated with grief that I had to leave her. But she was powerless to tell me to stay or to tell me to go! She never contested the matter. It was all very clear this was "the God call," because neither she nor I could prevent what seemed like the inevitable.

I was able to get a traveling bag and pack my few things along with any paraphernalia and bric-a-brac I could find. I came up short since we never had much of anything of value to begin with. Mama gave what little traveling money she could spare. I can't forget the fact that she always tried, no matter how tiny.

Morning dawned cloudily, and the chilly June air nipped at my cheeks as I walked outside to see the area I had lived in for fifteen years. I went back inside and got myself together to depart alone. Mama and I both knew it wasn't goodbye, so we refrain from tearing up over the circumstances. I gathered up my things, and my mama walked with me to catch the market bus underneath the broken streetlight so I could finally be delivered to the unknown place to which I was bound.

I felt like the Apostle Paul when he said, "And now, behold, I go bound in the spirit to Jerusalem, not knowing the things that shall befall me there:" (Acts 20:22). Most assuredly, I know I was led by the Holy Spirit because I wasn't capable of such a bold, human move of my own accord.

As we arrived under the streetlight in the shadow of the brisk early morning country breeze, I quickly gave mama a huge hug to refrain from crying. While she hugged me, she softly uttered, "May Massa God go with you, and send word when you reach the place."

This is the most heartrending part of this book to compose. I honestly don't know if it would be easy for me today to part ways from my child—let alone not knowing where my child would end up. Though it was painful and difficult, she yielded and released me with the hope that God would keep me, and I would have a far better life than she could offer. Looking back, that was a very surreal moment in my life. This makes me think of the narrative about Hannah in 1 Samuel 1:2-2:21. After years of waiting on a child from the Lord, God finally answered Hannah's prayers and gave her

Samuel… but Hannah brought Samuel to the temple when he was weaned and gave him back to God. You need to understand at that particular time in Israel, there were no prophets and God needed a willing man to serve. Samuel was that man. It was no coincidence that Hannah had the good desire of her heart to give the child back to God. Psalm 37:4, said, "Delight thyself also in the LORD; and he shall give thee the desires of thine heart." I now know that it doesn't matter what condition you were born or raised in. God has a good purpose for your life, and He can and will use your life — if you let Him, just like He used Samuel's life.

I asked mama long afterward why she did it, and I believe she said, "Maybe I felt like I was releasing you back to God."

After all, it was inevitable! If Hannah had only one son, and she was able to release him back to God, then so could mama.

I boarded the market bus that was already waiting. It was filled with higglers (people who go to the marketplace to trade or buy and sell). They were packed like sardines in a can, everyone in their designated area. They owned their space because they paid a premium fare for it.

I sat on the edge of the seat beside two elderly women around my mother's age who were making the trip to the downtown Kingston market to sell all sorts of ground provisions.

Daylight broke, and so did my heart for leaving mama behind. The grey clouds hung low in the sky, looking still and as sad as I was.

I set out for the city of Kingston without any prior knowledge of exactly where I would end up. I couldn't let the ladies beside me see my tears — so I hid them. I had just driven away from my mama and the only life I knew. And what made it worse was that I didn't exactly know where I was going. (By virtue of this story, you can definitely call me a true descendant of our father, Abraham, by the end of the book!)

I felt awkward. I was both terrified and confidently strong. The Holy Spirit was my copilot, and reading my Bible was my roadmap. I made up my mind and believed with all my heart that if God called Abraham to leave his family and go to a place he's never been, and if He kept him there along with the promise, then surely, He can keep me, too!

As we traveled the miles, the sun began to peek out from behind the clouds and the rolling hills. I remembered what I read in 2 Timothy. As I reminisced, I became convinced that God was powerful enough to protect what He had placed in me, and I am certain that he is able to keep that which I committed unto Him. (2 Timothy 1:12).

So, there I was, bound to Kingston. Doesn't this sound like a story from out of the book of Acts? The driver took a circuitous route through a place called Spanish Town to pick up a passenger. Man, my glad bag almost burst from excitement that he was stopping for a short break! Insufficient legroom had numbed my legs. Like a worm, I wiggled my way out from the back of the bus to use the facilities—and then I had to hurry back because time was of the essence. Once I boarded again, my body began to shiver—not because I was too cold but because the fear of the unknown began to wrestle with my faith. I silently begged Jesus to hold me because I was shaking terribly like a leaf. I clutched my little duffle bag for dear life. The lady sitting beside me may or may not have felt my unsteadiness and the killer potholes made the ride dangerously horrendous!

Thank God I arrived in Kingston safely and in one piece. I know how a fish out of water feels—very frightened and confused. People normally described some parts of Kingston as more wicked than Sodom and Gomorrah—I cringed at the thought. I held my breath, bit my lips, and let out a huge sigh. I uttered loudly, "Holy Spirit, help this dear child!" I added, "Dear mama, sweet Jehoshaphat, dear Jesus of Nazareth, pretty please, pray for me; don't let me end up among the scoundrels!"

The lady beside me was kind enough to give me a few traveling tips. I withheld from her the fact that I didn't know exactly where I was going. I don't know why; maybe I thought she would freak out at my mama or me since I was alone. She pointed me to the street that led to the buses heading into the

Portmore/St. Catherine bus depot and she gave me precise instructions on where to walk as if we had been mother and daughter. It almost sounded like she was giving me instructions on how to navigate the rest of my life's journey, too! At the moment, I had wondered if I could give her a message to convey to my mother once she made it back home—that I made it safely to Kingston. I knew I had more miles to go, so the thought remained futile, and besides, I didn't want her to judge my mother.

I grabbed my bag, threw it over my squared shoulders like a confident soldier preparing to charter into an unknown war zone to fight for justice with the determination to win! I started walking towards the bus depot, but the place remained foreign to me. Thank goodness I could read and follow instructions—those barefooted days at school surely paid off. You learn to appreciate an education once you have to read street signs to help you arrive at your destination.

So many buses headed into Portmore/St. Catherine, all lined up—like a fleet of ships in the harbor getting ready to set sail. A sea of people moved to and fro in every direction. For once, I wasn't afraid, which I considered very odd. The drivers called out the names of the areas in Portmore to which the bus was headed. One driver said, "Braeton Phase Three," and another hailed, "Greater Portmore," and another one yelled, "Portsmouth and Waterford."

I looked carefully back on the address the lady had given me, and it said Portsmouth.

When I walked up the stairs into what appeared to resemble a luxurious tour bus with padded seats and air conditioning, it felt like it was meant to be. Though in that moment, the future was still far off and very unclear. I retreated to the back aisle since I could just drop my bag under the seat for a more comfortable ride. I sat down and let out the loudest sigh I could muster—I still wondered where I was going. I still wondered how I developed the nerve to board a bus and escape from the only life I ever knew. Who did I inherit this gumption from? Like Anne of Green Gables states, "The future is yet an untrodden path full of wonderful possibilities."

I sat there, brooding. When I was a little girl, I always desired a good life. I never accepted what I saw in and around me. No matter what, don't settle for what you see period. I had dreams and distinct ideas about how my life could be better. I would imagine the most beautiful life night and day. Never forget that your dreams, voice, imagination, love, and prayers are the most powerful force in the universe. But it's up to you to use these forces to elevate, innovate, and uplift yourself and others. The words you speak over yourself give life to dreams. Think it. Speak it. Write it. Live it.

The conductor beckoned one last time to the sea of people. He was looking for more passengers—even though the bus was already packed.

Finally, it was time to travel again into my future. This reminded me of Marty and Doc Brown excitedly getting ready to board the DeLorean car to go back to the future that was bound to change the trajectory of both their futures forever. We started on our way, and it was destination Portmore. As I sat in complete stillness, glaring through the window and dreaming of my new life (which felt like a close reality), I took advantage of the opportunity to fully immerse my body in the scotch of summer heat piercing through the tinted window onto my brown ginger melanin skin. I had a real flashback to my past and the first possible glimpse of hope for my future. The bus was traveling as fast as possible since there was no speed limit at the time but thank goodness the road was mostly pothole-free. I had managed to ask the conductor discreetly, and he promised to oblige me and let me know when the bus arrived at Portsmouth, which is located inside the providence of Portmore.

I wasn't at all frantic at this point. I felt tranquility and peace. The Holy Spirit had helped to conquer my fears. I was in fellowship with the Holy Spirit the entire journey and He provided guidance and comfort. Every now and then, my heart would race a little because of where the unknown path in front of me would lead. I prayed and read from the book of

Genesis about Abraham leaving Ur of the Chaldees to borders of the unknown—this story gave me so much courage. Truly, if we read the written Word of God long enough, we're bound to find answers for life's questions there.

In between reading and peeking through the window, I was a little afraid when the bus began to drive over across the Portmore Causeway Bridge. I have a phobia for large bodies of water (Confession is still good for the soul…amen). But the Holy Spirit brought to my remembrance, "For God hath not given us the spirit of fear; but of power, and of love, and of a sound mind" (2 Timothy 1:7), which I held on to for dear life.

Nothing looked familiar. The air felt thicker than what I was used to. We drove deeper into the Portmore housing area, which stretched for miles and miles. It was amazing how it just metastasized the more inland we drove. All I was used to seeing were lots of scattered houses, hills, trees, valleys, and farmlands. The view wowed me. Everything was meticulously joined together like husbands and wives.

I was paying close attention when I saw a gigantic sign that said, "Welcome to Portsmouth." The conductor then summoned the passengers who needed to get off, including me. I debarked from my very first coach ride, which I enjoyed immensely! When you're used to tiny buses that have busted windows, and broken doors in which conductors pack passengers like sardines, you can feel the difference in a "regular" bus with padded seats; it feels like a luxury bus.

I walked confidently into the bus stop with my belongings and then I looked around as far as the eyes could see. Before I made my move, I intentionally spied out the land, like Caleb and Joshua did before they entered Jericho. For a fleeting moment, I let myself dream out loud again. And as my mind drifted towards the future, I closed my eyes and my mind was flooded with a feeling of relentless hope and joy of my new future.

In her directions over the phone, the lady told me I would see the Portmore Community College. When I spotted the building, a flood of new joy burst out inside of me again. I knew I wasn't lost—and right there at the bus-stop, I began to praise God, as I cried tears of joy. I crossed over to the other side of the street and walked towards the phone box. I called the lady to inform her of my arrival, but I didn't get her; I got her son who was a little bit younger than me. He instructed me where to walk and told me he would meet me halfway since his mother was in the shower and because they lived near the bus stop.

I was the happiest country girl in all of Portsmouth that day! Oh, sweet Mary and Joseph! I can't express the thoughts that flooded my soul; it was transcendent! I could only attribute it to Proverbs, "Trust in the LORD with all thine heart; and lean not unto thine own understanding. In all thy ways acknowledge him, and he shall direct thy paths" (Proverbs 3:5-6). The Lord had directed my path.

I walked several blocks until I saw a young boy coming towards me. He saw my duffel bag, and we didn't have to exchange pleasantries because he knew it was me, somehow. He helped me with my bag, even though the house was literally right around the corner. I arrived at my destination on Monday, June 23, 1997, sometime after 10 am.

Joy bubbled inside me as I walked inside the house that was a part of the Portmore housing scheme. The young man showed me to my room and then called his mother to alert her that I had arrived. I asked him immediately if I could use the phone to call my sister, Shelly, at school. She was the head girl at the time, and I knew if I called her, I would get her. On the first try, I got her, and she was elated that I had arrived safely. She said she would pass the message to mama.

Once the lady was available, she greeted me and introduced me to her eleven-year-old son and her one-and-a-half-year-old daughter. She showed me around the house. It was a modest three-bedroom home with one bathroom, one kitchen, a large living room, and dining room conjoined with a small wash area. It was a delight to live inside of a house that had an inside bathroom and electric power! It was nothing like the primitive life I was accustomed to.

We shared plans and my story. She agreed again to help me finish high school, and I was quite delighted at the interest she took into me. She said she would need me to help babysit her daughter in the daytime until she returned home from work. I was happy and complied because she took me in as a stranger, and she was going to give me an opportunity to finish high school.

Things went well for the first couple of weeks. I had food to eat and a safe place to sleep. I was very grateful. I babysat, did the laundry, and cooked with pleasure. I didn't feel like it was a burden because it was barter — exchange labor for room, board, and schooling.

In mid-July, my sister, Shelly, called me, and she burst out in excitement that she got my school report. She said, "Gal, you came in first in your class!"

I was floored. We had fifty-six very bright students in my class. I wept, remembering how difficult it was to get to school to sit my exams. The hardship and pain of poverty doubled up on my mama around the last lap. Some nights, I had to pray that God wouldn't let the kerosene oil in the lamp run out before I was done with my studying. (I can't begin to tell you how many times I experienced the Shunamite woman miracle. There were times I would look at a dry lamp wick still burning. Who could it be but God?) My mother sacrificed every penny she had left for me to have transportation so I could do my exams. It was rough, but I studied as best I could, and I made good grades. Will God not keep what you commit unto Him? "Commit to the LORD whatever you do, and He will establish your plans" (Proverbs 16:3, NIV).

The end of July fast approached, and I wanted to check out some of the best schools in Kingston. Since my report was excellent, I thought I stood a good chance of getting into a good school. Time moved fast, so I prayed about the situation and asked the Holy Spirit if it was time to approach the lady. One day, I made it home from a local church I had visited for the first time since I arrived in Kingston. From the looks of things, the lady believed in God but didn't appear to be a devout Christian.

That Sunday evening, the week of July 27, as I walked into the house, I decided it was time to dialog about school. She was sitting on the sofa and I sat beside her and asked if she could help me get registered for school. She quickly said, "Oh, I was going to tell you, you can go register at Heart Trust Institute; they have an evening school program."

My heart leaped into my throat, my mouth dropped, and my eyes popped wide open, and I responded by telling her a resounding, "No! You said you'd help me finish high school, and Heart Trust is for people who didn't get a chance to finish high school."

(I mean no disrespect if you are reading this book and you dropped out of high school or didn't have the opportunity to go and so you finished at Heart Trust—it's a wonderful institution.)

I firmly said to her, "I'm sorry, but I'm not going to any evening classes. I would like to finish high school and graduate please!"

She responded with disdain, and she blatantly said, "I'm only trying to help you because I feel sorry for you." Oh no she didn't! Can you tell that I'm upset?

In that precise moment in time, I felt like I had a promise from God, and that wasn't the promise. I had made the journey to Kingston so I could be given the opportunity to finish my high school education. The situation left me with an unfavorable taste in my mouth. How could it be now that the trajectory was changing course against my will and God's? I didn't want to settle for the alternative. At first glance, I didn't understand why God would open the door and why he had chosen her only for her to deny me my heart's desires. Jeremiah 29:11 stirred my heart so wonderfully, "For I know the thoughts that I think toward you, saith the LORD, thoughts of peace, and not of evil, to give you an expected end." This was not the plan nor the end I was hoping for.

All promises made by God captured my heart. Whenever I can recall any promises of God, I'm able to tap into the power of God. By the end of this chapter, you will understand that all of God's promises are true. According to 2 Corinthians 1:20, "For all the promises of God in Him are yea and in Him amen." Can I tell you something? I tapped into some power that Sunday evening. I thought it was just pure evil for her to make me a promise and lie to me. So I got off the sofa and I responded back to her very bluntly, too. I was like "Listen, lady, I mean you no disrespect, but I don't want you to feel sorry for me. I just need you to help me as you promised over the phone."

Did I shock her? Yes indeed. This little country girl had to stand up for something, or she would fall for everything. The lady repeated that the only way she could help me is if I watch her baby during the day and then attend classes in the evenings. I felt conned, and I foresaw an onerous downward spiral, so I rejected her offer. Have you ever felt conned?

She must have been mad at me because I wasn't her ideal country girl. Though I was beyond grateful she took me in. It seemed she had a plan for me, and I had a plan for myself, too, and God also had a plan for me, and only one plan could prevail and that was the ultimate God plan. Her plan wasn't going to come to fruition in my life. Oh no! Can you believe the nerve? I was a fifteen-year girl who so desperately wished that someone would take me up, help me, hold my hands, nurture me, and mother me so that I could become the very best version of myself, but no. Good stranger lady wanted me to be a stay-at-home mom all day long taking care of her baby girl. And ain't nothing wrong with all that, but I said, "Nope, and thank you! Homegirl needs some education! I am fifteen."

I wasn't going to allow my life to be marginalized or defined by her agenda for me. Clearly, her plan had backfired because she wanted me to babysit permanently in the daytime and then go to evening remedial classes—not on my watch. Not that anything was wrong with that in itself. My sole purpose in leaving my mother's house was to finish high school and that's what I was going to do some way, somehow.

I know you might be thinking that going to evening classes is better than nothing. But being poor and needy doesn't mean you should be a pushover and let anyone silence your voice and your dreams. Besides, when you decide to live a life of faith, you can't settle for a mediocre life. God made over three thousand promises to the believers, and I believed Him to make me the head and not the tail. I knew what God said about me. I knew I had authority and I was willing to exercise my faith in Him.

When you're poor, people always try to take advantage of you. That's why my heart goes out to the poor and needy in our society. Take, for example, my mother, who never had a proper education. She suffered greatly in people's hands—because she couldn't break the cycle of poverty over her life. Today, education is one door to rise above poverty. If one door closes, try another one or crawl through a window.

While she was gushing over her failed plans, right there at that moment, the Holy Spirit refrained me from speaking any further on the matter with her. It was closed. The Holy Ghost instructed me that my time was up! It was time to leave. I replied, "Oh God, are you kidding me now?" I began to freak out. "Oh, God," I cried, "now what? What's going to happen to me? Oh, sweet Jehoshaphat! God, exactly where should I leave and go?" I cried and shook my head. "God, either You're mad or I am. One of us is crazy!"

I figure this must have been nothing but a test. Was God testing my faith? The words "Time's up" hit me like a ton of bricks, and I managed to walk away, trembling before the words could fully soak in. Tears gushed like an uncontrolled fountain. A wave of hopelessness swept across my hope. It was only a few weeks ago that I was bathing in the sea of what seems like an eternal hopefulness! My hope was crushed! And then right away the Holy Spirit brought to my remembrance this verse: "Now the God of hope fill you with all joy and peace in believing, that ye may abound in hope, through the power of the Holy Ghost" (Romans 15:13). The Holy Spirit also nudged me to read about the young man Joseph. I read about how his young life was turned upside down until God turned it upright once again. (You can read the full encouraging story here. Genesis 37:18-36). And this is why we are urged to, "Study to shew thyself approved unto God, a workman that needeth not to be ashamed, rightly dividing the word of truth." (2 Timothy 2:15). Read on to see God's divine intervention.

CHAPTER 19

A Call to Faith

In order to comprehend the full reality of what transpired on the day God sent me to listen to the radio and upon my arrival in Kingston, it is vital to grasp the importance of the two elements that made all of what happened possible: faith and the work of the Holy Spirit. In this chapter, let me share about faith. In chapter 20, we'll examine the work of the Holy Spirit.

If you're unfamiliar with the account of Abraham, here is the backstory:

> *I encouraged myself that if Abraham did it, so could I.*

"Now the LORD had said unto Abram, Get thee out of thy country, and from thy kindred, and from thy father's house, unto a land that I will shew thee: and I will make of thee a great nation, and I will bless thee, and make thy name great; and thou shalt be a blessing: and I will bless them that bless thee, and curse him that curseth thee: and in thee shall all families of the earth be blessed. So Abram departed, as the LORD had spoken unto him; and Lot went with him: and Abram *was* seventy and five years old when he departed out of Haran. And Abram took Sarai his wife, and Lot his brother's son, and all their substance that they had gathered, and the souls that they had gotten in Haran; and they went forth to go into the land of Canaan; and into the land of Canaan they came.

And Abram passed through the land unto the place of Sichem, unto the plain of Moreh. And the Canaanite *was* then in the land. And the LORD appeared unto Abram, and said, Unto thy seed will I give this land: and there builded he an altar unto the LORD, who appeared unto him. And he removed from thence unto a mountain on the east of Beth-el, and pitched his tent, *having* Beth-el on the west, and Hai on the east: and there he builded an altar unto the LORD, and called upon the name of the LORD." (Genesis 12:1-8).

Please understand that I'm no Abraham here; I'm just a lowly country girl who simply believed what God said. When I was seven years old, God prompted me to read the story of Abraham several times. If it wasn't for Abraham's faith as a mere man, I wouldn't have been bold enough to have the faith to decide to leave my mother's house. I encouraged myself that if Abraham did it, so could I. We must truly grasp what God's Word says, "For we walk by faith, not by sight" (2 Corinthians 5:7).

Initiated By God

In our journey of life, we can navigate in one of two ways: on the basis of what our eyes can see, which is walking by natural sight, or on the basis of what we cannot see—that's walking by faith. I implore you to choose the latter.

God desires each person's journey to be one of faith. According to Hebrews, "But without faith, *it is* impossible to please *him*: for he that cometh to God must first believe that he is, and *that* he is a rewarder of them that diligently seek him" (Hebrews 11:6). Through the life of Abraham, we learn what walking the journey of life by faith looks like.

God reached out to Abram and called him away from his native home. "Now the LORD had said to Abram: Get out of your country" (Genesis 12:1 NKJV). In the life of faith, God always takes the initiative. Somebody once said, "I sought the Lord until I finally found Him." In reality, if you ever sought the Lord, it's because the Lord previously searched for you. "No one can come to me unless the Father who sent me draws them" (John 6:44, NIV). At the time, I wasn't thinking that God was calling me away. I was going because I wanted to finish high school, and I needed some divine help. Little did I know that God had a bigger and better plan for my life. Jesus said, "You didn't choose Me, but I chose you" (John 15:16, WEB). God always takes the first step and makes the first move.

Total Surrender

Somehow, a cost is also involved with God. God told Abram he had to leave his city, Ur of the Chaldeans, and his father's house. Most of the time, going after God, will require us to leave our comfort zone. Following Him will cost each of us something.

Abraham had gotten married and settled down with his bride. He was prosperous in his business. Maybe everything was going well for him. One day God spoke to Abram, telling him to follow His instructions to become a blessing to the whole world. Abraham obeyed and departed.

Faith is based on God's Word. "So, then faith *cometh* by hearing, and hearing by the word of God" (Romans 10:17). Faith is demonstrated by obedience. Total obedience means giving all your time, talent, and treasure. It means giving your totality to Christ. I whole-heartedly encourage every believer to never settle for being a mediocre Christian. The entire journey should be traveled with the Lord Jesus Christ, giving Him everything we have.

When God sends us, sometimes, He doesn't tell us the whole story or show us the big picture of what corner to turn left or right on, but we are expected to go, trust, and believe God without doubting Him—that's what faith is. It's the ability to open your spiritual eyes to see beyond the present and the norm. In fact, James tells us that we can't get anywhere by wavering with God; we just have to believe. "But let him ask in faith, nothing wavering. For he that wavereth is like a wave of the sea driven with the wind and tossed" (James 1:6). To waver is to be unstable in your mind and thinking. Either you believe God or you don't.

God gave Abraham a covenant filled with promises—no blueprint and no map. Today, even though God has given us the Bible as our blueprint, hardly any of us would leave on a long journey without our GPS. But somehow, Abraham took God up on his offer even though he had no evidence of this prophecy. God said, "In you, all the families of the earth shall be blessed," and through Abraham's obedience to answer the call of God by faith, this act ultimately ushered in the Savior through his lineage. You and I have a Savior whose name is Jesus today because of God's promise to Abraham. I received my personal Pentecost because of Abraham's faithfulness—and I am able to enter the Kingdom and have dominion once more. With just one act of obedience, God will bless you!

The Author and Finisher

When Abraham arrived where God had sent him, the Lord was there waiting to greet him. "And the LORD appeared unto Abram, and said, Unto thy seed will I give this land: and there builded he an altar unto the LORD, who appeared unto him" (Genesis 12:7). "Looking unto Jesus, the author and finisher of our faith" (Hebrews 12:2).

This means that the same Jesus who called you to follow Him by faith will meet you where He calls or sends you. He goes before you, paving the path towards your destiny.

Faith Without Works is Dead

"But wilt thou know, O vain man, that faith without works is dead?" (James 2:20).

Notice the first thing Abraham did once he moved away from his house and livelihood. He decided to settle down, so he built an altar and pitched a tent. That was Abraham physically working to demonstrate his faith. The altar and tent also symbolize his devotion, commitment, and trust in God. He had no intention of turning back. He was sold out to the call, and he did not waver.

I know this talk of faith sounds nothing but boring at times, but if we ever seek an audience with God, we must first have faith. I'm a living proof that faith can move mountains. I have evidence that faith will get God's attention and make doors open.

CHAPTER 20

The Work of the Holy Spirit

The Holy Spirit and the truth of Acts 2:38 changed my entire life. "Then Peter said unto them, Repent, and be baptized every one of you in the name of Jesus Christ for the remission of sins, and ye shall receive the gift of the Holy Ghost." (Acts 2:38).

> When you fast for five days, the Holy Spirit can give you a phone number and a whole new life.

The apostle John tells us, "But the Helper, the Holy Spirit, whom the Father will send in My name, He will teach you all things, and bring to your remembrance all that I said to you" (John 14:26, ESV). The Holy Spirit is our Helper! I wouldn't have these testimonies or this life without the Holy Spirit.

In this chapter, I will share fourteen works of the Holy Spirit—fourteen ways that the Holy Spirit manifests and operates in us. Don't close the book now! The final part of the story is just ahead.

The Holy Spirit **regenerates** the believer. He's the new birth. The way He birthed Jesus is the same way He births you and me. "Not by works of righteousness which we have done, but according to his mercy, he saved us, by the washing of regeneration, and the renewing of the Holy Ghost" (Titus 3:5).

The Spirit **indwells** the believer. He not only birthed you, but He lives in you. "Don't you realize that your body is the temple of the Holy Spirit, who lives in you and was given to you by God? You do not belong to yourself" (I Corinthians 6:19, NLT).

The Holy Spirit **seals** the believer. "In Him you also *trusted*, after you heard the word of truth, the gospel of your salvation; in whom also, having believed, you were sealed with the Holy Spirit of promise, who is the guarantee of our inheritance until the redemption of the purchased possession, to the praise of His glory" (Ephesians 1:13-14, NKJV). The word *seal* means two things in Greek: stamp of approval and preservation.

The Spirit **adopts** the believer. "For ye have not received the spirit of bondage again to fear; but ye have received the Spirit of adoption, whereby we cry, Abba! Father!" (Romans 8:15).

The Holy Spirit **fills** the believer. "And they were all filled with the Holy Ghost and began to speak with other tongues, as the Spirit gave them utterance" (Acts 2:4).

The Holy Spirit is the **author of scripture**. "Knowing this first, that no prophecy of the scripture is of any private interpretation" (2 Peter 1:20). "All scripture *is* given by inspiration of God, and *is* profitable for doctrine, for reproof, for correction, for instruction in righteousness" (2 Timothy 3:16). God breathed into men, and they wrote.

The Holy Spirit **interprets** scripture. "But the natural man receiveth not the things of the Spirit of God: for they are foolishness unto him: neither can he know them, because they are spiritually discerned" (1 Corinthians 2:14). In other words, without the Spirit, you can't understand the Bible nor what God is saying. A lot of people know the Bible, but they don't really know who God is. The Holy Spirit gives revelation. We must ensure that we don't just read the Bible with our minds without understanding. "For the letter killeth, but the spirit giveth life" (2 Corinthians 3:6b).

The Holy Spirit **guides** the believer. "For as many as are led by the Spirit of God, they are the sons of God" (Romans 8:14). "This I say then, walk in the Spirit, and ye shall not fulfill the lust of the flesh" (Galatians 5:16). Jesus said that when the Holy Spirit comes, He will guide you into all truth. Never ignore the guidance of the Holy Spirit. He has led and guided me in a very tender, loving way. Sometimes He guides in a difficult way, screaming inner conviction.

The Holy Spirit **anoints** the believer. This means He releases an enabling power and sets aside believers for the work of the Lord. "But the anointing which ye have received of him abideth in you, and ye need not that any man teach you: but as the same anointing teacheth you of all things, and is truth, and is no lie, and even as it hath taught you, ye shall abide in him" (1 John 2:27). The anointing teaches me, opens up scripture, edifies, and magnifies the Word of God in my life. The next chapter will reveal this work of the Holy Spirit in my life.

The Holy Spirit **sanctifies** the believer. To be sanctified means to be set apart by the Lord for a specific use. "According to the foreknowledge of God the Father, by the sanctifying work of the Spirit, to obey Jesus Christ and be sprinkled with His blood: May grace and peace be yours in the fullest measure" (1 Peter 1:2, NASB).

The Holy Spirit **provides fruits** for the believer's life. The fruit of the Spirit brings about God's character in our lives. "But the fruit of the Spirit is love, joy, peace, longsuffering, gentleness, goodness, faith, meekness, temperance: against such there is no law" (Galatians 5:22-23).

The Holy Spirit **empowers** the believer. The Holy Ghost gives believers the ability to do what God created as our purpose.

The Holy Spirit comes with spiritual gifts as well to edify the body. These gifts include: The Gift of Wisdom, The Gift of Knowledge, The Gift of Prophecy, The Gift of Discerning

Spirits, The Gift of Tongues, and the Gift of Interpretation of Tongues (1 Corinthians 12:7-11). These spiritual gifts are given to each of us according to God's ordain Kingdom purpose for our lives. It's very essential for us to operate according to these spiritual gifts in order to walk in our full potential and fulfill our God given assignment here on earth. Our ultimate goal is to use all these gifts to bring glory to His name and not for self-gains.

When you fast for five days, the Holy Spirit can give you a phone number and a whole new life. God called me towards whatever plan and purpose He had for my life—not because I was poor and needy, but because He created me with a life purpose. He created your life with a purpose—and a good plan. I promise you that the Holy Spirit will change your life—if you trust, believe, and give Him a chance.

CHAPTER 21

The Holy Spirit Gave Me a Phone Number

"And Jesus said unto them, Because of your unbelief: for verily I say unto you, If ye have faith as a grain of mustard seed, ye shall say unto this mountain, Remove hence to yonder place; and it shall remove; and nothing shall be impossible unto you." (Matthew 17:20).

The moment I walked away from the lady and retreated to my room, I broke down and set a fleece before God as Gideon did. I didn't understand, nor did I know my next move. I had no Plan A, B, or C! Jesus carrying me all the way through was my ultimate plan. With God, it's always Plan A. He's never confused for a moment about His plan for your life. So let me implore you to trust God's Plan A.

> *I knew God wouldn't have me travel almost a hundred miles to just leave me alone.*

I pondered the thought that no matter what happened to me, there had to be a glimmer of light for me somewhere. I knew God wouldn't have me travel almost a hundred miles to just leave me alone. Through the eyes of faith, I saw a blurred vision of that light, but I remained ever so optimistic.

Returning home wasn't an option. The thought didn't even enter my mind. Going back would have been way too easy, even though I didn't have enough money to make the journey home.

This was only a setback, I thought. This was a warning sign, telling me that life wasn't a bed of roses. I would have to fight through roadblocks, potholes, and all sorts of hills and valleys just to reach my dreams. I tried very hard to gain some composure, but my body continued to tremble from the knowledge that I couldn't stay there, and I had nowhere else to go. What would you have done? Would you have packed up and returned home?

I needed solace, so I turned to the book of life and ingested the Psalms for refuge and encouragement: "I know the Lord is always with me. I will not be shaken, for He is right beside me" (Psalm 16:8, NLT).

The Word of God is our handbook for living. When I don't know what to do, I usually go to the Word and listen for what He's asking me to do. I knew He was with me, so I submerged myself further in looking for divine intervention.

I laid prostrate all night long. I cast my concerns and my burdens upon Him. I fully trusted in the God of my father, Abraham. As the night stretched on, I wept before Him because He said that His burden was light and His yoke was easy (Matthew 11:30). I hoped and pleaded that somehow, He would miraculously open another door or even a window.

When hope is dim, even a window serves its purpose. "Hope deferred maketh the heart sick: but *when* the desire cometh, *it is* a tree of life" (Proverbs 13:12). I had to encourage myself in the Lord. His word became my only food. When I was seven, and I first met the Lord, He gave me Psalm 37 to feast on, and verse 25 had become a bedrock for me: "I have been young, and *now* am old; yet have I not seen the righteous forsaken, nor his seed begging bread." I declared verbatim over myself, "Lord, You won't let me beg; You promised to provide."

As you're reading this, you might have a true and great need, but let me remind you that God is so much bigger and greater than any need.

Broken, contrite, and vulnerable, I bawled and told God, "I have faith that You can deliver me. I know You didn't bring me this far to abandon me." I prayed for His divine will.

Sometime during the wee hours of the morning, the Holy Spirit prompted me to enter into a time of fasting and prayer — for five days.

Can I testify again on how powerful fasting really is? This is the pivotal point. Fasting releases God's power. One of the ways that the Holy Spirit prompts us to fast is through a need in our lives. If you need stronger prayer about a matter, that's an invitation from the Lord to fast. If you need God's guidance for an issue in your life, that's an encouragement to fast. If you need deliverance or protection, that's a time to fast. Will you do it? Or will you miss the unique opportunities for the grace that He will extend to you through fasting?

I strongly believe in the power of prayer and fasting because that's what got me safely to the capital city in the first place. I decided to enter an Esther-type fast, even though I had no one to back me in prayer like the people of Shushan who prayed and fasted with her (Esther 4). I wished I had someone, even a Mordecai, to join in with me. I felt a bit lonely and outnumbered, but still, I decided I would seek the face of my dear Lord alone.

It was quite fortuitous that the lady was on vacation for that whole week and so she was able to watch her daughter. Since I didn't have that responsibility, I was at liberty to seek God night and day. I prayed for five days straight (of course, I fell asleep at times), and the only thing I had was a little water. I cried out to the God who brought me from my mother's house into a strange place. I sobbed and asked Him to deliver the help I needed. I earnestly prayed until all my physical strength was spent.

Exhausted, I didn't know what more to pray. The Holy Spirit began to pray and make intercession on my behalf. "Likewise the Spirit also helpeth our infirmities [weaknesses]: for we know not what we should pray for as we ought: but the Spirit itself maketh intercession for us with groanings which cannot be uttered. And he that searcheth the hearts knoweth what *is* the mind of the Spirit, because he maketh intercession for the saints according to *the will of* God." (Romans 8:26-27). This is why believers need to be filled with the Holy Spirit of God—because the Spirit leads the believers into *all* truth. Praying in the Spirit is our prayer language.

On Friday, August 1, 1997, I found myself lying in a fetal position, still sobbing over my unmet needs. I was heavily perturbed that I was alone in that big city without help. This weighed heavily on my spirit. I wondered what I would do if she told me to leave before God opened up a way of escape. I wondered what would become of me, but I gave no room to fear. Instead of begging and pleading with people when a sudden situation comes up against you, sometimes all you can do is to declare a fast like Esther and Ezra and wait on God to intervene (Ezra 8:21-22). When a challenge has risen against you in your marriage, your health, your finances, or your family that you cannot change on your own, and you begin to humble yourself before God in fasting and prayer, you will begin to see the effects of God's intervention. The Bible's definition of fasting is to humble oneself.

Fasting is a scriptural mandate. David said, "I humbled myself with fasting" (Psalm 35:13, 69:10, NKJV). When you humble yourself with fasting, God will give you grace, wisdom and elevate your spirit to get through. When you fast, you open the door for God's supernatural intervention in your circumstances! I saw the power of God firsthand when I humbled myself and fasted for my school fee.

During my fast, I declared Ephesians 3:20 over my life: "Now unto him that is able to do exceeding abundantly above all that we ask or think, according to the power that worketh in us." "And we know that all things work together for good to them that love God, to them that are the called according to his purpose." (Romans 8:28). I believed God for miracles.

All of a sudden, I heard a still, small voice. The audible voice of God said to me, "I'm your help, child; get up and go dial this number."

First, I hadn't put any food in my mouth for approximately one hundred and twenty hours, so my knees were weak, and my body gaunt like David's in Psalm 109:24. So I didn't move at once due to a lack of strength.

Second, I thought I might be delusional since my body was pretty weak and without nutrients. Third, I pondered the thoughts at length because the voice sounded familiar. I heard the audible voice of God saying again, "Get up and go dial this number." This time I sat up quickly, and it was as though God had quickened my spirit and body with renewed strength.

The Holy Spirit reiterated a third time, "Get up and go dial this number." I got up. While I was walking towards the kitchen, I was tickled, trying to comprehend the phone number part in my mind. With tears streaming down my face, I said, "Lord, are you mad or am I mad? You know I have no one here in this city to call."

As I stood at the kitchen counter, the Holy Spirit brought to my remembrance Acts 16:6-7, and I tried to contextualize the scripture. "Now when they had gone throughout Phrygia and the region of Galatia, and were forbidden of the Holy Ghost to preach the word in Asia," The Holy Spirit communicated with Paul and Silas about going into Asia, and now, the same Holy Spirit was bidding me to dial a number I didn't know.

It was then that I clearly saw the parallel. This was God's divine strategy. The Holy Spirit prompted me to pick up the phone, and as I obeyed, He gave me a seven-digit number to dial. I didn't write down the numbers; He gave them to me individually, and I dialed one by one. When I finished dialing the phone number, the line began ringing within seconds. Immediately, I heard a lady's voice on the other end of the phone and she straight away asked me to stop crying.

My stomach dropped into my lap, and I felt blood begin to pound in my head. I bawled softly, "Oh God, You've got to be kidding me; You've got to be kidding! I know you are mad!" I was so caught off guard, and I was momentarily speechless!

We managed to express pleasantries—and it was like my heart leaped into my throat, cutting off my breathing. I went into utter shock.

She heard my sobbing and pleaded with me to stop again. Then I heard the most profound words. She said, "The Lord brought you before me while I was in prayer this morning, and He instructed me to pray fervently for you and told me that I should expect a phone call and make plans for your coming."

Say what! Oh man! What in the world. You can just imagine the beating of my heart and the expression on my face! My mouth dropped, my eyes popped wide open, and I started to hyperventilate. Maybe I fainted. I felt as though I was in a different dimension. My heart was pounding out of my chest.

Was I having a vision? Where was I? What was happening to me? I wasn't sure if I was still mortal, so I pinched myself hard just to make sure God didn't transfigure me somehow as He did with Enoch and Elijah. In my shock and silence, she cried out to me, "Are you still there?"

After a lengthy pause, I said, "Yes!" and I realized I was still among the living!

She said, "Don't cry anymore, dry your tears, and would you like to come today?"

Ugh! In my mind, I thought to myself, "Come where exactly?" I gave a resounding yes with no hesitation!

Once again, I said yes to another stranger over the phone with absolutely no idea of where I was bound. She asked for my location, I gave it to her, and as providence would have it, we were only a few blocks away from each other. I was flabbergasted! My body shivered; my hands trembled as I wrote down my new address then we hung up.

I stared at the phone in disbelief. What's up with God and this phone thing?

Thankfully, I just so happened to be in one of those spontaneous, adventurous seasons in my life, and I thought to myself, "Oh well, this really can't hurt." If this was how God defined faith, then surely, I had faith; plenty of faith! A cup full! So, I was going!

I found myself laughing like Sarah and crying simultaneously. I was happy and scared to death! I began to sing, "Lead me, Lord, I'll follow." God tried to calm my human nerves by reminding me of how He used my Sunday school teacher, Sister Regent, on my behalf because of prayer and faith. My faith felt so inspired that my spirit soared all over Kingston in the joy of the Lord! I could feel the sweet presence of the Holy Spirit. The Holy Spirit is like a wingman who cheers us on! It was so extraordinary! I began to pack up my few belongings again in utter amazement and disbelief at what seemed like a coincidence.

Just as the children of Israel ate the Passover in a hurry to make their exodus out of Egypt toward the Promised Land, I made haste and did not tarry. After packing, I entered the veranda, and this very kind lady sat there attending to her daughter and son. I had tears rolling down my face, yet I was laughing at the same time. (It's possible that her last impression of me is that I was crazy!) She had no idea she was a conduit for God's plan, and I had no idea she was a conduit. God just blew my mind. When you exercise brave faith in God, He can and will use just about any vehicle or channel to bring about His will in your life. The Word of God says in John 14:13, "And I will do whatever you ask in my name, so that the Father may be glorified in the Son" (NIV). Hallelujah!

So I thanked her from the bottom of my heart for allowing me to stay in her home and for allowing God to use her home to help me get to my destiny. (God used her without her knowledge. Never underestimate our God. Oh glory!) We said goodbye, and I left. I asked her son to push my duffle bag half of the way on his little bike and he complied. I didn't know exactly where I was going or what was going to happen next—every step was one of wild faith.

As I walked, I stopped to capture the beautiful wild roses of August blooming in the meadow behind the football field. The midafternoon sun shone down so gracefully. It was the most beautiful day! My heart filled with gladness. I was completely mesmerized and astounded by the mighty move of God. I wasn't confused over whether I had done right or wrong. Two Scriptures came to my spirit: "For we walk by faith, not by sight" (2 Corinthians 5:7). "But without faith *it is* impossible to please *him:* for he that cometh to God must believe that he is, and *that* he is a rewarder of them that diligently seek him." (Hebrews 11:6). I had prayed and fasted and believed God with all my heart.

Fear and gloominess still lingered. But sometimes, you must face your fears head-on like David facing Goliath. What I love about the victory of David is not that he fought well but that he believed well. Did it cross my mind at the moment that this new stranger lady could double-cross me, too? No, actually! I didn't know what God was doing, but I trusted in Him and believed His plan completely.

We all know that there's a reason for every disappointment. But when you see it as a stimulus, it can only propel you further. I felt the power of the Holy Spirit at work at that moment. Never doubt that we serve a God who works miracles. I must have prayed a hundred prayers that week and cried a thousand teardrops, not knowing my fate or where life was taking me next.

If you're praying for a miracle right now, no matter how impossible that miracle seems, please, trust that God knows the full story. He is working out every detail even when you can't see how. He is ironing out all the loose ends, shifting things into place, intervening, intertwining, and preparing a place of refuge for you. He's setting up people to work in your favor and to bless you. He's allowing your name to be called in rooms you have not yet entered. He's opening doors that no man can shut. Don't worry when you can pray, because God does some of His best works when your spirit prays.

CHAPTER 22

My New Home

All the houses go by numbers. As I walked, I focused my eyes forward so that I wouldn't miss my new home. In the near distance, I could see the landscape of the outer layer of the house. It had a very nice and fresh curb appeal to it. The beautiful hibiscus flowers that Jamaicans call shoe block were dancing above the artistically manicured front hedges.

As I drew closer, I caught a slight glimpse of the lady and her husband waiting on the veranda. Apparently, she saw me too, because as soon as I arrived at the front gate, she opened it promptly, to welcome me in, and helped to unburden my load.

> *I didn't have to carry water on my head from miles away to wash...*

We exchanged pleasantries again, and she introduced me to her husband, who was sitting and holding a little black AM/FM radio (He was a lefty just like my mama!). He was listening to Mr. Perkin, a very popular radio personality, and watching the fish in their tank.

I couldn't believe I was standing in front of her. I was so glad I had obeyed God's voice and dialed that number.

My life is a living proof that obedience to God is better than sacrifice. It's like a magnet that only attracts God's blessings. While I stood on the veranda chitchatting with the two strangers, I began staring at the fish tank—and just like that, I became engrossed in my thoughts. I arrived shortly after the noon hour, just in time to see her husband feed the beautiful fishes swimming around in their safe haven, so carefree and happy.

Have you ever had nonsensical wishes? I don't know where the crazy thought came from, but I wished at that moment that I was a gold fish. I thought to myself, "They have no problems; their bellies are big; they have food and a place to sleep at night, free of charge." I am very thankful God didn't listen to my thoughts and turn me into a fish to make me swim with whales like Jonah. Ha!

The lady invited me inside her pristine home and offered me a seat on her luxurious upholstery settee. The fabric was so exquisite and nice, like a beautiful Parisienne dress I'd seen in an antique magazine and wanted in one of my dreams. The quaint and modern blend with a touch of eclectic style took my breath away and gave me a positive vibe.

It was always such a delight to be offered a seat since the normal place for me to sit at home was either on our broken-down bed or on the floor. The lady handed me a box of tissues since I was still crying over the whole ordeal. Soon after, she offered me a tall, refreshing glass of lemonade with ice. She asked me to share my story, and so I did, chapter by chapter.

She reiterated that while she was in prayer, the Lord had brought me before her. "The Lord told me to expect a phone call from you, and that I should make plans for your coming, and that I should pray fervently for you." She said.

Again, I was floored. I was quickly reminded of what we're commanded to do in James 5:16. "Confess *your* faults one to another, and pray one for another, that ye may be healed. The effectual fervent prayer of a righteous man availeth much." I could sense a great transformation taking place right before my eyes. It blew my mind. It felt and sounded like an experience straight out of the book of Acts. This was the most astounding move of God yet. I sat there, speechless. I had no idea what to do next. I was so glad that I had decided to step out on a limb and follow the voice that had called me there. I tried to talk more, but I was overcome and drenched in rivers of tears cascading down my face like a slow, rainy day. This providential happening triggered memories of what the Lord had done in my life before. Gratitude for the Lord flooded my weeping soul, and I worshipped Him.

As we got more acquainted, we talked about how she could help me, and we specifically discussed school plans. I proudly told her about my report card, how I had come first in my class. She was thrilled for me. First, she recommended Kingston Technical High School and Bridgeport High. She said her nephew works at Bridgeport High School, which was only twenty minutes away. She got him on the phone, and he told her they had orientation going on.

She made plans for us to go by the school and for me to get registered by the following Monday. This was the happiest I had been for a good while because of the uncertainty that had surrounded my life. I felt such confidence in God's plans. Philippians says, "Being confident of this very thing, that he which hath begun a good work in you will perform *it* until the day of Jesus Christ" (Philippians 1:6).

I asked her about the church, and she mentioned Wildman Street. It was in affiliation with my former church in the country—but somehow, I'd never heard of it until that moment. What was so amazing about that moment was how God orchestrated my life to be connected with these Apostolic Pentecostal people of the truth, the Name, and the oneness of God. They believed the exact same thing I was called to. They, too, had the Acts 2:38 experience. The husband was an international evangelist of the gospel.

How very intuitive and wise of God, I thought. I laughed and cried because I witnessed and experienced the written

Word of God happening in my life. When God places a vision or an ambition in your imagination, He will find a way to connect you to it. Whatever God calls you to, He will make provision for you. And the Holy Spirit will lead, teach, and guide you into all truth (John 16:13). I was in awe of the work of the Holy Spirit and the greatness of our God!

I managed to gain composure, and she decided to give me a full tour of the house. Like the previous house, it was also a three-bedroom, with one bathroom, a living/dining room, and a beautiful laundry room in the back. During the tour, she stopped and introduced me to her daughter, who had walked out of her room, directly in front of the kitchen area. She appeared much older than I and had apparently been sleeping when I arrived.

Everything was still so foreign to me, but these were things I'd dreamed of. Everything was so pretty—nothing was broken, no scratches, no stains or cracks on the walls. I could use the inside toilet and flush it. I could use the refrigerator and the warm water inside the shower. I didn't have to carry water on my head from miles away to wash—I saw two white washer boxes with buttons that I was totally unfamiliar with.

And the very best thing of all was that they had electricity. I wouldn't need to strain my eyes to study. I could iron my uniform with an electric iron without getting coal stains all over it. I was in Kingston heaven, y'all! Or let's just say I'd never stepped foot inside of a house so glamorous before. Of course, I'd seen nice houses in the country, but not with so many uptown perks. It was hard to grasp that it was now going to be my home. The little girl inside me was beyond happy.

On our way out from the back area, she pointed me to my room. It was located directly in the middle, between her room and the bathroom. When she said I could unpack my things, I literally wet myself—oops! I was like a little puppy that was totally overwhelmed by the circumstances and couldn't contain itself! That just broke me all over again. I hardly had anything that was mine. I wasn't an orphan, but most of my life I felt like Anne, the orphan girl of Green Gables, who had nothing more than her imagination and her wit. I tried to imagine her excitement the moment Marilla Cuthbert told her she could stay at Green Gables for good.

The feeling was exhilarating! My hands trembled while I tried to unpack my little things from the duffle bag that had become like a friend. I looked around my room—paused and wondered what Abraham must have felt like once he reached his destination. I recalled that the first thing he did was build God an altar. So, I thought that I, too, should pattern myself after him. I looked around the room and saw that no place was suitable, so crazy me looked under the bed. It had a lot of space, so that's the place I decided to be consecrated to the Lord for my altar.

There, I worshipped Him for being Jehovah-jireh to me (The Lord who provides. Genesis 22:13-15). Truly, I am no

Abraham, but the word of God says, "For whatsoever things were written aforetime were written for our learning, that we through patience and comfort of the Scriptures might have hope" (Romans 15:4). I was feeling more than a bucket of hopefulness!

It was the very first time I had a bed or a room to myself in my life. At the previous place, I shared a room with the lady's daughter. Here, I had my own bed, dresser, and closet. I'd always wanted to have my own closet, dresser and looking mirror. Oh, it felt like I had it all! The moment was surreal, and my life had moved swiftly to the beat of contentment. Finally, my life had spontaneously been filled by the things I had believed and imagined having by faith. Can I just tell you that when you least expect it all, the things you've been praying for all these years will come true? Only have faith and believe.

My bed was neatly and nicely made with a pink quilted bedspread. It had pillows — two whole pillows with matching cases and pillow shams. My earth-toned mahogany closest was a delight — it had mirrors on either side of the doors. I didn't really have anything to hang in there, but it didn't matter because I had my very own closet. I could just stare at it and dream of the day I could hang all sorts of fancy dresses and French slips for church. My dresser had six empty drawers and a large fancy-looking mirror. I had a flashback to all those days I used to look into our piece of broken mirror in which I was unable to see the full contour of my face. Oh, it was a dream come true.

I sat directly in the middle of the bed in front of the mirror and stared at my frail body and my beautiful self. My body looked gaunt from the fasting. I was down from one hundred and ten pounds to about ninety-five pounds, but everything was like a dream. The fast was totally worth a few pounds. When Job was afflicted and in agony and his body wasted away, he prophesied that even though worms destroyed his body, one day, his redeemed body would put on an incorruptible one and he would still see God in his glorified body.

Don't be afraid to be led by the Spirit to fast. Knowing God on a different level is going to cost you something. (Make sure you consult with your physician before you plan to go on an extended fast.) Sometimes, when we need to hear from God, we have to surrender our bodies to Him. Put your body on the altar of sacrifice and yield it totally to Him—and let the Spirit lead and control. Why should I worry over my flesh when God knows the path I take (Job 23:10)?

Back in my room, the little girl inside me came out to help put away my few things, and she cried happy tears. I couldn't believe this was happening to me. God had opened a new door. Have you ever dreamed of something and it happened, and you simply could not bring yourself to the reality of it? It took me months to accept my new reality.

Everything was such a treasure. One of the perks of my room was the skylight. I enjoyed saying "my this," and "my that," but I so loved that skylight. It took years before I had anything that was actually mine—even though nothing in the house was technically mine, except my personal belongings, but it was mine for that moment in time. Because Kingston was humid, they had inserted a window above my room. It was dreamy. Some nights, I would gaze up into God's romantic celestial expanse, so beautifully decorated with shiny jewels of the sky, her moon and stars. Sometimes, I would do the waltz with God underneath the moonlight, like Cinderella and her prince! Quirky but cool! You should try waltzing with God sometimes!

I had finished unpacking my things when the lady called and knocked on my door, she announced that dinner was served. Oh, for love of honesty, it didn't occur to me that my bedroom had a door until she knocked. I almost choked on happiness before dinner. I was so happy about the room in itself and overjoyed about my nicely displayed furniture that I didn't even notice it came with a door (poor girl problem, hey!) Shoot, I wasn't even hungry! I had fasted for over a hundred hours, and I still wasn't hungry. I was filled up with happiness and joy! Nevertheless, I washed my hands, made it promptly to the table, and sat down nervously and gently.

The smell was heavenly. The presentation was superb. I pondered the thought that maybe this was a one-day deal in heaven. I pushed the thought out of mind, but it was hard to keep at bay. I was now telling myself, "I'll never go to sleep because if this is heaven, I don't want to wake up from it."

Did I mention the fine china and well-polished silverware, so neatly set in their places? The fancy placemats...I'd always dreamed of buying mama some fancy placemats one day. The heavy crystal serving bowls contained Escovitch Red Snapper, and another platter held deep-fried chicken coated in seasoned wheat flour. The sides were mixed vegetables along with rice and peas.

For a moment, I felt as though I was getting realigned with my royal roots. I felt like Sista Queenie! (I thought, "Mama, if only you could see your royal daughter now!") I managed to self-serve myself properly, but I was worried sick about eating because I'd never used a knife and a fork together before. I remember sitting on the floor at home trying to cut my big tire-wheel dumplings with forks that were made from cheap metal, so most times we ended up biting into them. And I don't remember us having eating knives—only the ones my mother used for peeling her ground provisions.

My knees rattled together underneath the table as I buckled under the pressure of what to do. It felt like my heart was going pop out of my chest. Man, if I could have made a swift escape from the table to the floor, I would have taken it. When we bowed our heads and clasped our hands to pray, I extended my prayer a bit longer. I said, "Lord, please don't allow these kind people to pull me in any conversation that might have anything to do with me, because I don't know how to be diplomatic around tables." I thought I heard God laugh. Later on, I realized that I meant to say, "Lord, I don't know any table etiquette." Yes, I knew some formalities, and I had good manners, but civility and proper decorum were not a part of my upbringing.

They started eating with their knives and forks together, and yes, I was willing to learn, but I was scared to death to touch my knife. I tried to follow along with the conversation in a diplomatic way, and I bit my tongue! I wanted to cry, but I was way too happy!

I can't deny I was nervous about eating my chicken. These people were so skilled at cutting meat off a bone, you'd think you were at the butcher shop. Man, they were too skilled! All along, I was wondering how in God's heaven I was going to get to suck and chew my juicy chicken bones. My inner voice chimed in, "Oh God, how could You do this to me? You know how much I love to chew my bones!"

Life is so funny—all my little life growing up, we could only afford to buy chicken once in a blue moon, and now I had access to quality chicken and fish. And it seemed that I was going to have to act lady-like and conceal my desire for wanting to suck and devour my chicken bones properly. They say you can take the girl out of the country, but you can't take the country out of the girl!

They never touched the meal with their bare hands. It was frightful. What planet did they come from? Who eats boned chicken and fish fancily? Seriously, who? Where I came from, chicken and fish were a luxury. We used our hands, and we ate everything—I mean everything! Fat, bones, and whatever meat you could afford to access from the one pound of bona fide chicken-back. Hey oh, hey! That's all mama was able to trust on credit again and again from Ms. Milly, and she might still owe her for a couple of pounds (of chicken-back parts), up until today! Ms. Milly was so kind to mama. Love you, Ms. Milly, may God continue to bless you with long life.

At first, I tried my best to stay away from the drumstick, but somehow it ended up on my plate. I didn't know how to be a lady and not suck and chew on my bones. I never felt so much pressure from a plate of dignified food in all my life! I was so glad when dinner was over.

Then I heard the word dessert. I didn't know what it was like to have dessert after dinner back at home. This was truly a heavenly experience! We had *grape nut ice cream* from the famous Devon House in Jamaica. (If you ever visit Jamaica, pay them a visit!) Man, it was so deliciously good. I savored every spoonful—while wondering if God could cause these good humans to adopt me. I had also imagined licking the ice cream residue from my little crystal bowl like ten times—no kidding. But I have no doubt they wouldn't want to adopt me if they knew I licked plates like a dog!

After a long day, it was time to retire to bed. In the bathroom, I took a nice warm shower with a body-wash that smelled like a beautiful field of lavender mixed with a touch of lilac and a hint of myrrh. Afterward, I slipped back into my dirty clothing (yuck!) and tiptoed inside my room. I put on one of mama's old blouse she had given me to sleep in because I had no proper nightgown or fancy duster. But who cares if it had holes and such? It kept me cozy and warm!

I was happy. I had a roof above me, food on the table, and a good place to rest. I had experienced a Biblical miracle—a supernatural miracle. I prayed and asked God to open another door in faith—with hope—that He would answer, and He did. For the first time, I was truly happy in the confidence of the Lord. (Hebrews 10:35).

I crawled underneath my bed like a humbled mouse before the Lord, and I poured out my heart again, filled with so much gratitude and thanksgiving. I was so incredibly blessed and inundated by everything He did for me within a day. It was a perfect day. God can truly turn your whole life around in just a moment, in just a day, or in a year—you merely need to continue to trust and believe in Him. He changed my life; He can change yours, too!

While I wept and prayed before the Lord that night, the Holy Spirit brought to remembrance the story of Cornelius and Peter in Acts 10. I turned to the chapter and read it again, and I clearly saw God at work in my life. I exercised my faith through fasting and praying, trusting God to work a miracle, and He did more than a miracle. When I decided to humble myself, submit, and surrender my will to God, He chose to operate through this lady—another believer—on my behalf. During this time, she was also praying in submission and obedience. When we as believers come into unity in the Spirit, there is great power there. There is power in unity, and there we will see the supernatural. Ephesians 4:4 says, "There is one body, and one Spirit, even as ye are called in one hope of your calling." "For by one Spirit are we all baptized into one body, whether *we be* Jews or Gentiles, whether *we be* bond or free; and have been all made to drink into one Spirit" (1 Corinthians 12:13).

God supernaturally connected Peter and Cornelius together by prayer and faith. They both came into alignment with God's Spirit and will—and Cornelius and his household received the gift of the Holy Ghost.

God used this story to get me to be fully at peace with myself and to trust the process. I am first generation Apostolic and God saw fit to connect me with a family whose household was already filled with the Spirit.

How marvelous is God? The Holy Spirit confirmed this. He reassured me that I need not worry and that all of heaven was behind me because of my prayer and faith. I was a bit concerned since the first lady didn't commit to her words. But this time, the Holy Spirit comforted me and showed me that just like Cornelius, my prayer came up like a memorial.

Heaven had heard me, and all would be well. Goosebumps and tears. People of God, our God is real!

As I continued praying, the Holy Spirit solidified this truth and comforted me yet again with these words before I fell fast asleep: "You believed God with all your heart and you moved heaven to operate on your behalf until your answer came. Be not afraid. Notwithstanding, you waited five days in prayer and you never flinched, wavered, nor doubted!" 1 John 5:14 says, "Now this is the confidence that we have in Him, that if we ask anything according to His will, He hears us" (NKJV).

My dear readers, I felt a bit like Daniel, the great servant of God. Do you remember how Daniel prayed and prayed until his answer came? Do you think you are any different from Daniel? No, my friend! You just need to persevere in your prayers. Never, never give up on any prayer you have prayed, for God hears them all.

The truth is that I couldn't do this alone. Moses, Esther, Ezra, Joel, David, Nehemiah, Jesus, and the prophets all helped, just to name a few. They all were there rooting in their testimonies for me to remain steadfast and faithful to prayer. And my biggest support of all is the Holy Spirit, who's ever-present and always abiding—who keeps on praying and making intercession on my behalf.

That night, I felt the same powerful presence that came into my room when I cried out to the God of Israel when I was seven. The Holy Spirit truly ministered to my spirit that night, like how Jesus was ministered to right after his fast in the wilderness by the holy angels. In the gospels, we see Jesus praying every chance He had. Every time, before He went out to minister, He prayed, and supernatural miracles took place. The answer, my friends, is in your prayer and your Kingdom authority!

The Holy Spirit showed and taught me how powerful consistent prayer and fasting can be, and He gave me strength for the journey ahead. If you ask the Holy Spirit, He will tell you that your prayer is your greatest weapon on earth! It's the fastest way into God's presence and to get His attention! If we want to see the full manifestation of the Holy Ghost's power in our lives, then we must always be praying and fasting. The word of God says, "And these signs shall follow them that believe; In my name shall they cast out devils; they shall speak with new tongues; they shall take up serpents; and if they drink any deadly thing, it shall not hurt them; they shall lay hands on the sick, and they shall recover." (Mark 16:17-18). Miracles, signs, and wonders *will* follow. As called believers, we just need to tap into the power and dominion we have in the Mighty Name of Jesus! Use your Kingdom authority! Hallelujah to the King!

CHAPTER 23

God Called Me to Bridgeport High

In one day, the fully operational power of the Holy Spirit in my life transformed my circumstances. He started to show me deep things in God. He gave me hope and insight into my future and told me that God was going to use me greatly. So, over the happiest weekend of my life, I prayed and asked the Holy Spirit to choose the best school for me. And I awaited His answer.

On Sunday, my new family took me to Wildman Street Pentecostal Church. I didn't have anything fancy to wear, but the excitement of going into the house of God welled up in me. It had only been five years since I'd received the gift of the Holy Spirit and was baptized, and I couldn't wait to go to my new church to learn more about God.

> She walked down to me, took my hands, and literally dragged me to the center of the auditorium.

As long as I live, I shall never forget my first Sunday experience at Wildman Street.

I had brought every decent piece of clothing I could find for my new life. When I dressed in the little suit that I used to wear as part of the youth choir back home, I felt so well put together. I put on my slip, the only slip I owned. It was my mother's old slip. I had lost count of all the times she had helped to stitch its waist, but it still didn't fit right.

That morning when we arrived at church for Sunday school, the family parked the vehicle directly in front of the sanctuary. Being driven to church was such a perk, considering I used to walk a few miles back home. While happily sliding into position to maneuver myself to step down onto the pavement, I looked down—and lo and behold, my skirt was lying down at my sanctified feet. Frightened, I cried out loudly for help since my hands were full, and since nothing about my slip was sanctified. In doing so, I drew full attention to myself from everyone that was heading to Sunday school. I felt so embarrassed! My slip was the "holier than thou" type—that is, my slip had holes everywhere! Poor country girl problem!

Nonetheless, Sunday school was entirely awesome! I learned about all of Jehovah's names in the New Testament for the very first time from my Sunday school teachers: Brother Beckford and Brother Dempster. Later on down the road, they both would help to nurture and foster me—as a father would a daughter—in helping me to become a godly woman. God knew I needed it.

Come Monday morning, the lady took me to register for school. We first went to Kingston Technical, but when I got to Bridgeport High, that's where God said He wanted me — and I was in, just like that. After the grand tour, I took a tour around the compound on my own. I hummed a little chorus when out of nowhere, the teacher in charge of school devotions and the Interschool Christian Fellowship (ISCF), heard me singing as I was walking. She blatantly said, "When school commences, I would like for you to minister with that song." Startled, my brow furrowed, and I gave her a weird look. Then she said, "By the way, I want you to be in charge of devotions."

In my mind, I said, "Look, lady, are you mad. You don't even know me, and who are you to be giving me orders? I won't be in charge of anything!?" I thought to myself, "How very rude of her. I'm not even on campus for an hour yet, and I'm her target."

But then I turned around and told this very strange and crazy teacher person that she was barking up the wrong tree. This happened to be a natural instinct of mine — sometimes, I just tell you exactly what I'm thinking.

I dunno — maybe my ugly 'red sister' was visiting that day. Since then, I've prayed and asked the sweet Lord to please help me to bridle my tongue! But this teacher was very determined. I plainly rejected her. I laughed and said, "Oh goodness gracious, no, madam! I won't be singing in front of all those students."

But in no time, September came around, and she called me out, not once, but three times. I just stood in complete noncompliance, muttering softly in defiance. "I'm not going up there!" My eyes sparked fury, my heart skipped beats, and the rest of my insides boiled over like a mad volcano. She refused to take no for an answer, and still, I refused to go! (I was very, very shy before God got a hold of me. Looking at me now, you wouldn't think so!)

I didn't know anyone. No one knew me either, except for her and the lady's nephew—so I didn't budge. I was very reluctant, but she was persistent. She walked down to me, took my hands, and literally dragged me to the center of the auditorium. (I thought that the students might have held me in high regard—thinking I was someone of piety or noble status.) I pressed my lips tightly together and expressed a slight grin. She raised a song to warm things up, and as I began walking back to my place, thinking I was off the hook, I felt a firm hand pulling me back to the center. I could only think of King Saul hiding from the people because he was too afraid to be king (1 Samuel 10:22)!

The following morning, she was at it again. I murmured to myself, "She has got to be kidding me! Didn't she hear my 'no' yesterday! God, from where did you get this crazy lady?"

She stepped down into the crowd of students again and invaded my privacy—and I just stood there like a stiff bamboo tree. She pulled me behind her to the center of the room. I decided to start praying and worshiping along with the song she had raised. Right there at that moment, the Holy Spirit reminded me of what He said to me two or three days prior: He wanted to use me greatly.

I froze, and I couldn't think of what to do. Then then the teacher said, "Ms. Kacey is going to minister to us tomorrow morning."

The nerve. Ugh! What? I just ran back to my place. (And oh, she was the first person to call me Kacey because most people couldn't pronounce Kasia—I didn't let it bother me, and it stuck.)

I didn't want to go back to school the next day. But the school term had just begun, so I had no choice. Wednesday was upon me, and I ended up going before hundreds of students that morning and every other morning after that to sing and lead in worship—before the principal, vice-principal, and every student in devotion before God. Sometimes, if it was a combined shift, there could be close to a thousand students. By the time I graduated in 1999, every student who attended Bridgeport High knew who I was, or they'd heard my name. I had evangelized the entire school community.

Please, understand that I'm not perfect, nor am I glorying in myself. I just want to share my testimony and brag about Jesus to all the world!

They enjoyed the devotions and how I shared the love of Jesus and the gospel of the Kingdom so much that they nominated me as the president for the Interschool Christian Fellowship (ISCF) within a few months. I was able to influence the entire school body with my apostolic zeal and faith in the Lord Jesus Christ. From the principal to the vice principal, God made Himself known through me to the entire school body.

I loved going to the library, and students would seek me out for counsel there. I counseled many students who just needed someone to talk to. I used to be inside the school library five days a week. The two places I felt most fulfilled at BH were in the library and inside the auditorium. Many students came to know Christ. Many students received the gift of the Holy Ghost and were baptized while I served, witnessed, and ministered there.

Looking back, Bridgeport High wasn't merited as highly as Kingston Technical—it wasn't any sort of "Ivy League" school. But attending it was a complete set-up by God Himself. I am sure of it. "In Him also we have obtained an inheritance, being predestined according to purpose of Him who works all things according to the counsel of His will" (Ephesian 1:11 NKJV). God always wants what's best for us in our education and every other area of our lives. In Genesis and Exodus, we see clearly in the young life of Joseph and Joshua that God purposefully wanted them to succeed in whatever they set out to do. We also need to understand Isaiah. "My thoughts are nothing like your thoughts," says the LORD. "And my ways are far beyond anything you could imagine. For just as the heavens are higher than the earth, so my ways are higher than your ways and my thoughts higher than your thoughts" (Isaiah 55:8-9 NLT).

There were souls at school that my light and testimony were supposed to reach. Don't ever doubt the location to which God has called you.

Where God leads you is exactly where He wants you to be. When the teacher followed quietly behind me and listened to me sing and then asked me to minister without knowing who I was, that was all part of God's plan. She was the one He'd used to call out my purpose. I got up in front of those students frightened and always trembling at best. I sang songs I'd listened to on the radio but didn't know how to sing properly, yet the Holy Spirit would choose a song and minister it through me.

At times, students told me I sounded like I was singing with angels, and by no means can I sing. Just so you know, the Holy Spirit is well capable of doing anything, even singing. He can teach you to cook, be an excellent wife, be a good friend, a great entrepreneur, or even be a great writer! The Holy Spirit can do anything through you when you yield yourself to Him! I still don't understand it all. All I know is that God will use any available vessel. He once used a donkey to speak to Balaam. He still does mind-blowing things today.

Do you remember the story of Phillip, in Acts 8:26-40, when the Spirit took Phillip into the desert to baptize the eunuch? After Phillip went down in the water with the eunuch and came up again, he was suddenly gone (transported) by the Spirit of the Lord. Phillip was taken to another place, called Azotus, to preach the gospel. This is the same Holy Spirit that used me to do and speak things I wasn't capable of doing in the natural realm, and He can use you too!

The Holy Spirit is very real. When I read these different accounts in the Bible, I would pray and ask God to use me.

A few times during devotions, I shared the testimony of how I had to leave my mother's house in the country and travel to Kingston alone to live with complete strangers. Because I needed much help, and I believed that faith in God could move mountains and do the impossible. I shared the reason why I was standing in front of them.

I told those teachers and students how the first lady had double-crossed me, how things didn't work out, and how it propelled me into an emergency fast for five days. I recounted the supernatural power of God at the end of the fast because I chose to believe in what God's Word said. I said, "My answer was a phone number and a brand-new home and family. People who didn't know me from Adam took me into their home without a background check. I was a stranger with absolutely no earthly biological relations to them except for the fact that we all share one common Holy Spirit. God gave me a phone number to call a lady I did not know. Doesn't God see and know everything?" (Proverbs 15:3). I continued, "It was that same stranger lady who registered me here, bought my school uniforms and supplies, and provided me with lunch money and transportation for school. The reason I am standing in front of you is that I prayed and believed God."

I watched as teachers and students surrendered to God in tears because of my testimony. This little country girl who was classified as a jacket back home had developed a heart full of faith and love for her God and was making a difference. She decided to seek after the God of her fathers: Abraham, Isaac, and Jacob. God chose to use her in spite of herself.

After a while, when I saw how impactful my life had become to hundreds of students on a day-to-day basis, I finally realized that God had called me to Bridgeport High. When God does it, it's well done! I decided to trust God by reading His Word and declaring what He said over my life, who would believe where I would end up! You need to know that you have Kingdom authority to speak things over your life, just like the Apostles did in the book of Acts and see it come forth into your life. You have full Kingdom rights and authority. Praise God!

I watched Him come through for me time and time again. Before my journey to Kingston, I didn't realize that the full power of my faith, the power of my potential, and that the power of fasting and prayer could be actualized fully in my life to that magnitude. Sometimes you're going to have to trust God and walk away from your comfort zone. The comfort zone is where destiny and dreams go to die.

By the end of my three-year journey at Bridgeport High, God had used me to evangelize my school district in a tremendous way. I don't say any of this to be braggadocious before you. I would be remiss if I didn't mention the former vice-principal of Bridgeport, Ms. Norma Plummer—the one whom God intentionally sent there decades ahead of me to be a destiny helper and a mother figure to me. She took me under her wing and treated me like her own daughter.

It was quite a surprising shock when it turns out that my new family members were also conduits. Because of this, Ms. Plummer became an essential part of my life's journey. It wouldn't have even been possible for me to register for college without her and Rev. John Mark Bartlett. I will share in book two the testimony of how they came to my aid just so I could get into college. I'm not saying the journey was easy—but it produced necessary spiritual and physical fruits in life. This story is just the tip of the iceberg.

When you walk by faith with God, He causes people to open impossible doors and make way for you. The love and kindness Ms. Plummer bestowed upon my bosom came from the very heart of God Himself because it was genuine and authentic. Today, I still bask in this never-ending love of Jesus. "Because he hath set his love upon me, therefore will I deliver him: I will set him on high, because he hath known my name." (Psalm 91:14). I pray that this testimony will help you stretch your faith and believe in God again.

CHAPTER 24

How the Holy Spirit, Faith, and Prayer Can Get You the Answers You Are Looking For

As I mentioned earlier, the Holy Spirit is the Spirit of God that He promised to give to you, to live in you, to enable you to follow Him, to be a witness, to be in possession of the promises of God, and to be a representative of Jesus Christ to live a Christ-like life in this world.

> *I give Him full permission to dwell inside me throughout my life.*

Jesus knows that the world we live in is anti-God in every way. As you know, it's very difficult to be a good Christian if you're trying to follow the Lord Jesus. Every day, you must swim against the currents of life. Jesus said He would not leave us orphans (John 14:18), and that He will go to the Father and send us the Comforter (Holy Spirit) to be with us, to guide us into all truth, and to give us peace. This is why it is vital to have the Holy Spirit in your life.

Where Is the Holy Spirit?

The Holy Spirit is in you, beside you, around you—He's everywhere. We understand that God is omnipresent, omniscient, and omnipotent: "Yahweh's eyes are everywhere, keeping watch on the evil and the good" (Proverbs 15:3, WEB). "And there is no creature hidden from His sight, but all things are naked and open to the eyes of Him to whom we must give account" (Hebrews 4:13, ESV).

Ever since Jesus returned to the Father, the Holy Spirit has gone out into the world. Since the day of Pentecost, we don't have to feel for Him; we just have to receive and believe Him. John tells us that "God is a Spirit, and they that worship Him must worship Him in spirit and truth" (John 4:24). When we say that we need to "seek the Holy Spirit," we don't mean that we have to go looking for Him, because He's not lost or far away. But of course, what we mean when we say "seek the Holy Spirit" is that we want you to focus on Him and entertain His presence.

Why Hasn't the Holy Spirit Come Into You Yet?

Let's look at an analogy: Why aren't you living in that beautiful house across the street? For obvious reasons, right? It's not your house; it's somebody else's house, and that somebody hasn't invited you in.

It's the same thing with the Holy Spirit. The Holy Spirit wishes to live in you, but He's a gentleman, and He will never force Himself in.

If He's not yet living inside you, you are not His. You haven't given your life to God, and as such, you haven't invited Him. Scripture says, "But ye are not in the flesh, but in the Spirit, if so be that the Spirit of God dwell in you. Now, if any man has not the Spirit of Christ, he is none of his" (Romans 8:9).

But you will say, "I have given my life to God, I have invited in the Holy Spirit, but He still hasn't come." The only reason He hasn't come in is that when you asked, you only did it by lips and not your heart. The Holy Spirit knows that if He comes in because you ask Him with just lips, it would be the same thing as you going to that house across the street, and once you got there, everyone ignores you, and no one attends to you, so you're left on your own. A lot of people say they gave their lives to Christ, but they do their own thing. They never listen to the Holy Spirit or follow His leading. Some people give Him access to certain areas, and that's it. You can't give access to the kitchen only and tell Him He's uninvited in the rest of the house. In order for the Holy Spirit to do the work that He was sent to do in this earthly realm and in all our lives, He needs full access to your spirit, mind, and body. We need to give Him the highest priority to sit on the throne of our hearts.

The only way to know what God intends to do is to allow the Holy Spirit to lead you by giving God His rightful place in your life. I was going through a difficult season in my life when

God proved himself to me through this Scripture: "For the LORD God *is* a sun and shield: the LORD will give grace and glory: no good *thing* will he withhold from them that walk uprightly." (Psalm 84:11). Dear ones, this is a promise to all of us. God's word is true! And this is why we all need the Holy Spirit: to walk uprightly before Him.

Jeremiah, the prophet, reminds us why. "I know, O LORD, that a man's way is not in himself, Nor is it in a man who walks to direct his steps" (Jeremiah 10:23, NASB). Once you give Him complete access to lead and guide your life, then everything that pertains to His will concerning your life will come into alignment.

"…according as his divine power hath given unto us all things that *pertain* unto life and godliness, through the knowledge of him that hath called us to glory and virtue" (2 Peter 1:3).

If you ask me how I know this, it is because I gave Him full reign a long time ago. I had no father to cover me, protect me, provide for me, lead me, guide me, or teach me, so I had to give God one hundred percent, twenty-four-hour all-around access in all areas to be the Father of all, bar none! All I do and say come through Him.

I had to be intentional! I do nothing, I go nowhere, without the Holy Spirit leading me. I give Him full permission to dwell inside me throughout my life. And please, no, I am not perfect, far from it. I mess up a lot, but God is merciful.

When I was thirteen, my mother shared her pregnancy stories with me. I was very afraid, so I prayed and asked the Holy Spirit to protect me from teenage pregnancy, and He did just that because the Holy Spirit is a keeper. When I had to leave my mother's house to travel miles and miles away into the unknown, He sponsored and guided my journey. He protected and kept me safe, just like He promised.

It Simply Takes Faith

The Apostle Paul wrote: "So then faith *cometh* by hearing, and hearing by the word of God" (Romans 10:17). I want you to understand what God caused me to understand. When Abraham heard the voice of God without even fully knowing and comprehending this new God, he obeyed. He trusted and followed God's instructions. And God counted him righteous! Like Abraham, by faith, I hear what the Word of God is saying to me every day and I try to obey and do what He's asking me to do. "But be ye doers of the word, and not hearers only, deceiving your own selves" (James 1:22).

Faith, obedience, forgiveness, and love got me my answers from God based on His Word. I saw where He led and blessed the patriarchs because they had faith in Him, so I decided to exercise my faith in God also. The writer of Hebrews lets us know that "without faith, *it is* impossible to please *him*: for he that cometh to God must believe that he is, and *that* he is a rewarder of them that diligently seek him" (Hebrews 11:6).

Unfortunately, we're living in a time when our faith can become lackluster! Many Christians opt-out on exercising their faith because everything they need is so easily accessible at the push of a button. This is the microwave generation. Yet some things that we want or need, we can only access from God, and it will take authentic faith to achieve such things.

Sister Margaret Banks said in her book *The Five Principles of Powerful Prayer*, "One must understand that you will not receive anything from the Lord without faith." If you're planning to ask God for anything, you will not receive anything from Him without faith, period. The Holy Spirit always works hand in hand with our faith. The only reason that I'm able to testify to you is that I've exercised my faith in God's Word and gotten results—not one result but many! I only boast in the Lord! My faith is based upon the truth that God is, and that He is a rewarder of them that diligently seek Him (Hebrews 11:6).

I have faith that God is always going to do what's best for me and you—do you believe? Throughout my life, I have found comfort in the abundance of the benevolence of promises God made to me, to us. God is interested in me, and He has our best interest at heart. I have faith in the solemn promise that He will never leave me alone nor forsake us. I have faith that He's coming again soon.

Praying for God's Will

The Bible tells us to pray and to have faith, according to the will of God. We should accept whatever answer God gives because He knows what's best for us.

There's a story in 2 Chronicles that is a good point of reference. King Hezekiah had a close relationship with God. He didn't follow after his father; instead, he trusted in the God of Israel and kept the Lord's commandments. He reformed Judah, he burned down all the false idols, and he restored the place of worship. Because of this, he was deemed a good king of Judah who pleased God.

One day, Isaiah, the prophet, delivered a word from God to him: "Set your house in order, for you shall die and not live." Hezekiah did not accept the will of God for his life at that time. Instead, he did what any Christian would have done today—pray and asked for healing and long life. Of course, God granted the king his request. Later on down the road, although some blessings came from Hezekiah's extra years of life, Hezekiah soon became lifted up in pride (2 Chronicles 32:24-25). Even though Hezekiak repented, during the extra fifteen years of life, his wife bore him a son named Manasseh, the heir to the throne. Manasseh would reign for fifty-five years as a terrible king who undid every good thing his father had done for Judah. He led Judah once more into sin and rebellion against God and caused the destruction of Jerusalem by the

Babylonians (2 King 24:4-10). One of Manasseh's gruesome acts of wickedness was murdering the beloved prophet, Isaiah.

I know that this story will help someone to understand the importance of praying for the will of God and accepting His answer even though sometimes, it's hard to do. We can always pray in faith and rely on the Holy Spirit to help us so that we're never led by our tunnel vision.

James said, "Ye ask, and receive not, because ye ask amiss, that ye may consume *it* upon your lusts" (James 4:3). We must make sure that when we ask, we ask in the Spirit. We also pray in the Spirit according to the will of God and not according to our flesh because our flesh cannot please God (Romans 8:8).

Sometimes, when I'm praying, I reflect on the three Hebrew boys who were placed in a difficult predicament. They had a choice: they had to either continue to stand on their faith in God or bow to evil Babylon. Many times, when I'm facing adversities, I want God to deliver me in this instance—but I still pray the will of God by faith, I say affirmatively like the Hebrew boys, "If He's chosen not to deliver me or heal me, He's still God, and He's still able."

Let me add what Jesus said Himself: "He went a little farther and fell on His face and prayed, saying, 'O My Father, if it is possible, let this cup pass from me; nevertheless, not as I will, but as You will'" (Matthew 26:39, NKJV).

Dear friend, we must remain steadfast and unmovable in our prayer life and faith. Here's a promise that you can rest on: "And we know that all things work together for good to them that love God, to them who are the called according to *his* purpose" (Romans 8:28).

Prayer Changes Things

Sometimes, we pray and pray, and we still walk away frustrated that our prayers aren't being answered. The truth is that certain prayers we are making may require a certain posture in our hearts before they provoke God in heaven. Jesus said that when you pray, pray in faith, believing that what you're praying for is going to come to pass. In the gospel of Mark, "Jesus entered into Jerusalem, and into the temple: and when he had looked round about upon all things, and now the eventide was come, he went out unto Bethany with the twelve.

And on the morrow, when they were come from Bethany, he was hungry: and seeing a fig tree afar off having leaves, he came, if haply he might find any thing thereon: and when he came to it, he found nothing but leaves; for the time of figs was not *yet*. And Jesus answered and said unto it, No man eat fruit of thee hereafter for ever. And his disciples heard *it*.

And they come to Jerusalem: and Jesus went into the temple, and began to cast out them that sold and bought in the temple, and overthrew the tables of the moneychangers, and the seats of them that sold doves; and would not suffer that any man should carry *any* vessel through the temple. And he taught, saying unto them, Is it not written, My house shall be called of all nations the house of prayer? but ye have made it a den of thieves. And the scribes and chief priests heard *it*, and sought how they might destroy him: for they feared him, because all the people was astonished at his doctrine. And when even was come, he went out of the city.

And in the morning, as they passed by, they saw the fig tree dried up from the roots. And Peter calling to remembrance saith unto him, Master, behold, the fig tree which thou cursedst is withered away. And Jesus answering saith unto them, Have faith in God. For verily I say unto you, That whosoever shall say unto this mountain, Be thou removed, and be thou cast into the sea; and shall not doubt in his heart, but shall believe that those things which he saith shall come to pass; he shall have whatsoever he saith. Therefore I say unto you, What things soever ye desire, when ye pray, believe that ye receive *them*, and ye shall have *them*. And when ye stand praying, forgive, if ye have ought against any: that your Father also which is in heaven may forgive you your trespasses. But if ye do not forgive, neither will your Father which is in heaven forgive your trespasses." (Mark 11:11-26).

On another occasion, a very desperate father approached Jesus, asking Him to have mercy on his demon-possessed son. He complained to the Lord that He already asked his disciples, and they couldn't cure his son. "And Jesus rebuked the devil; and he departed out of him: and the child was cured from that very hour. Then came the disciples to Jesus apart, and said, Why could not we cast him out? And Jesus said unto them, Because of your unbelief: for verily I say unto you, If ye have faith as a grain of mustard seed, ye shall say unto this mountain, Remove hence to yonder place; and it shall remove; and nothing shall be impossible unto you. Howbeit this kind goeth not out but by prayer and fasting." (Matthew 17:18-21).

The message that Jesus is trying to get across to us is this: what it takes to get answers and see results is faith, prayer, fasting, and His Word. If we're going to see anything happen in our prayer life, we must have faith. Jesus clearly states that if you have faith like a mustard seed, you can ask your mountains to move.

I testified earlier how I didn't have any money to start high school, and I decided to exercise my faith by entering into a period of fasting and prayer. I saw my faith move that financial mountain. God answered my prayer and provided me with $3,800—This happened the very same day I prayed, fasted, and asked in faith.

We must have faith in God's ability and His willingness to operate on our behalf. Jesus admonished us to pray, and when we pray, we should also forgive. If you don't take anything from this book, please take the word *'forgive.'* Jesus personally taught me the art of forgive from a tender age. Forgiveness is one of the keys to getting the Kingdom of God to operate on our behalf.

Forgiveness and obedience walk hand in hand; they're like magnets that attract God's blessings. When you willfully forgive those who wronged you, it unlocks doors. I heard what Jesus said, and I've tried to practice the "leaving my gift at the altar" principle, and it has worked for me.

"Therefore, if you are offering your gift at the altar and there remember that your brother or sister has something against you, leave your gift there in front of the altar. First, go and be reconciled to them; then come and offer your gift" (Matthew 5:23-24, NIV).

"For if you forgive other people when they sin against you, your heavenly Father will also forgive you. But if you do not forgive others their sins, your Father will not forgive your sins" (Matthew 6:14-15, NIV).

Since we're on the subject of forgiveness, let me encourage you to go ahead and send those texts, make that phone call, write the letters, pay that person a visit, and say, "I'm sorry." Do whatever you have to. Ask for forgiveness. Just release it.

Jesus taught His disciples to pray "After this manner therefore pray ye: Our Father which art in heaven, Hallowed be thy name. Thy Kingdom come, Thy will be done in earth, as it is in heaven. Give us this day our daily bread. And forgive our debts, as we forgive our debtors, (forgiving others rather than retribution and competition). And lead us not into temptation but deliver us from evil: For thine is the Kingdom, and the power, and the glory forever. Amen" (Matthew 6:9-13).

The attributes to have your prayers answered by God are simple things like having love for each other, your belief, having faith, your obedient to God's Word, having a clean heart, prayer, fasting, and your ability and willingness to forgive. These attributes coincide easily with the fruits of the Spirit: love, joy, peace, forbearance, kindness, goodness, faithfulness, gentleness, and self-control. The apostle Paul in 1 Corinthians said, "…though I have all faith, so that I could remove mountains, but have not love, I am nothing." (1 Corinthians 13:2b, NKJV).

You must understand that you will not receive anything from the Lord without faith. And according to Jesus, unless we can forgive each other, He will not hear or answer our prayers. I know this for sure. God encouraged me to forgive a lot of people—and I couldn't do it without first being human and feeling His love.

We can't forgive without love. It's impossible! You can give without love, but you can't forgive your neighbor without first feeling love or some type of empathy towards them. We are commanded to love first; that's the highest calling of any Christian, for God is love. He said in John, "If you [truly] love me, you will keep my commandments" (John 14:15, NASB). There are requirements when we walk with God, wouldn't you agree? I discovered this when I was thirteen, and the first person I had to forgive was my father for not loving me or wanting me, and it changed my life.

I'm not saying any of this is going to be easy, but if we want to see divine manifestations in our lives, if we need God to answer those prayers, we must be willing to take up our cross and follow in the steps of Jesus all the way to Golgotha and learn how to love and forgive.

CHAPTER 25

Author's Note:

To Encourage You to Pray, Fast, and Exercise Your Faith

You may be familiar with the book *Shoutin' on the Hills* by Nona Freeman. I must have read this book about a dozen times because it resonated with me and helped my faith to grow exponentially! In the book, Nona shared a story about her mother, Carrie Eastridge. It was Thanksgiving Day, and her mom had no money. To make things worse, the pantry was empty. The only food they had was a little bit of oatmeal. Carrie fed the children skimpy portions of oatmeal for breakfast and the last bit at noon. She then led her family in an urgent prayer for Thanksgiving dinner and concluded: "Please, Lord, make it by one o'clock. Thank You. Amen."

> *When it comes to having faith, no twelve-step program is required.*

Immediately after the prayer, she was moved by faith and told Nona to set the table. Of course, Nona grumbled at the instructions but pulled out the china anyway. With the table set and no food in sight, they waited.

Sometimes, when I see or read what God has done for His people, I just want to run and dance and do cartwheels — because He's a faithful God! What do you think happened? At exactly one o'clock and not a minute later (when we pray, we need to be specific), a knock sounded on Carrie Eastridge's door. It was her neighbor who lived a couple of miles away. The neighbor said, "Sister Carrie, when we thanked God for our dinner, the Lord told me you didn't have any, so we have decided to share with you."

Chills and tears. What a God! Dear friends, I can't stop the tears from falling. The first time I read this book was in 2005 — it made my heart glad because I realized even more who I have the same divine connection with the same God that provided for Carrie Eastridge and her family. She was bold enough to take authority in the Name of Jesus Christ and use her Kingdom authority, the weapons of prayer, fasting, faith, and the Word of God.

For a long, long time, all I had for my companions were faith, prayer, fasting, and the Word. I can't seem to shy away from the topic of faith because I'm afraid this is where most of us fall short. But I know this is exactly where we will obtain answers, and I want to help you to obtain your answers. As you conclude this book, I pray that you will remember some of the things God did for this poor little country girl who decided to trust Him with all her heart.

I invite you to invest all your faith in Him even if it's smaller than a mustard seed—because that's the requirement. In Matthew, Jesus said, "Because you have so little faith. Truly I tell you, if you have faith as small as a mustard seed, you can say to this mountain, 'Move from here to there.' and it will move. Nothing will be impossible for you"(Matthew 17:20 NIV). When it comes to having faith, no twelve-step program is required. You just need to apply practical principles and obey the Word of God. Just do what God's Word said to do!

The miracles that He performed in my life, they're not some made-up fairytales—they're very real! He's still doing them today. Faith still moves mountains, but you've got to believe! "Jesus said unto him, If thou canst believe, all things *are* possible to him that believeth" (Mark 9:23). If Carrie believed God, you can, too!

I want to reiterate these key areas of my faith journey to remind you of what faith in God can do. My life would have a very different narrative today if it weren't for my faith in the Lord Jesus Christ.

When I first cried out to God in 1988 at the tender age of seven because of a disadvantaged life, I had no idea that He would show up in my bedroom with the host of heaven. He declared and made a promise covenant to me from His own written Word that He would be a father unto me.

My friends mocked and jeered me for wearing the only decent dress I had to wear to Sunday school Sunday after Sunday. I had no idea that God would use the situation to make Himself known to me. He showed Himself to me as God Almighty; omnipotent, omniscient, omnipresent, the all-powerful one with the ability to work through others for anything on my behalf.

When I fasted for the very first time in 1995, I prayed and declared the Word of God in Mark 11:24 over my life. I declared it to be so by faith because I truly didn't know how to fast. For five or six hours, I prayed the Scriptures in faith, believing God would provide my school fee. I had no idea that God would respond to my request within hours. I still don't mind that He put my answer inside a purse lying in the middle of the street! Only God would do something like that!

One year after the money ran out, He raised up my two sisters, Juju and Shelly to help, to prove Himself to me that He can always make a way out of no way. My sisters were poor as well, but God used them to bless me nonetheless because I put my faith and trust in Him alone.

When my sister, Juju, suddenly passed away in 1997, I prayed and fasted in faith because I had no one else to help me finish up my high school education. In response to my prayer,

God sent me to Sister P's house to listen to the radio—I thought maybe God was mad, or maybe I was hallucinating—but like a child, I obeyed and went. By divine providence, a lady announced she needed a girl from the country, and by faith, I wrote down her number. I had no idea why God was sending me to listen to the radio, but later on, I realized He was testing, teaching, and helping me to fully recognize His leading—and what the power of being obedient to His voice will do.

I waited fourteen days to call this lady because I had no money to spare for calling time. When I finally did call her, she said I was the "only one" who had called her since the day she made the announcement. I almost fell over dead. Shocked and in disbelief. I started bawling when it hit home that I had become the next Abraham. A woman Abraham! Ha!

I still believe that God could have provided for me at home, but my faith was at work—Now I am more than convinced that He called me away to really demonstrate His power in my life, not just to save me from a life of poverty.

In June of 1997, shortly after I was done with school, the Holy Spirit nudged me that it was time. Only fifteen years old, I took this leap of faith and journeyed into the unknown. I had no idea where I was going, but, like Abraham, I packed up my few belongings and left my mother's house for the city of Kingston. This is how I proved that the Holy Spirit is really our guide. He protected and kept me safe until I arrived at my destination.

Once I settled in with the lady of providence, I came to understand that she had a plan for me that I didn't have for myself. She didn't want to register me for high school as she had promised over the phone—she wanted me to take care of her baby in the day and take classes at night. God only used her as a conduit—a small part of the puzzle. The Holy Spirit nudged me to fast and pray for five days. During my fast, the Holy Spirit prayed through me. I asked God to help me and let His will be done.

At the end of the five days, God supernaturally showed up, and the Holy Spirit gave me a phone number to dial. I was so frightened I thought my heart would stop beating! Within an hour of receiving this phone number, I was with my new family. I dialed the number, and God instantaneously and supernaturally opened a new door and connected me with an Apostolic Pentecostal family. They were complete strangers to me. I moved in with my new family right away. Only God can work miracles like that.

My new family gave me hope and a room of my own, and they got me registered for high school without a hassle in three days' time. I was privileged to live with my new family until I graduated from high school and started college. Only God can perform such acts.

In all of this, please, don't ever think that I'm perfect or that I am better than anyone or that I am being at all a braggadocio! I fail God every day. I'm a royal mess most days!

Don't think for a minute that I'm portraying myself to be self-righteous or holier than thou. I'm just a country girl who met and became friends with an incredible, magnanimous God! He assured me that every promise in His book is mine. They're mine and yours—every chapter, every verse, every line.

Dear friends, they are mine and yours, all three thousand promises that are Yes and Amen. But the question is this: how will we attain all these promises? We must first do what the promises require of us to do. God told Joshua, "This book of the law shall not depart out of thy mouth; but thou shalt meditate therein day and night, that thou mayest observe to do according to all that is written therein: for then thou shalt make thy way prosperous, and then thou shalt have good success" (Joshua 1:8).

God was not joking about what He said to Joshua, and He's not joking with us either. The Psalmist David said, "O fear the LORD, ye his saints: for *there is* no want to them that fear him" (Psalm 34:9). No wants, absolutely none!

When we fear the Lord, keep his commandments, and walk in complete obedience before Him, He will honor and bless us. That's exactly what I've been trying to do all my life. If we would have what the good book promised, we must move away from making lazy excuses but instead apply and comply. Yes, we fall short daily. Each time we make mistakes, we tell ourselves, "Self, you aren't perfect." (I do that all the time, too).

Even though Job was broken and fallen just like you and me, God said Job was perfect, blameless, and walked uprightly before Him (Job 1:8). I believe God wants us to move from the norm into perfection in Him by faith. (Hebrews 6:1-6). With all our flaws, God will help us overcome them so we can walk uprightly to reap the fatness and the benefits of the land.

In Deuteronomy 28, God gave Israel an outline. He laid out the blessings and the curses before them. In the New Testament, Jesus made it very clear again: "Whatever a man sows, that he will also reap" (Galatians 6:7, WEB).

Let me be honest with you. Growing up, I had no one to teach me about faith except for the Holy Spirit. The book of Hebrews is where He taught me from scratch for the very first time, and everything stuck with me until today. I believe in the written Word of God and that it is true (2 Timothy 3:16). When I started out on this journey of faith, I had no idea what I was doing or where it would take me. It took me on the same path of faith as Abraham and the others, but a different journey in time. We simply cannot please God without faith.

I couldn't do any of my life without faith. Faith in Jesus Christ saved me. Faith became my bulwark for the rest of my life. Dear friends, I wouldn't have had any testimony without my faith. All of what I shared is intentional. My prayer as well as desire for all of you is to come up higher in God — because our faith is the seed of greatness, miracles, testimonies, authority, dominion, and power! Your faith will take you to deeper depths and higher heights in God. None of us can get to the next level in God without faith.

I've read the entire book of Hebrews. Each time I read this book, it sets my soul ablaze! I'm blown away by the names of every individual who was mentioned in the "Hall of Faith." It is recorded that some had great faith and some small, but they all had faith! James said that faith without works is dead. "For as the body without the spirit is dead, so faith without works is dead also" (James 2:26).

If we look at all the heroes, we see that they did some type of works to demonstrate their commitment to God by faith. I'm afraid it's the same requirement for us New Birth Christians. If we want to see God manifest Himself in our lives and around us, we've got to move by faith! For example, if you need a job, you can't stay in bed all day—you get up, get that resume updated, and start looking and applying.

We can't afford to resort to feebleness in faith. We must earnestly contend for the faith. (Jude 1:3) So let the spirit of your faith arise to the occasion! We're reminded in Philippians to, "Only conduct yourselves in a manner worthy of the gospel of Christ, so that whether I come and see you or remain absent, I will hear of you that you are standing firm in one spirit, with one mind striving together for the faith of the gospel" (Philippians 1:27, NASB). I command your faith to arise! You can't take your rightful place in the Kingdom until you learn to walk by faith and not by sight (2 Corinthians 5:7-9). Call your faith to arise out of obscurity, because that's where my faith arose from. I write this book to challenge and increase your faith!

Can I call on you more than ever to pray until your spirit really prays? The Word of God says that Jesus prayed so profusely in the garden of Gethsemane before His Passion that His sweat became like drops of blood falling to the ground (Luke 22:44). How else can we access the throne of God if we don't pray and worship? The veil was rent in twain; we have full access to the throne room of God continuously! The secret of all failure is prayerlessness! The secret to prevailing with our God is through much persistent, persuasive prayer and fasting.

Can I urge you to pray and take God at His Word? Prayer became like oxygen to me the moment I learned how vital it was for a healthy, thriving relationship with God. It became my personal philosophy. The more time we spend in prayer, the more prepared and experienced we become to handle the glory and manifestation of God.

When you pray, don't be afraid to ask God for exactly what you need. Be specific like Carrie Eastridge. Tell him the type of house, car, job, husband, wife, children, family, and investment you desire. He loves us, and He's more than willing to give us what we need.

If you don't know how to pray or fast, ask the Holy Spirit to teach you. Or you can start with *When Ye Pray* and *When Ye Fast* by Joy Haney. I already mentioned Margaret Banks' book *The Five Principles of Powerful Prayer*. To learn more about faith, you can read *The Power of Faith* by Smith Wigglesworth.

Please bear in mind that prayer is necessary to maintain closeness with God. Prayer is the greatest weapon on earth — it's more powerful than any atomic bomb!

The patriarchs fasted, the apostles and Jesus fasted, and Queen Esther fasted. We don't fast enough, we don't pray enough, and we must — I am speaking to myself, too! Like I expressed before, we don't fast to beg or twist God's arm. We fast to humble ourselves and become more like Him. We fast to know His will and plans for our lives. Seeking God in prayer will bring the things we desire, for He said, "But seek ye first (Seek me first), the kingdom of God, and his righteousness, and all these things shall be added unto you" (Matthew 6:33).

Praying and fasting are beseeching God, and by doing these, we access the heavenly realm. Sweet friends — I hope to drive this point home — and here is the caveat. Our prayer and our worship are the keys to access God. I'm speaking from experience. Your faith, along with fasting and prayer, can catapult us into a spiritual realm that can't be attained otherwise.

If you don't have an altar at home already, please pick out a place for only you and God to meet. Establish it now! You'll be glad you did. For years, while I was in high school, my prayer altar was underneath my bed.

Can I challenge you to build back up your fasting life? I want to encourage you to re-build that broken-down altar and pray again, fast again, believe God again, and activate your faith so that God can demonstrate His power through you by the power of the Holy Spirit!

Remember what Jesus said to his disciples in Matthew 17:21: "Howbeit this kind goeth not out but by prayer and fasting."

CHAPTER 26

The Faith of Kasia

Wherefore seeing we also are compassed about with so great a cloud of witnesses, let us lay aside every weight, and the sin which doth so easily beset *us*, and let us run with patience the race that is set before us (Hebrews 12:1).

Now, faith is really what is hoped for, the proof of what is not seen.

By faith, when I was seven years old, I cried out to God because I was poor, I didn't have any shoes, and I didn't have a father. God showed up, gave me Psalm 27:10, and said He would be a father unto me. And He kept His promise.

> *By faith, I graduated from Bridgeport High at nineteen years old…*

By faith, when I was seven years old and I was ridiculed because I only had one dress to wear to Sunday school, Sunday after Sunday, I prayed a simple prayer, and God provided a brand-new dress.

By faith, when I was eleven years old, I asked God to fill me with the baptism of the Holy Ghost, and He answered and baptized me with the Holy Ghost and fire, with the evidence of speaking in unknown tongues just like Peter and rest of the apostles on the day of Pentecost (Acts 2:38).

By faith, when I was thirteen and had no money to start my first year of high school, I prayed and fasted for the very first time in my life, and God provided $3,800 for my tuition the same day.

By faith, when I was fourteen, the Lord showed me a vision of myself jumping over the dark hole my mother had fallen into—to be saved from teenage pregnancy.

By faith, I prayed and fasted for God to help me finish my high school education when my sister passed away. And He used strangers hundreds of miles away to open up a way for me to have an education.

By faith, when I was fifteen, I left my mother's house following the leading of the Holy Spirit, who supernaturally made provision for me to travel to a city that I'd never been to before to live with complete strangers.

By faith, I fasted for five days for God to open a new door, and God supernaturally gave me a phone number that I never knew to connect me with my new family (destiny helpers), who would help to change my life and help me walk into my destiny.

By faith, I graduated from Bridgeport High at nineteen years old and started college because God made way for me.

"Now faith is the substance of things hoped for, the evidence of things not seen. For by it the elders obtained a good report.

By faith, Abel offered unto God a more excellent sacrifice than Cain, by which he obtained witness that he was righteous, God testifying of his gifts: and by it, he being dead yet speaketh.

By faith, Enoch was translated that he should not see death; and was not found, because God had translated him: for before his translation, he had this testimony, that he pleased God. But without faith, *it is* impossible to please *him*: for he that cometh to God must believe that he is, and *that* he is a rewarder of them that diligently seek him.

By faith, Noah, being warned of God of things not seen as yet, moved with fear, prepared an ark to the saving of his house; by which he condemned the world, and became heir of the righteousness which is by faith."

The Faith of Abraham

"By faith, Abraham, when he was called to go out into a place which he should after receive for an inheritance, obeyed;

and he went out, not knowing whither he went. By faith, he sojourned in the land of promise, as *in* a strange country, dwelling in tabernacles with Isaac and Jacob, the heirs with him of the same promise: For he looked for a city which hath foundations, whose builder and maker *is* God. Through faith also, Sara herself received strength to conceive seed and was delivered of a child when she was past the age because she judged him faithful who had promised. Therefore, sprang there even of one, and him as good as dead, *so many* as the stars of the sky in multitude, and as the sand which is by the sea shore innumerable.

These all died in faith, not having received the promises, but having seen them afar off, and were persuaded of *them*, and embraced *them*, and confessed that they were strangers and pilgrims on the earth. For they that say such things declare plainly that they seek a country. And truly, if they had been mindful of that *country* from whence, they came out, they might have had the opportunity to have returned. But now, they desire a better *country*, that is, a heavenly: wherefore God is not ashamed to be called their God: for he hath prepared for them a city.

By faith, Abraham, when he was tried, offered up Isaac: and he that had received the promises offered up his only begotten *son*, of whom it was said, That in Isaac shall thy seed be called: Accounting that God *was* able to raise *him* up, even from the dead; from whence also he received him in a figure."

The Faith of Isaac, Jacob, and Joseph

"By faith, Isaac blessed Jacob and Esau concerning things to come. By faith, Jacob, when he was a dying, blessed both the sons of Joseph; and worshipped, *leaning* upon the top of his staff. By faith, Joseph, when he died, made mention of the departing of the children of Israel; and gave commandment concerning his bones."

The Faith of Moses

"By faith, Moses, when he was born, was hidden three months of his parents, because they saw *he was* a proper child; and they were not afraid of the king's commandment. By faith, Moses, when he has come to years, refused to be called the son of Pharaoh's daughter; Choosing rather to suffer affliction with the people of God, than to enjoy the pleasures of sin for a season; Esteeming the reproach of Christ greater riches than the treasures in Egypt: for he had respect unto the recompense of the reward. By faith, he forsook Egypt, not fearing the wrath of the king: for he endured, as seeing him who is invisible. Through faith, he kept the Passover, and the sprinkling of blood, lest he that destroyed the firstborn should touch them. By faith, they passed through the Red sea as by dry *land*: which the Egyptians assaying to do were drowned.

By faith, the walls of Jericho fell down after they were compassed about seven days."

The Faith of Many

"By faith, the harlot, Rahab, perished not with them that believed not when she had received the spies with peace.

And what shall I more say? for the time would fail me to tell *of* Gedeon, and *of* Barak, and *of* Samson, and *of* Jephthae; *of* David also, and Samuel, and of the prophets: Who through faith subdued kingdoms, wrought righteousness, obtained promises, stopped the mouths of lions, Quenched the violence of fire, escaped the edge of the sword, out of weakness were made strong, waxed valiant in fight, turned to flight the armies of the aliens. Women received their dead raised to life again: and others were tortured, not accepting deliverance; that they might obtain a better resurrection: And others had trial of *cruel* mockings and scourgings, yea, moreover of bonds and imprisonment: They were stoned, they were sawn asunder, were tempted, were slain with the sword: they wandered about in sheepskins and goatskins; being destitute, afflicted, tormented; (Of whom the world was not worthy:) they wandered in deserts, and *in the* mountains, and *in* dens and caves of the earth.

And these all, having obtained a good report through faith, received not the promise: God having provided some better thing for us, that they without us should not be made perfect." (Hebrews 11:1-40)

Our ancestors won God's approval by their faith. Therefore, I pray that all of our names will be numbered amongst them whose faith was approved by God.

"For the righteousness of God is revealed from faith to faith; as it is written: BUT THE RIGHTEOUS man SHALL LIVE BY FAITH." "But that no man is justified by the law in the sight of God, *it is* evident: for, The just shall live by faith." "Now the just shall live by faith: but if *any man* draw back, my soul shall have no pleasure in him." (Romans 1:17, Galatians 3:11, Hebrews 10:38).

Now, tell me, is there anything too hard for our God to do!?

"Behold, I am the Lord, the God of all flesh; is anything too difficult for me?" (Jeremiah 32:27, NASB).

References

I Montgomery, L.M. *Anne of Avonlea,* Grosset & Dunlap, New York, New York, U.S.A, 1919. Public domain. p. 55

II Banks, Margaret, *The Five Principles of Powerful Prayer,* Pentecostal Publishing House (April 29, 2011).

III Smith Wigglesworth, The Power of Faith, Whitaker House (November 1, 2000).

IV Daddy How Could You, Dr. Alice M. Millsap

V The Fatherless Daughter Project: Understanding Our Losses and Reclaiming Our Lives, Denna D. Babul, RN and Karin Luise, PHD, Avery (June 7, 2016).

VI Shoutin' on the Hills, Nona Freeman, Word Aflame Press (January 1, 1985).

VII Father Absence https://www.psychologytoday.com/us/blog/co-parenting-after-divorce/201205/father-absence-father-deficit-father-hunger

VIII Father Absence And Its Effects On Daughters
http://library.wcsu.edu/dspace/bitstream/0/527/1/Final+Thesis.pdf

IX Fatherless Daughters, Pamela Thomas, Simon & Schuster (May, 26, 2018).

X https://aspe.hhs.gov/further-resources-poverty-measurement-poverty-lines-and-their-history

XI https://www.census.gov/library/working-papers/2001/demo/POP-twps0052.html

XII The Purpose of the This Storm, Nadia Nembhard-Hunt, Ease Education Consultancy (August 3, 2018).

Editing Services and Contributions

Steven Nimocks – steven@stevennimocks.com

Erika Mathews – Resting Life Editing – www.restinglife.com

Talina Pyne – pynetalina871@gmail.com

Tina Harris – www.pepperedplum.com

Cherie Foxley – Cheriefox Book Design - www.fiverr.com/cheriefox

Stay Connected With Kacey

Connect with Kacey on her social media to receive daily inspiration and encouragement:

Website: www.kasianimocks.com

Facebook: www.facebook.com/kacey.howell.37

Instagram: www.instagram.com/kaceynimocks

We Would Like To Hear From You

If this book has minister to your life in anyway and you would like to share your testimony or contact the author, please send us an email at:

info@kasianimocks.com

Available on Amazon Unlimited, Kindle, Amazon

About Kacey

Kasia has a burden for souls and has been witnessing and ministering to Christians for over 20 years. Using her own life as an example, she has shared her experiences on her blog at Kacey's Korner touching lives in multiple countries with overwhelming success. She strives to equip, encourage, and provide inspiration for others from a personal place of experience. *The Girl in the Little White Dress* is a result of the years she has shared portions of her testimony and life. With the many requests to write a book with all her experiences walking with God, this book came into being.

As a successful published author, Kasia is the founder of a fast-growing community called the *Royal Academy for Singles*, *Royal Academy for Single Sisters*, and *Dear Christian Singles* reaching souls around the globe. On her storytelling platform (Facebook), she shares God's truth about salvation, holiness, marriages, courtship, and most importantly, the love of God while providing practical tools for Christian living in a very refreshing, down-to-earth way. She narrates her first-hand spiritual encounters and impacts people's hearts, thoughts, mindsets, and everyday struggles. Using the written 'Word of God' as the authority, she shows her readers evidence by sharing her personal testimony in a relatable way, which makes her an undeniable force that many in this generation relate to. Kasia is also a lover of modest fashion. For this ideal she established Kasia's Royal Rose Boutique. She is a rare gift from God who is willing to help and serve those that are hungry for real answers to real questions

www.ingramcontent.com/pod-product-compliance
Lightning Source LLC
Chambersburg PA
CBHW031056080526
44587CB00011B/708